Dreams Come True, and Mine Will Too:
A Memoir of Renewed Hope
Danielle Ndende

Copyright © 2024 Danielle Ndende
www.daniellendende.com

ISBN: 978-1-7390317-3-2

DCTMWT / RDRMDA Ltd.
Montreal, Canada

CONTENTS

CONTENT WARNING

This book contains material that may
be distressing to some readers.

Depression, suicidal thoughts, panic attacks.

For Ming Mang Moung, for being the
kindest and absolute best mom.

For Sylvie, for encouraging me to pursue my passions.

And for my thirteen- and twenty-two-year-
old selves: there was always another side.

PREFACE

I've been putting off writing this book because I don't know where and how to start. Today is Friday, May 22, 2020, and it's about 10:30 p.m., as I finally have the courage to start working on this project. This is scary, very scary, but here we go.

As you can tell by the title, this book is about dreams and my conviction that they come true. I know—pretty cliché, but still true. This title came to me long before I even knew I wanted to write a book. *Dreams come true, and mine will too* was initially a personal mantra, something I started repeating to myself after going through the hardest times of my life, making it to a better side, and eventually feeling like I could achieve my goals and make my dream come true. As of today, my dream hasn't come true yet, but my hope is that it will.

Throughout our time together in this book, I will share my life experiences, especially the most painful ones, and some lessons I've learned along the way. My hope is that my journey will give you the courage to go for what you want and pursue your dreams, regardless of your circumstances.

This book is mainly inspired by my recollection of events that have occurred since 2017. I will also dive into my journals (yes, I am an adult, and I keep a journal), share how I started journaling again, and how it has helped. Spoiler alert: It is one of the reasons I am able to write this book.

Welcome to my journey, and happy reading.

CHAPTER 1:

OH, HEY!

Driven: the kind of word people put on their resumes or cover letters, sometimes without giving much thought to it. I've been guilty of doing that too—from cover letters to the tell-me-about-yourself interview question, I've described myself as a driven candidate to hopefully ingratiate myself with recruiters at the other end of the phone or with interviewers across the table. I substantiated my self-description, but I didn't always fully appreciate the meaning behind the word "driven."

Since I was a teenager, I've had goals I wanted to achieve, and I've pursued them. This wasn't about appearing driven to others; my goals simply mattered to me, enough not to let people's opinion get in the way. For example, I didn't let anyone, not even my father, deter me from pursuing my chosen educational or professional path. I say *not even him* because in patriarchal cultures like mine, most of the important decisions in a household (including children's education) tend to rest in the hands of the father. That was true to a certain extent in the house I grew up in.

During our last year of middle school, my classmates and I had to pick a major we wanted to study in high school. Although at that point,

I didn't have a dream career yet, I knew whatever path I followed in the future would be business-related. So, when orientation forms started circulating in class, asking students to indicate their preferred field of study, I chose economics rather than one of the other three options: literature, mathematics, or biology. The school was going to make a final decision based on the student's choice and academic performance. The problem is, it didn't seem like these orientation forms served their purpose, at least not for some students, and especially not for those in my cohort.

I grew up in Yaoundé, Cameroon, where I attended one of the top three middle schools in the country, the best in my city. The school had this process of classifying students, and I think wrongfully so, according to how "smart" they were. The basis for this was their academic performance. Each grade consisted of five cohorts, with all the "best" students being placed in a single cohort while the rest were distributed among the other four. You could tell who the "smart kids" were by looking at the cohort letter embroidered on their uniforms.

I happened to have been "smart enough" to attend Grade 9-E, the cohort with the brightest students. A common belief among students, especially those in my cohort, was that only the best could study math in high school and would be oriented to do so. This was further pushed onto us by teachers and the administration. Studying math in high school was effectively a status symbol, and obviously everyone in my cohort wanted to be part of the elite. And ideally, they would further be funneled into Grade 10-C4, the cohort of the "brightest" math students. Everyone except me.

Despite choosing economics as my major, my orientation decision letter indicated I was going to study math. The letter required parents' approval and signature, but I never showed it to mine because I knew my dad wanted me to study math and wasn't going to let me appeal the decision. So, I took care of it myself.

After weeks of back and forth to the principal's office to have my orientation decision changed, my major was finally approved. I was going to study business, to many of my classmates' dismay. The day my orientation decision was updated, I remember being so happy that I spent almost the entire lunch break marveling at my letter. The words *Economics and Social Sciences* looked so good next to my name, and I couldn't wait to be in high school.

"Why aren't you crying?" A classmate said while walking by as I stood on the balcony of Grade 9-E, daydreaming about the following year and smiling at my letter. She posed the question as soon as she saw my orientation decision and sounded and looked very concerned.

"Why would I cry?" I replied. "This is exactly what I wanted!" I made sure to emphasize that this was my own decision, but she didn't seem to believe me. I didn't care. She left me on the balcony, and I resumed my daydreaming.

As soon as word got out that I was going to study business, I started to get comments such as, "What a waste of your intelligence," or "Why did they even allow you to study in this cohort in the first place?" Pretty much everyone in my cohort was going to study math. What a disgrace that a student from Grade 9-E was going to study something else! Some people laughed at me; some suggested I just didn't have what it takes to succeed in a more scientific field, while others truly didn't understand my decision. For someone who cared a lot about people's opinion in other aspects of my life, this did not bother me at all—I already believed in choosing a path that works for you, regardless of what people think. I believed in being fulfilled in your own choices.

When I showed my updated letter at home, my dad insisted I request a change of major. I didn't. A few months later, after school was out and it was too late to make the change at my middle school, he arranged for me to transfer to another school to study math. I was not going to do that either. I had already started reading the accounting book I had asked my mom to get when I told her I wanted to study business. That was back when I thought I was going to like accounting, which I ended up hating in high school. But that's beside the point.

I didn't want to change schools, even to study economics. And I certainly didn't want to study math anywhere. I spent the entire summer fighting for my major at my current school at the time. I pleaded with my mom and asked my older siblings for help. And finally, just a few weeks before classes started in September, my dad agreed to let me study what I wanted at my school. I was lucky my spot hadn't been taken already.

It wasn't until years later when I shared this story with a few people, and they thought I'd been brave, that I realized I had done something other students couldn't. They either didn't have the courage or were too worried about what people would think, or a combination of both.

This set the tone for the rest of my academic life, as I navigated broader options for college and what to study in grad school. I fell in love with management consulting when I was in high school, and it became my dream at that point. I don't quite remember how that happened, since no one around me was a consultant and no one I knew at school wanted to be one, but I know I've always wanted to fulfill my desire to help others. In the context of companies, consulting sounded like a good match. As soon as I figured this was my dream career, I started doing my research on the education needed to get in the field. Once again, I picked a major in college that didn't align with my dad's initial vision, but as you can now imagine, the major I picked is the one I graduated with.

Speaking of college, it was an altogether interesting experience for me, as I'm sure is the case for many people. Looking back on my college years, and because my life subsequently took a different turn as you will read, I can say those years were the closest thing to *living my best life*. To date, some of my best memories date back to that time. There was always something going on, and I was always up to it. From traveling nationally and internationally, to going to social events and parties, to being involved on campus while trying to maintain good grades … I didn't run out of things to keep me busy and entertained. I was grateful for it all, but it's only later I realized that there were things I unconsciously took for granted. I say *unconsciously* because sometimes I did pause to appreciate what I had and thanked God for what my life looked like, especially since parts of my childhood were also a bit different. But then I rushed back into my busy life.

My life wasn't perfect—of course not. I had challenges here and there, but they were manageable; had arguments with friends and went through breakups. I had bad grades sometimes, and some semesters were more challenging than others. I struggled sometimes with body image and with self-confidence; cried, sometimes for no reason. In short, I had bad days. But no day was bad enough to make me question my existence. I was actually … *happy*. A word that later left my vocabulary, and that I thought would never come back, at least not to be used in the context of my own life.

CHAPTER 2:

WHY NOT ME?

As mentioned, I was grateful for my life. Sometimes I compared it to that of the less fortunate or to people who were facing challenges, and I empathized. At the same time, I wondered what hardships I would experience, what they would look like, when they would happen, and more.

Some people repeated classes, and it took them longer to graduate either high school or college; that was their hardship. Others lost a close friend or family member or both; that was their hardship. Others struggled financially, could not afford tuition, books, or social activities, and that was their challenge. Still others were ill and dealing with a chronic disease while in school; that was their challenge. I know the list goes on, and I cannot begin to understand what some people were going through, even as I saw them every day and they looked fine to me. Some were probably dealing with a combination of everything I just listed or more. Some talked about their challenges; others didn't.

I sympathized and helped whenever and however I could, but I didn't completely understand their hardships. Though I was grateful for living a somewhat stress-free life, I couldn't help but wonder why my "grown-up struggles" hadn't occurred yet; that was scary to me.

I wanted to know what it felt like to have adult problems and wasn't satisfied with my smaller issues.

I never wished to fail a class or an exam and always studied hard so I wouldn't, but maybe if I had repeated a class, I would've had better words to comfort those who had stayed a year behind me. I never wished for anyone's death, but maybe if I had lost someone very close, I would've had the right words to comfort those who were mourning a loved one. I never wished to be broke, but maybe if I hadn't had enough money to afford necessities, I would've known how it feels not to have enough money to eat. And as I grew up and realized how much of a blessing being healthy was, I no longer wished to be ill (more on that later). I was thankful for my health, but maybe if it had been disrupted, I would have better related to people enduring pain.

Relate: that's exactly what I wanted. To relate to people more. I didn't feel comfortable not being able to assist my friends or other people who were going through tough times as much as I wanted to because I didn't know how they felt. I wasn't in their shoes, but I wanted to be in their shoes. I wanted to have a *story* to tell.

After obtaining my bachelor's degree from the Catholic University of Central Africa (CUCA), it was time for me to attend graduate school. I decided to pursue a master's degree in management, according to what I thought was required to become a management consultant. My dad had told me about DePaul University, a university in Chicago. I liked the city, and the Kellstadt Graduate School of Business–DePaul University's graduate business school–offered a master of science in management, which I liked as well.

I applied and was admitted to DePaul University's in-house English Language Academy (ELA), where I would take my English as a

Second Language (ESL) classes. Once I completed my studies at ELA, I planned to apply to the master of science in management program.

I packed my bags and said goodbye to family and friends. My childhood dream of studying in the United States was about to come true. I had hoped and longed for it since high school, and although it came years after what I originally wanted, I was happy and grateful it was finally happening.

I left Cameroon for the United States of America in February 2017, and that is when my *story* began.

CHAPTER 3:

NOT WHAT I EXPECTED

Tiny crystals of snow were drifting down from the sky when I exited the airport. They landed on my black wool coat and seeped into my skin, crisp and cold, sending chills across my body. I didn't care. I wasn't cold, or maybe I was. But my first interaction with snow was totally worth it. After two ten-hour flights, I was finally in Chicago. I was smiling from one frozen ear to the other. I was … *happy*. My dad had arranged for one of his acquaintances, Father Andrew, to pick me up at the airport. He then helped me move into my place and provided general guidance about the city.

I lived in a student apartment complex in the West Loop neighborhood of Chicago, on South Peoria Street. The building was close to DePaul University's downtown campus.

DePaul had two main campuses: one in the Loop–Chicago's downtown area–and the other in Lincoln Park. My building was a thirty-minute walk to the downtown campus where ELA was located, three subway stops away. My mom and I had researched a few places and decided on this apartment complex because it offered a good combination of comfort and proximity to school and other places I would probably frequent. I'd been living alone since graduating from high school and wanted to keep that going, but accommodation prices in Chicago, especially for studio or one-bedroom apartments closer to my school, would not make that possible. Most units rented for upwards of $1,400. And they were unfurnished.

We went for a furnished four-bedroom, four-bathroom apartment that I would share with three other students. The important thing for me was that I have a private bathroom, and I specified in my application that I only wanted girls as roommates. The building had some pretty good amenities, and I remember wondering if all apartment buildings in Chicago were similar.

On the ground floor, there was 24/7 security, on-site management and leasing office, a study room, a game and entertainment room with a pool table, a computer lab with free printing, a vending machine, and a gym. All apartments in the building were furnished. Mine was on the third floor and came with a black leather sofa in the living room, a 32-inch TV, a coffee table, and a two-seat dining table set. The kitchen was open concept and came with an ice-maker fridge, a stove, microwave, oven, dishwasher, and more cabinet space than I would know what to do with if I lived in that apartment alone. I liked the apartment, though the dark floors combined with the black furniture and appliances gave it a bit of a dismal look. The sunlight coming through the four tall windows in the living room attempted to dispel that look.

There were also laundry and garbage rooms on every floor. A single wash load cost $2.50, while a dryer load was $1.75. All residents had access to reloadable laundry cards. Garbage disposal, on the other hand, was free. Well ... a more appropriate way to say this is the cost was included in the rent.

My bedroom was the only one with an in-suite bathroom. Others had their bathrooms across the hallway, which wasn't a big deal, but I liked that I wasn't going to have to get out of my bedroom to shower. My bedroom was furnished with a queen-sized bed, plus a desk and a chair, while the bathroom had regular bathroom stuff. Maybe not so regular to me was the fact that it had a tub; most bathrooms I'd seen back home that were not in hotels only included a shower. The single window in my bedroom was tall and wide enough to let in a substantial amount of sunlight. And for all this, my mom would pay about $1,100 per month, excluding utilities.

I stayed alone in that apartment for my first few months in the city and for the duration of my ESL classes. I had the entire kitchen to myself, so I wasn't too bothered.

As an international student whose first language was French, I needed to demonstrate English language proficiency to be admitted to the Master of Science in Management program at DePaul. I would achieve this by providing results for either the TOEFL (test of English as a foreign language) or the IELTS (international English language testing system). Because I had taken none of these standardized English language tests before leaving Yaoundé, I had to take ESL classes first.

DePaul's ELA offered intensive ESL classes at five levels of academic English—Foundations, Intermediate, High Intermediate, Advanced, and the fifth was a bridge between the program and university, University Bridge. As an incoming student into the program, I took the initial TOEFL screening exam that was used to determine each student's level. Luckily for me, I already had a solid foundation in English, so my screening test results allowed me to enter the program directly at the University Bridge level. That meant I would only need to complete one term—ten weeks—before starting "proper school." I actually got a higher score on that screening TOEFL than was required to enter the master's program directly, but because I hadn't applied to that program yet, I couldn't join. That didn't bother me—I saw this as an opportunity to warm up to Chicago without too much pressure.

My plan was to apply to the master's program only after completing the ESL classes because I wasn't aware DePaul offered conditional admissions. I was already well into language classes when I found out it was possible to be admitted to a program based on academic records and be required to take ESL classes if the English language proficiency requirement was not met.

Another reason I applied to ELA first was that the documents required to obtain a student visa (F-1 visa) were easier to get for ESL classes than for the master's program. For example, Form I-20, "Certificate of Eligibility for Nonimmigrant Student Status," or I-20 for short, was a document issued by a government-approved school. It provided personal and financial information about an international student. For the remainder of this book, I will refer to this form simply as I-20.

The I-20 was proof that a student had been admitted to a school and had sufficient financial resources to live and study in the U.S. for the duration of the program or at least one academic year, whichever was shorter. The form had three pages: the first one contained general student and school information; the second one, employment and travel authorization, if any; and the third, general instructions about the form.

The I-20 was issued for the duration of the program and ultimately determined a student's status in the U.S.

For example, let's say you were an international student who had been issued a five-year F-1 visa, and had been admitted to a two-year program. You would only be allowed to stay in the U.S. for two years because that is the duration of your program that appeared on your I-20. Conversely, if you had only been issued a six-month F-1 visa for the same program, you could stay in the U.S. for two years.

This is obviously a simplified example; a lot more goes into getting and maintaining status. That said, students could only receive an F-1 visa if they had first obtained an I-20, and only government-approved schools could enroll international students and issue I-20s.

Several documents were required when applying for an I-20, the most important of which probably being proof of funds. To receive my I-20, I needed to provide evidence that I had enough funds to cover tuition fees and living expenses. Since the ESL program was considerably shorter and cheaper than the master's program, it was easier to provide proof of funds to get my F-1 visa application processed on time. I was issued a six-month F-1 visa in January 2017 based on an I-20 that would also expire in June of the same year.

My classes at ELA started in March 2017. As we were nearing the end of the term, I started putting my application together for the master of science in management program. Since I had graduated from high school and college in my home country, I needed to do an evaluation of my transcripts and degrees to determine their U.S. equivalent. DePaul required a course-by-course evaluation, and I remember browsing the school's list of preferred providers on the website and being shocked at the $250 average evaluation cost. They didn't accept external providers, so I had no choice, but I obviously picked the cheapest available. By the end of May, my application essay, resume, and other relevant documents were ready. I was only missing the results from the additional TOEFL I was going to take at the end of the ESL program.

I submitted my application for the master's program on June 12th. By then, I had successfully completed the ESL program—stellar grades and an even higher TOEFL score. I was *happy*, and so was my mom when I told her. I was confident but not too much. *I can get in, but you never know.* My stomach was tight with anxiety. *I know this feeling.* Almost every time I'd felt that way about an exam, I'd ended up passing it. This time felt different, but then again, every time before had also felt different.

⌁⫘⌁

Days and weeks went by, during which I impatiently waited for a response. My heart skipped a beat every time I saw the words *DePaul University* somewhere, and it raced every time I got a Gmail notification on my phone. I didn't want to see a notification from the Kellstadt Graduate School of Business, but at the same time, I did. Some days, my stomach was aching; other days, it wasn't. This time definitely felt different. It may have just been because this was something new and bigger than anything I'd done before, so I chose to listen to my mom and to everyone who thought I would *definitely* be admitted.

By the end of June, I had been in the U.S. for about four months but hadn't been feeling the best. I felt lonely at times, spending my days in my bedroom watching movies and TV shows. I didn't have friends in the city. The ones I made in my ESL program left Chicago right after the program ended, and we didn't really stay in touch. I didn't get to celebrate my twenty-first birthday either, even though I had imagined something big to mark the occasion. I went out for walks and to the gym sometimes. I also went to Old St. Patrick's church—or

Old St. Pats as we called it—on Sundays and to the grocery store after mass, but that's about how much going out I was doing.

At that point, my I-20 had already expired, and I needed a new one to legally remain in the U.S. I was already well into my grace period—the sixty days you get after your I-20 expires and during which you must either change your status, transfer your records to a new school, or leave the U.S. Mine expired on August 1st. I needed to transfer my records from ELA to the Kellstadt Graduate School of Business, but I needed to be admitted first. Once I got my admission letter, I would request a records transfer when I applied for a new I-20. The transfer would only be complete once I got that new I-20.

Things were not going as I had imagined, but I kept telling myself it was just the beginning. I spent my first three months in Chicago alone in the apartment. Some days, I tried to offset my low mood with the fact I had the kitchen all to myself. And it worked. But my feeling of loneliness progressively grew more intense. I also lived on my own throughout my time at university back home, but at least some of my friends and I lived in the same building and others lived nearby. It was never too hard to find people to hang out with. If anything, it was hard to be alone.

I would choose living alone anytime, but I have to admit I had been fantasizing what life with roommates looked like. Movie nights, parties, outings of any kind, travel, adventure and lifetime experiences, shopping and beauty appointments … this is what I had seen on TV and YouTube. If I wasn't going to have that exact experience, I hoped it would be somewhat similar.

It wasn't.

My first roommates moved into our apartment in June and moved out in August, which wasn't enough time to become best friends, especially since all three were already friends and went to the same school. I didn't miss home yet, but it sure would have been nice to have people to hang out with. *It'll be fine. I just need to be admitted to my program; then I will make friends and live the life I'm dreaming of.*

⟁

One afternoon in July, I woke up from a nap to some news. I hadn't done much that day, not unlike the days before. I pressed my eyes shut and opened them back up, attempting to see more clearly. *What day is it? What time is it? Am I in New York yet?* I swept my hand across the bed and below my pillow to find my phone. I pressed the button in the middle. The time was approximately 2 p.m. on July 3rd. A red-and-white envelope icon appeared on the screen, indicating that I had gotten a new email. My eyes were still foggy and my mind in a haze as I opened the Gmail app.

> **From:** *Director of Recruitment and Admission*
> **To:** *Me*
> **Subject:** *DePaul University Kellstadt Graduate School of Business*
> **Date and Time:** *7/3/2017 at 1:45 p.m.*
> *Hello Danielle,*
>
> *Thank you for your application to the Kellstadt Graduate School of Business. The admissions committee has completed the review of your application for admission to the Kellstadt Graduate School of Business. Due to the competitive nature of the applicant pool, the committee is not able to admit all applicants. We regret to inform you that we are unable to offer you admission to the program this quarter.*
>
> *If you would like to receive feedback about ways to strengthen your application for admission, please do not hesitate to contact us.*

Thank you for your interest in the Kellstadt Graduate School of Business at DePaul University. We wish you much success as you pursue your academic and professional goals.

Sincerely,

Director of Recruitment and Admission

I was now wide awake, sitting upright on my bed. I wasn't sure how to feel so I didn't immediately react. I put my phone away to get ready to leave for New York City where my older sister Naomi lived.

I failed. The reality finally kicked in as I was walking through security at the O'Hare International Airport. My stomach was hurting and twisting into knots. *What am I going to do? I only have a month left and applied to just one school. Should I just leave? Then I'll go home and do what? A master's degree a whole year after everyone? I can graduate late as long as I am getting my degree abroad and as long as language classes justify the delay. If go back home, what was the point of coming all the way here? Take ESL classes I could have taken back home? They won't even be useful, and I'm still going to be a year behind. What is everyone going to think? What am I going to tell them? I have to stay here. I have to find a way. I'll be fine. Maybe this is just the challenge I have been asking for. Once I fix this, it'll be over, and I am going to live the life I am dreaming of.*

I fell asleep with those thoughts swimming in my mind and woke up when we touched down. While I was outside waiting for Naomi to come pick me up, I posted a picture on my Snapchat with the location filter and the caption, *"What better place to celebrate the Fourth of July than NYC?"*

My phone vibrated a few seconds later, and I opened Snapchat to look at replies to my story.

> **Lucas:** Living your best life!
>
> **Danielle:** Yes sir!

I smiled. Lucas and I had been in a relationship for a little less than a year at that point. Before I left home, we decided we were going to try and make this long-distance relationship thing work. We hadn't spoken in a few hours, so we jumped on a call. I was not doing great, and I didn't want to lie to him, so I told him about DePaul. He didn't know what to do besides being an emotional support. We talked about this and other things until Naomi got there, and I had to hang up.

———⬤———

I stayed in New York for about a week, and it was great. I managed not to worry too much about my situation, telling myself I would sort it out once I got back to Chicago. I didn't even mention anything about it to Naomi—I didn't want to bother her or ruin the vacation. Plus, I was going to fix this.

No one ever got back to me when I replied to my rejection email, asking for ways to strengthen my application. I only had a few more weeks left in my grace period, so I decided to call the school to schedule an appointment and get feedback on my application. After multiple failed attempts, they finally got me an appointment with an admission coordinator.

When we met on July 13th, he told me one reason my application was rejected was that they couldn't verify that I had an undergraduate degree. The transcript evaluation service provider I'd used had not determined that my previous education was equivalent to a U.S. bachelor's degree. My evaluation report, which was sent directly to DePaul, indicated that I had the U.S. equivalent of three years of post-graduate studies.

The education systems in the U.S. and Cameroon are different. I got my bachelor's degree after three years of university, while it typically takes four years to complete the same degree in the U.S. I explained these differences to the coordinator and asked if the school would be willing to reconsider my application if I could provide proof of my undergraduate degree. He agreed, but his expression led me to believe that simply validating my credentials wouldn't be sufficient to get me in. At the end of our conversation, he informed me that if I didn't provide that proof, I would need to be accepted into an undergraduate program to complete the missing courses and obtain the U.S. equivalent of a bachelor's degree.

Looking back, I know the issue wasn't just about my credentials. My application wasn't strong enough, and I didn't have much experience writing a strong resume, let alone one for the U.S. market. I later discovered that resume formats differ widely from country to country, and the one I had used for my application didn't fit the U.S. standards.

When I got home that day, I emailed the evaluation service provider, detailing my conversation with the admissions coordinator. I also asked if they could reevaluate my transcripts. They said they couldn't, and that even if they did it, the outcome would not be different.

Time was running out and the pressure was mounting, so I started contemplating the idea of applying to an undergraduate business program at DePaul, hoping I would transfer directly to the fourth year. That was clearly not the ideal situation, but at that point, I didn't know what other choice I had. I also told my mom, who I had kept uninformed until now. She was sad I wasn't admitted to the graduate program but had no more information than I did on how to proceed next. So, she did not object to the idea of applying to the undergraduate program, as long as I didn't have to start over.

———— ⟨▦⟩ ————

I started preparing another application the next day, on July 14th, mostly reusing the documents from my graduate application and making the necessary changes. I uploaded everything to my online account and hit submit. *Maybe this is good. Maybe this is what God wants for me. Maybe He wants me to experience undergrad student life here before going to grad school. Maybe this is better than going straight into my master's.* I lay down and let myself drift away into daydreaming about what my life as an undergrad student would look like. I smiled at the scenes of happy me. *It is going to be alright.*

I snapped back to reality when I remembered I also had to continue to look for another place to live, because my current lease was going to expire at the end of the month. I had purposely missed the deadline to renew it because it was getting uncomfortable for my mom to pay around $1,200 each month for rent and utilities, and uncomfortable for me to remind her of my bills. Instead of living with roommates, I now wanted to move into a studio apartment, which meant relocating to a more affordable part of the city. That didn't bother me at all—I could live pretty much anywhere as long as I had a place to myself. Nothing wrong with my roommates; I just wanted more privacy and an entire kitchen to myself. Also, we weren't best friends anyway.

As I looked for apartments, I soon realized how different the process of getting a place in Chicago was compared to back home. I didn't expect things to be the same, but I had no idea getting an apartment in Chicago required submitting an application that could potentially be rejected.

The apartments I was interested in required proof that I was making at least three times the monthly rent. I would also undergo a background and credit check, the results of which would determine my eligibility. This is when I learned about credit scores for the first time.

A credit score is a number that is used to determine someone's creditworthiness and ability to make on-time payments. It is calculated and assigned by credit bureaus, which gather information from different sources, including financial institutions. In the U.S., credit scores range from 300 to 850. A higher score signals less risk, while individuals with lower credit scores are viewed as more likely to default on their payments. Many factors affect credit scores, but the five most important are: (1) payment history (whether you've made past payments on time and how long it took you to make those payments); (2) credit utilization (how much of the credit available to you has been used); (3) length of credit history (how long you've had credit); (4) credit mix (the types of credit accounts you have); and (5) recent activity (how many new credit accounts you've applied for)[1].

One way to build credit is often through a credit card, using it to make purchases on credit and then making consistent payments to pay off the balance. A social security number, or SSN, is required to apply for a credit card.

At the time, I knew nothing about credit and was not yet eligible for an SSN, so I could not apply for a credit card to start building my credit. With no credit, personal income, or SSN, I needed a co-signer or guarantor to back up my rental applications. So, I would have to ask my mom for her personal and financial documents to include in my applications. I also needed to show proof of legal status in the U.S., for which I needed a valid I-20. Other requirements included paying a non-refundable application fee ranging from $50 to $200,

---

1   "What Is a Good Credit Score?" *Experian*, 2023, https://www.experian. com/blogs/ask-experian/credit-education/score-basics/what-is-a-good-credit-score/. Accessed March 2024.

depending on the apartment, and providing reference letters from previous landlords.

Back home, verifying your identity with your national identity card and being able to pay for rent each month is usually all it takes to get a place.

The process in the U.S. was lengthy, costly, time-consuming, and stressful, especially in my situation. I had no document that proved I was in a grace period and, therefore, could still legally reside in the U.S., even though my I-20 and visa had expired. Not everyone knew immigration laws, let alone the specifics around the F-1 status.

<hr />

As of July 18th, all my rental applications had been rejected. All except for one pending application for a studio apartment in Rogers Park, which I hoped would be approved. Rent and utilities were going to average $1,000 each month. Still expensive, but less than my current rent in a shared apartment.

When I was not stressing over my situation, I was dreaming about that apartment. I could definitely see myself living close to the beach. The apartment building was about forty-five minutes north of downtown by train, which wasn't too bad. Not as convenient as my current ten-minute train ride downtown, but I didn't care as long as I got to live on my own. The leasing agent I was in contact with was nice and understanding of my situation. I didn't share the details; I just told her I was waiting for a new I-20 to be issued to me, and she let me apply without one. I hoped to be admitted to the undergrad program and be issued a new I-20 in time to add it to my rental application for that studio apartment.

Each passing day brought an additional unit of pressure as we neared the end of the month, which was the end of my grace period. I kept telling myself that everything would be fine and that this was just the challenge I'd been hoping for, pushing through this weird feeling that had been weighing on me for months. But the anxiety gradually grew unsettling, and it showed on my face.

I'd noticed a few pimples on my face back in June but thought nothing of it. Well, I obviously did everything under my power to get rid of them, but I didn't think beyond that. As what I refused to call acne for a long time got worse, and through my research, I discovered that acne *could* be stress-induced or get worse because of it. This was a revelation for me and to be honest, it took me some time to accept that I not only had acne but also that stress had caused it.

This idea of stress causing acne sounded too farfetched, and I didn't think *my* acne could have anything to do with how I was feeling. To me, acne was the result of hormonal changes during puberty. I remember being shocked at the number of acne-fighting products I found at Target, Walgreens, and other stores on my first few trips there. I used to wonder if there were that many teenagers in the U.S.

Skin issues were not a concern for me growing up. My puberty manifested in ways other than pimples on my face. Some would appear here and there, but it was nothing to worry about. At least nothing *I* worried about. The only mark on my face was a scar from when I had chicken pox, but you had to come really close and pay attention to even notice it. I, and most people around me, had clear skin by the time we got to university. Or maybe I did not pay attention. What I do know is that people did not talk about stress, much less its effects on health. Some said stress and anxiety were "White people stuff." I personally didn't believe that, but then again, I only experienced stress in the context of exams or asking for permission to go out. I'm sure this was not the case for everyone, and some people had more serious issues, but I'd never heard anyone say they got acne because they were stressed out.

⸺⊶⊷⸺

Four days before the end of July, I got an email from the Driehaus College of Business at DePaul University. I'd been admitted to the undergraduate program starting in the fall. I was … *happy*, though I didn't know what year I would start at. I needed to pass some tests and provide an original syllabus, together with its English translation for each course I had taken prior to coming to the U.S., so the school could determine my level. My admission was great news, but it was only half the battle—I still had to transfer my immigration records from ELA to the Driehaus College of Business and get a new I-20.

I opened the attached documents to examine the requirements for requesting a transfer and a new I-20. The transfer release form looked straightforward. The I-20 checklist did too, especially since I wasn't seeing it for the first time. There was just one big problem. Tuition for one academic year was about $40,000, and the estimated living expenses for the same period were $15,000. To satisfy the proof of funds requirement to receive a new I-20, I would need to show at least $55,000 in liquid funds. *Great!* As a transfer international student, I wasn't eligible for a scholarship. And as simply an international student, I wasn't eligible for government-sponsored financial aid programs. *Where am I going to find this much money in less than a month?*

My mom was happy to hear about my admission to the school, but, as expected, she was a little distraught by the financial implication. "We'll do our best," she said, and I could tell she sighed, even though we were texting. I don't like asking for money. I like it even less when it involves my mom, and it bothered me that the amounts of my requests were now exponentially higher than when I was back home.

Considering the Driehaus College of Business was also part of the downtown campus, she thought it might be better if I stayed at my current student residence.

I silently disagreed. Although the studio apartment I was eyeing was unfurnished and farther from downtown, it cost less money and provided more space. I had even already bought a bedframe in anticipation of my move. My mom insisted that I stay where I was, so I reluctantly agreed to renew my lease, secretly hoping my rental application would still be approved.

———— ⬦ ————

On July 29th, I finally received an update on my rental application for the studio apartment in Rogers Park. It'd been denied. All my décor ideas went down the drain while I ran downstairs to the leasing office. I had missed the renewal deadline, but no one had rented my room yet, so there was still a chance. My monthly rent under the new contract increased by $10 because I hadn't renewed my lease on time to lock in the previous rate before they did their annual rent increase.

"I'll probably have to move out six months from now," I said, while the leasing specialist and I were going over the contract.

"So, we only offer annual contracts, so you won't be able to get out of it before the end of the next year unless you experience unforeseen circumstances. In that case, you would need to break the lease and pay the associated fees," she responded, pointing her pen to the section regarding early contract termination. I clearly hadn't read that.

"And how much would the fees be?" I imagined something like $100 or $200.

"Well, it depends on how early you end the contract," she said, "but it's usually an amount equivalent to three months of rent or the balance on your contract."

Wait what?! I internally exclaimed. I swallowed and nodded slowly before grabbing the pen at my right to sign the contract. Once more, I was shocked at how different—and much more expensive—it was to live in that city. Clearly, going to the U.S. for summer vacation was not the same as living there. I already had my keys and reloadable laundry card; I also knew my way around, so after signing the contract, I went straight up to my room without doing a tour of the premises.

As of August 1st, my grace period was over. Although I'd been admitted to a new program, I still didn't have an I-20 yet because of the challenge of providing proof of funds. I'd been filling my days with re-watching *Suits* or *Gossip Girl*, or scrolling my life away on Instagram, Snapchat, and YouTube. I was also looking for scholarships, grants, or other types of funding ahead of the fall term that would begin the following month. I still went to church on Sundays but didn't go out for walks as much anymore. It slowly became a sad experience to go out only to watch happy people have fun doing happy things in a beautiful and lively city. And although that didn't change anything substantially, my roommates had also already moved out.

Money was getting tighter and saving harder. With everything my mom had to pay for and other people she was taking care of, my allowance was shrinking, but I obviously did not complain. Most of my money was now going into skincare products. My skin condition had gotten worse, and switching up products every couple of weeks when I saw no improvement certainly did not help. My self-confidence took a hit. I didn't take pictures of myself and didn't show my face on video calls anymore. Not even for my boyfriend Lucas. Taking selfies had become a tedious task I didn't want to force myself to perform. Olivia was probably the only friend who video-called me almost as much as Lucas, and even to her, it became hard to show my face.

I wasn't feeling well either. A chaos of anxious thoughts about how I was going to remain in the U.S. and where I'd go to school kept me up at night. My situation felt like a mountain had dropped on my head, and nothing I did to push it off was working. There was also this pain in my left shoulder that I usually felt around exam time when I got really stressed, except it now extended to my neck, and I could never seem to find a comfortable position to sleep.

Most nights, I felt nauseous, dizzy, and my nose bled. I would run to the bathroom to throw up, clean up my nose and wipe my tears, then go back to bed to get one hour, maybe two, of sleep. I would then wait for the sun to rise and start the same cycle over and over again. I literally watched the sun rise and set before my eyes. Every. Single. Day. I chatted here and there with friends from back home, but the time difference didn't exactly play in our favor.

———— ⊂⠶⊃ ————

Before the month ended, on a day that I do not recall and did not log, I wrote to myself on the back of the last page of the August section of my planner. This was the earliest occurrence of me journaling post-childhood—I was around thirteen years old when I last wrote in a journal. I didn't write to myself again until about a year after that day in August 2017, at least not in an actual journal, because I didn't expect journaling to become a thing again for me.

It is not yet the end of the month as I am writing. This is just a note to myself and a reminder that I should stop worrying so much. Maybe there really is a link between my sudden acne and stress. I am going through a difficult time in my life. However, whatever happens, I should never forget that God has EVERYTHING under control, and prayers are ALWAYS answered. God's timing is just different but so much better. Danielle, I wish you strength, faith, and confidence for whatever is next and whatever your status is at the end. Peace and love. ♥

The status I was referring to was my immigration status. I still didn't have all the required documents to request a new I-20, and the deadline to complete my transfer was five days after the start of the school year. And even if I could attend DePaul, I didn't know what year I would transfer to. Finding all my previous course syllabi had proven harder than expected, and my transcripts and evaluation report were not enough. The school wanted a description of every single course I had taken to determine what courses were remaining for me to complete. Olivia and I had done the same undergraduate program back at the CUCA, so she helped me find course descriptions for some of the classes we had taken, but the program had evolved over the years. Some courses had been altered, added, or removed, so it was nearly impossible for me to retrieve all my syllabi since 2013; that is exactly what my dad was told when he went to my previous school.

I'd been looking for cheaper schools too, but the deadline to apply for the fall term had already passed almost everywhere. I'd found a graduate program that was going to start in October and was still accepting applications, but there was still an issue with the cost of attendance and getting an I-20. The good thing that came out of applying to that program was the school had requested another transcript evaluation report, since the provider I'd used for my DePaul applications was not one of their partners. So, despite the frustration of having to pay about $300 for my transcripts to be re-evaluated, I submitted them to another evaluation service. This time, the report recognized my three-year bachelor's degree as equivalent to a U.S. four-year bachelor's degree.

The reason for this was that my high school diploma was equivalent to a U.S. high school diploma, plus one year of undergraduate general studies. This may have had something to do with the courses I had taken in high school, such as economics, accounting, business management, and law. I guess sticking to my decision to study business in high school was paying off. In any case, it was a relief to know that I wouldn't have to start over if I were to join that program. Unfortunately, unlike the process at DePaul, the I-20 application was an integral part of the overall admission process at that school. This meant that even if I met all the other requirements, if I couldn't receive an I-20, I would not have been admitted to that school. And I wasn't.

———————⟶⟵———————

I had gone to orientation for transfer students at DePaul earlier in August. I'd met with my academic advisor, who helped me register for the only two classes I was eligible to take because they didn't have prerequisites. As I went from one session or workshop to another throughout that day, my heart was beating a little faster at all the things I was seeing and hearing. I kept thinking to myself that DePaul was definitely my dream school. From academics to extra-curricular activities to networking opportunities and career outlook after graduation, it just had it all. And it was located in downtown Chicago. I mean … you can't beat that. I attended a session with the career center, during which I learned more about upcoming events and the types of companies that recruited directly from DePaul. When I heard that one of them was Deloitte, my dream firm, and that it would host events on campus as well, I knew I didn't want to go to another school. Sure, DePaul wasn't the only school Deloitte recruited from, but it was the only one I'd been admitted to.

Please, God, help me go to this school. It's my dream.

CHAPTER 4:

DRAW CLOSE

" I don't think it's a good idea," Olivia said on the other end of the phone while I was getting ready. She thought it was going to hurt me more to go to school, knowing I would have to drop all my classes just a few days later because I couldn't prove my level of education. She didn't know I couldn't afford to go to DePaul. By then, my mom had confirmed she wouldn't be able to pay the tuition fees, but this was not information I felt comfortable sharing just yet.

I continued to get ready for my first day of classes on the morning of September 7th, ignoring Olivia's speech on the other end of the line. She definitely had a point, and I appreciated her worrying about me just like I appreciated her being there for me, but I also needed to get out of my room more often and see what it was like to attend classes other than ESL.

I moved my full-length mirror from the corner between my desk and my bedroom window, then leaned it against the window for better lighting. And for the first time in months, I lined my brows, and applied eyeliner and some lipstick. Olivia had to go, and I did too, but before I left, I stared at my reflection for a few minutes. My eyes were still swollen from the tears I had cried the night before, thinking about my future, wondering if I would make it to the other side, and where that other side was. I wasn't wearing foundation, so my dark spots and acne were visible. However, I liked the way my turquoise sweater looked tucked into skinny jeans. My hair looked good too, still styled from my trip to the hair salon three days earlier. I wished I'd done my nails too, but I had to save money, especially since my friend Sarah was going to visit soon.

I took a step back, turned around, then back around. I grabbed my phone to take some pictures. *I don't look that bad.* Before I knew it, tears were rolling down my cheeks in disagreement with that statement. I quickly dabbed my cheeks with the back of my hand, packed my stuff in my favorite Aldo bag, and off to school I went.

The day had gone well. I even made a friend, who I wasn't going to see again because that was my first and last class with her. I wasn't going to do the assignment either because there was no point. Instead, back at my room, I started preparing my application for this master of business administration (MBA) program I'd recently come across. The next available program start date was January 2018. It was still far out, but I thought I'd still try.

The MBA program was at Roosevelt University, a school I often walked by, just a couple of blocks from DePaul's downtown campus. The school didn't offer a master's in management, and because I'd been told that MBA degrees were for experienced professionals, I wasn't sure I would be accepted into the program. Despite having limited work experience with just one internship, I still wanted to try. Though less than DePaul, Roosevelt was still expensive, and I didn't know where I'd find the money and proof of funds to apply for an

I-20. But at that point, I didn't have anything to lose but the $100 application fee. At least I now had a new transcript evaluation report stating my bachelor's degree was "valid." I also took advantage of my admission to DePaul to get help with resume writing from the career center, so my resume looked much better than when I applied to the Kellstadt Graduate School of Business.

Because of all the doubt about whether I would get in or not, I applied without telling anyone. I didn't want to keep hearing that my chances were small because I had no full-time work experience. I didn't want to be rejected again and have to tell my mom or anyone else about it. If it didn't work out, at least no one else would know.

———— ⌀ ————

A few days later, I started thinking about what Sarah and I would do once she came over. I barely knew what there was to do in Chicago because I hardly ever went out. I eventually decided I'd just take her to the movies and see what she wanted to do once she was in the city. I wanted her to have a good time, but I also hoped that spending time with her was going to fix my acne.

Sarah and I had known each other since high school, after which she went to university in Germany. We kept in touch, though we didn't speak or text very often. She was visiting her family in another city and since I was also in the U.S., she thought she'd come say hi.

I took the train to the O'Hare International Airport on the afternoon of Thursday, September 14th to pick her up and took her back the following Sunday morning.

We didn't talk much that Sunday morning, and I hadn't realized it was my fault.

"Is everything okay?" she asked, concerned and looking up from her suitcase. "You're so quiet today."

"Oh, am I? So sorry! I'm usually very quiet when I wake up, but everything is fine, don't worry." I smiled and handed her a folded T-shirt.

That was such a bad lie. We'd spent the past three days together, so she'd seen me in the morning. That's just all I had for not having to tell her that the time we'd spent together was the happiest of the year for me. That for three nights in a row, I'd stayed up not because I was worried but because we were chatting and laughing. That watching *Girls Trip* and having Oreo milkshakes at the AMC Dine-in Theatre was my first time going to the movies with a friend in Chicago. That I was going to miss our nightly walks downtown. That I was sorry we hadn't gone to a bar or a club like she wanted because I didn't know much about the city's nightlife. That I was thankful she didn't comment on my skin before I told her I had acne. And that once she was gone, I was scared to go back to my empty room and to the reality of my situation she unknowingly helped me escape from. So, I lied and hoped she believed me.

———⬤———

I dropped my classes on September 18th, then emailed my International Student Service (ISS) advisor, informing her I wouldn't attend DePaul anymore, giving no specific reason. She replied two days later.

From: *International Student Services (ISS) Advisor*

To: *Me*

Subject: RE: *Update*

Date and Time: *9/20/2017 at 3:53 p.m.*

Hi Danielle,

Thank you for your email. I'm sorry to hear you will not be continuing your studies at DePaul. Can you please tell us if you have plans to study at another U.S. school or plans to leave the country soon? Our SEVIS reporting deadline is quickly approaching, so we'll either need to report that you did not enroll, which would be a negative SEVIS termination, or report that you've left the country, which would be a positive termination.

If you would like to transfer your SEVIS immigration record to another U.S. school, please provide me with a copy of your admission letter and a complete "intent to transfer" form. If your new school requires us to complete a transfer verification form, please provide me with this form as well. You may drop these forms off at the International Student Services front desk or scan and email them to my attention no later than 4:00 p.m. on Monday, October 2, 2017.

If you plan to leave the U.S., or if you already left the country, please provide us with proof of your departure, including a departure form along with your flight itinerary showing the date you will leave or already left the U.S.

I want to help you avoid problems with your non-immigrant status and your timely response/action is needed. Failure to maintain lawful student status

> **may lead to serious immigration-related problems,**
> **including detention and removal.**
> *Thank you,*
> *ISS Advisor*

The Student and Exchange Visitor Information System (SEVIS) is one that stores, tracks, and monitors international students' information in the U.S. When an I-20 is issued, it comes with a fixed and unique SEVIS ID. As an international student, I could only have one SEVIS number (and file), which explains the need to transfer immigration records when changing academic programs.

The SEVIS system was managed by the Student and Exchange Visitor Program (SEVP), which acted as a bridge between the U.S. government and schools. So, earlier when I stated that only government-approved schools could issue I-20s and enroll international students, I meant SEVP-approved institutions.

How did this happen? Why is this happening to me? Why am I going through this? Why isn't God listening to my prayers? He knows how much I wanted to study in the U.S. and how much I want to go to school. Why did He make me come all the way here only to experience this?

This couldn't possibly still be the challenge I'd been asking for. This must have been punishment for something I'd done before. Maybe going to the U.S. was a mistake. Maybe I should have stayed home and completed my master's there. Had I known all this was going to happen, I wouldn't have left.

My sight was still blurred by tears when I replied to the advisor's email.

> *From:* Me
> *To:* ISS Advisor
> *Subject:* RE: Update
> *Date and Time:* 9/20/2017 at 4:10 p.m.
> Hello ISS Advisor,
> Thank you for your e-mail. I do have plans to leave the U.S. soon, but I haven't booked my flight yet. As soon as I do, I will send you the itinerary, along with the departure form.
> Thank you,
> Danielle

I didn't know what else to say. My time in the U.S. was over, and I needed to come to terms with that. How was I going to find a way to stay in Chicago in just ten days? What school was I going to apply to that was not already in session and would get back to me soon enough to still have time to process my I-20 transfer request? And, most importantly, what school was I going to find that did not cost an arm and a leg? I hadn't heard from Roosevelt yet, and even if I had, and the decision was positive, the January 2018 start date was too far away, and the school was too expensive to get a new I-20 in time.

I texted my mom later that day to let her know we would need to prepare for my return home, and I explained why. She asked if there wasn't some kind of professional certificate I could do to buy me some time until I found something more permanent. The answer was no. I had previously researched these types of programs and although their affordability made them appealing, the ones I'd found were not offered by SEVP-approved schools. She told me not to lose hope and that we would figure something out once I got home.

I was sitting on the bottom edge of my bed, with my head against the wall, gazing out the window and thinking about what I would do once I got home. I'd, for sure, hide from everyone because of how my skin looked, but I guess it wouldn't hurt to see my family again. I tried to convince myself that this wasn't the end of the world, but it didn't seem like God was on my side. *I'm so sorry for all the bad things I did for which You are now punishing me.* It didn't seem like He was happy with me; it all felt like punishment. I must have done something wrong in the past. I didn't know exactly what it was, but I knew I was now paying for it.

About an hour went by before I got up to grab the decorative wooden sign on my windowsill; I'd gotten it for $3 at Target the first time I went shopping there. It was a 3D triangle, approximately the size of a pear, made with a type of wood I don't know. Its sides were painted with a peachy-orange color and on the front, the words **DREAMS come TRUE** were written with gold foiling. The word **TRUE** was in all caps with pink, turquoise, yellow, and the peachy-orange colors painted in the hollows of the letters. A white-and-turquoise feather was painted at the peak of the triangle, looking like it was falling from the sky.

The wooden sign itself was not very pretty, to be quite frank. I bought it mainly because of the quote and because my favorite color is turquoise. I was so excited to finally be in Chicago and when I saw this little thing at the store, I had to get it as a reminder that my dream of studying and living in the U.S. had finally come true; that my dream career would also become a reality.

I looked at the sign for a few seconds and half-smiled before putting it back down. *Maybe they don't.*

———— ⬥⟋⟍ ————

The next day, I texted Naomi to let her know I would soon leave the U.S. She already had a basic idea of my situation at that point, but I didn't talk about it all that much. She knew I hadn't been admitted to grad school and instead to an undergrad program, but she didn't know about my deadlines and the specifics around my status. No one did, really.

When I told her everything, she was convinced I wouldn't have come all the way to the U.S. just to take ESL classes and leave right after. As much as I wanted to believe her, I just didn't see how a solution would emerge in less than two weeks. Plus, I had started looking for programs in other countries, and I was fine leaving the U.S., as long as I came back. She suggested we start looking at language programs again as they were more affordable, easier to get into and, most importantly, they were SEVP-approved.

I wasn't exactly thrilled with the idea of taking additional ESL classes, considering my recent intensive program at ELA and my already excellent TOEFL score. I felt like that money could be put to better use. And to be honest, I wanted to start "real school" already and stop feeling like I was running behind compared to my peers. It'd already been a year since my last "real class," so doing yet another ESL program would only delay me further.

I didn't have a better idea and knew this was a temporary fix, so I spent the weekend scouring the Internet. I was trying to find an ESL program that would process my application and issue me a new I-20 in time for my DePaul ISS advisor.

———— ⚬═══⚬ ————

On September 26th, six days before my deadline, I was admitted to Berlitz, a language center in the Loop. It was smaller than DePaul's ELA and had fewer enrollments at the time. I was even going to be the only student in my class for my level. This had nothing to do with my proficiency level; the center just didn't have many students enrolled. I wasn't going to study there for longer than one term. The fees for my level were a little under $3,000 for the entire ten weeks, about $500 less than ELA.

The location of the center and the cost of the program worked out well for my mom, so I started preparing the paperwork for my SEVIS transfer application and I-20 request. I first needed to provide Berlitz with the transfer form signed by my ISS advisor before they could give me an admission letter. That is because my ability to attend the program was contingent on DePaul's confirmation of my eligibility to transfer. However, I needed to show an admission letter to my ISS advisor before she could release my SEVIS record and sign the transfer form. That was another tricky and stressful situation, and I spent the week leading up to my October 2nd deadline going back and forth between Berlitz and DePaul. At last, my ISS advisor agreed to sign the form, but Berlitz had to send her my admission letter directly for my SEVIS record to be transferred.

When I woke up on the morning of October 2nd, and very much like every day before, I checked my email to see if Berlitz had finally sent my admission letter to DePaul. They hadn't. I got out of bed to take a shower and get ready to go nowhere.

Why is this happening? Why isn't God listening to me? What's the point of all of this? I was bathing in sorrow, lathering up the soap with my tears. I don't know how long I stayed in the shower. Once I came out to put my clothes on, I checked my phone again to see if there were any updates. Twelve-fifty-two p.m., still nothing. *That's it for me.* My eyes roamed the room as if they were seeing it for the first time, blurred behind the tears. *I should have started packing over the weekend when I realized my transfer was still incomplete.* The tears spilled over my face when I realized I had less than three hours to leave.

Though I didn't have that many things to pack, I knew I wasn't going to manage to vacate the apartment and leave the country by 3 p.m. That's if I even had a flight ticket already, which I didn't. The thought of having to rush my mom to get me a ticket in the next few minutes broke me down even more. I began packing but the pounding in my head, the dizziness, and the nausea made it impossible to continue. I needed to lie down. I did not find the courage to tell my mom what was going on, so I just lay down on my bed, unsure what was going to happen next.

The vibration of my phone pulled me out of my thoughts a few moments later. It was a Gmail notification. I thought it could be *the* email, but I wasn't a hundred percent sure.

From: Berlitz Learning Center Manager
To: ISS Advisor
Cc: Me
Subject: Admission Letter — Danielle Ndende
Date and Time: 10/02/2017 at 3:24 p.m.
Dear ISS Advisor,
Thank you for sending me the signed transfer form. As requested, I am attaching the acceptance letter so you can transfer Danielle's SEVIS record to us. Please let me know if you have any questions.
Regards,
Berlitz Learning Center Manager

I let out a heavy sigh of relief and sent a thank-you email to the manager. That was close. Too close. About an hour later, as I was putting my stuff back in place, my ISS advisor emailed me.

From: *ISS Advisor*

To: *Me*

Subject: *SEVIS transfer*

Date and Time: *10/02/2017 at 4:31 p.m.*

Hi Danielle,

I received your admission letter from the new school. However, the SEVIS government database will not allow me to transfer your (electronic) SEVIS record because DePaul did not issue you a new internal "transfer" I-20 form based on your earlier transfer request. And we were not able to generate this I-20 because you did not submit the supporting documentation to DePaul. I will have to call the SEVIS help desk to find out what we can do in this situation and will keep you posted.

Best,

ISS Advisor

I did not reply to her email because I did not know what to say. And quite frankly, I didn't fully understand what the implication of her email was. I knew this wasn't good news but wasn't sure how bad it was.

The week went on, and my stress level shot up to new heights while my self-confidence dropped to new lows because of my acne and dark spots. My shoulder pain never went away, and I was still nauseous at night. However, the nose bleedings weren't as frequent anymore.

I'd resolved not to talk about my late-night sickness anymore because when I did, people asked if I was pregnant. Nothing wrong with being pregnant, of course; I just wasn't. It took a lot of courage to finally give a truthful answer when people asked how I was doing, so when I opened up and their first reaction was to ask if I was pregnant, I decided to go back to answering "Great!" every time someone would ask how I was doing.

The question may have been warranted, but it wasn't what I needed to hear, especially since there was no way I could have been pregnant. I wasn't seeing anyone. Literally. I spent my days and nights alone in my bedroom and barely went out for walks anymore. And I didn't qualify for miraculous conception either.

My relationship with Lucas had actually been deteriorating. By October, we had already broken up twice but still got back together, though it honestly did not do any good to either of us. I had changed. We both had, and so had our relationship. With my lower self-confidence, I constantly worried that he would leave me for a girl with no pimples, though I didn't specifically tell him that. We barely saw each other since I didn't pick up video calls or take pictures of myself anymore. I had also become *very* irritable—the slightest things would make me cry. Then I started struggling with something I had never dealt with before and never thought I would: anger. There were times when I would fly into a rage during an argument, yelling at my phone before breaking down into tears. My anger issues were episodic and lasted from July to August, long enough to create damage and make me want to take a step back to figure myself out. Lucas often pointed out how my situation was affecting me. I knew I wasn't myself anymore but because I had always been in control of my emotions and pretty much everything else in my life, I refused to admit the obvious. So no, I was not pregnant.

The next time my ISS advisor emailed me, she had good news.

> **From:** *ISS Advisor*
> **To:** *Me*
> **Subject:** *RE: SEVIS transfer*
> **Date and Time:** *10/06/2017 at 4:32 p.m.*
> *Hi Danielle,*
> *The SEVIS help desk just approved the cancellation of your earlier transfer, allowing us to transfer your SEVIS record out to Berlitz Languages, Inc. – Chicago. Please report to your new school as soon as possible to obtain your new SEVIS I-20 form and to enroll in classes. Please be reminded that you'll need to start classes at Berlitz Languages, Inc. – Chicago within five months of your last date of full-time enrollment at DePaul, or the next available term at Berlitz Languages, Inc. – Chicago, whichever comes earlier. Good luck in your future endeavors!*
> *Best wishes,*
> *ISS Advisor*

My last date of full-time enrollment at DePaul was in September and my program at Berlitz was set to begin on October 11th, so I was good. I thanked the advisor and hoped in my heart that this time was real, and that nothing was going to ruin it. I didn't want any more heartbreaks. I gathered, then submitted the required documents when I applied for my new I-20, which would be ready for pick-up at the start of my classes. I informed my mom and sister and thanked them for their support. They were both relieved and happy for me, as was I. What an emotional roller coaster the past four months had been!

My I-20 was issued for the duration of the program—from October 11th to December 29th. I had class every day from 8 a.m. to about 3 p.m. and being the only student for the entire duration of the program didn't make for a very fun experience. I learned new things and was glad I could practice speaking English with native speakers, but a lot of the study material was review.

I wanted to work to help support myself while I was in the program, but as an international student only doing language classes, I wasn't eligible to work. I still felt lonely but at least I had a reason to get out of my room every day for two months.

Money was still tight, and I was running out of the savings I had accumulated over my university years at the CUCA, but I have to admit I could have done a better job of managing what I had. The thing is, I was trying to quench my many frustrations with shopping. I bought clothes and shoes for no reason. Or maybe not for no reason: I was hoping to soon have a social life. I bought the clothes and shoes and tried them on in my room, creating different outfits for different occasions. But my excitement quickly faded when the reality of having nowhere to go and no one to go there with kicked in. Sometimes I returned the items to the stores; most times, I didn't.

I've always loved walking and would take walking over public transit any day, as long as the weather is nice, but there were times when I walked to Berlitz not because I wanted to, but because I'd spent all my money on clothes and couldn't afford transit passes anymore. It was only toward the end of November that I decided to stop wasting my money on clothes. I didn't want to keep spending what I had on things that only made me temporarily happy. I especially needed to save for when my mom was going to come visit in December. I wanted to buy her Christmas and welcome gifts and take her out to eat at least once.

———— ⌾ ————

Later in November, on a day I do not recall, my relationship with Lucas officially ended. *Officially* because it'd been over on my end for a while, but I held onto it. On that day, I finally acted on a thought I'd been mulling over for approximately three months. My hesitation came from not wanting to hurt or lose him, and from wanting to prove to everyone–including myself–that we could make our long-distance relationship work. When I left home, so many people bet that our relationship would not last much longer. I wanted to prove them wrong so bad that I stayed longer than I needed to in the relationship. But with everything I'd gone through since coming to the U.S., I felt like I was losing myself.

While I still loved Lucas and was thankful for his support throughout the summer, I was no longer happy, and I knew he wasn't either. We tried to stay together but it didn't work out. He also had his own faults and shortcomings. Other things intensified my desire to leave, but I mostly needed time, space, and, ironically, I needed to be alone. I wanted to refocus, figure myself out, and discover or rediscover who I really was.

I can't say things got better after our breakup, at least not right away. When I didn't cry because I felt lonely or because of my skin, I cried because I was heartbroken and didn't seem to make myself understood. People–including Lucas–did not believe me when I said we'd broken up because I needed to work on myself.

"Why don't you just say you found someone else? You don't have to lie." "You must have gotten tired of him." "He must have cheated on you. And if not, why did you leave him? Don't you know how hard it was to find a good one?" "Who else do you think is going to put up with all your requirements?" "Did you even think about him?" "You're going to end up alone if you keep leaving people who love you." "He should have never stayed with you in the first place." "What more space do you need when you're already thousands of miles away?" "What kind of self-work do you need that requires you to be single?" "How can you say you still love him and yet break up with him?"

These are some of the comments I received day after day and unfortunately, back then, people's opinion on certain aspects of my life still mattered a whole lot to me. Not enough to make me doubt my decision or want to get back with Lucas, but enough to make me doubt myself and believe that I was selfish and mean, and that maybe I wouldn't find someone else.

God, I hope You too are not mad at me. I hope You understand my decision and won't punish me for it. I didn't mean to hurt him; I just haven't been feeling well. Please don't be mad. Please allow him to be happy. Please, God, understand and don't punish me.

I made this little prayer one day, laying in my bed, replaying people's comments in my head and crying my eyes out. I felt so guilty that I thought God was also mad at me. Back then, I wrongfully believed He would punish me for every single thing I did not do right, just like I believed challenges were His way of punishing me.

When the time difference didn't make it too difficult, my friend George stayed up with me on the phone for a few hours to help fill the new void that had been created from not speaking with Lucas as much anymore. He helped me feel better about my decision and reminded me it was okay to take time for myself, regardless of what anyone thought.

George and I had been friends since high school, after which he went to study in Switzerland. We did not speak all the time but stayed very close friends. And once I told him what was going on with Lucas, he became more present. He did not know about the other things I was going through. I'd only vaguely mentioned having to change schools. I felt uncomfortable admitting to him that I was having money issues and couldn't afford to pay for school. So, we talked about everything but school.

———————⌀———————

Part of working on myself was getting closer to God and knowing Him better. I'd been thinking about reading the Bible for months, but I didn't have one, and I kept putting off buying it.

Back in July, amid what was going on with DePaul, Lucas told me about a verse that stuck with me. One day we were on the phone, and I was telling him how lost I was feeling. He told me to pray about my situation, to forget about it but to believe God would take care of it. He couldn't recall the exact verse, but he was certain it was in Mark. So, I Googled his explanation and found this:

"Therefore I tell you, whatever you ask for in prayer, believe that you have received it, and it will be yours." (Mark 11:24)

Lucas confirmed it was the one. We didn't talk much about God, so I was quite surprised when he mentioned this. But most importantly, I was intrigued and curious to know what else I could find in that book—I had no idea there was practical advice in the Bible. But if I'm being honest, this verse didn't really work for me; however, it was a magnet that attracted me to many others that did.

I wasn't as close to God as I thought I was. I attended Catholic schools all my education (including my stint at DePaul), grew up in a pretty religious family, but didn't know much about the Bible. I read parts of it multiple times when I was forced to do so at home or in school, but I retained very little. I only knew "basic" and popular verses. I prayed in the morning, before eating, and at night. I went to confession at least once a year for Easter (though that changed in college), went to church every Sunday and Catholic feast day. I prayed for my family and friends, for the people around me and for the less fortunate. I prayed to pass my exams and to be granted visas for travel. I tried following the Ten Commandments and everything else I was taught about God. But I purposely kept Him at a distance, not so much because I didn't think I needed Him, but because I believed more important issues in mine or others' lives needed His attention. I called on Him for what I deemed important, and I took care of the rest. Admittedly, I enjoyed the feeling of being in control. Keeping God at a distance ensured that I stayed in the comfort zone where everything was under my control and I could predict most outcomes because *I* was the orchestrator of my life.

Since I did not know how or where to buy a Bible, I reached out to Father Andrew, the priest who picked me up at the airport at my father's request when I arrived in Chicago.

Danielle: Hello Father, how are you?

Father Andrew: Hey Danielle. I am good. How are you?

Danielle: Good too, thanks! I am writing because I need your help with something. Don't worry, it's nothing too complicated or time-consuming.

Father Andrew: Sure!

Danielle: I'd like to buy a Bible, but I don't really know where to go. I don't want to order one online because I am afraid it's not going to be a "good" version, and the church I go to doesn't have a shop. So, I figured I would ask you.

> **Father Andrew:** I perfectly understand. Maybe one of these days we can go to a Catholic bookstore?
>
> **Danielle:** Sounds good, thanks!

He picked me up one day, and we went to the bookstore to get my Bible. On our way there, he was curious to know why I wanted to buy a Bible. Without going into the details, I mentioned not being able to attend DePaul, feeling lost and overall wondering what was in the Bible. He liked my little story and decided to gift me the Bible once we got to the store.

On our way back, I was staring and smiling at my new Bible on my lap. It was a pocket-size book with a hard but flexible white faux-leather cover. Along that cover, a cross was imprinted, and the words "New American Bible" were written with silver foiling across the horizontal bar. There was the usual publishing information on the side, while the back only had the ISBN number. It was an unsurprisingly thick book, and all the thin and flimsy pages were coated with the same silver foiling. *I love my new Bible.* It was definitely cuter than the ones I was used to, with their black or brown covers that didn't make me want to open them. This one felt like my first Bible, but it wasn't.

The book was so thick and the pages so thin and the font size so tiny.

"So, how do I read this?" I asked Father Andrew, as if the words had escaped my mouth without my permission and unsure this was a valid question.

He smiled, as if he'd been expecting that question.

"Start with the New Testament and read a chapter every day, then let the Holy Spirit guide you forward."

That is almost exactly what I did.

CHAPTER 5:

TURNING THE PAGE

Why isn't she out yet? I glanced at my watch: 2:48 p.m. My mom's flight had landed at 2:30 p.m., yet she was nowhere to be found. I paced up and down O'Hare Airport's terminal 3, impatiently waiting. After what felt like an eternity but was probably a couple more minutes, I saw and recognized my mom from the back. She was fixing her grey beanie, then zipped up her beige jacket, getting ready to tackle the two degrees Celsius weather of December 3rd. She was probably less than five meters away from where I was standing—too long a distance to walk. I ran toward her, barely avoiding anyone or anything on my way.

"Ming Mang Moung!" I screamed when I jumped and wrapped my arms around my mom, slightly tipping her over. When she turned around, her eyebrows were raised to the top of her forehead, her eyes wide open. After a moment of confusion, she hugged me back and squeezed me in her arms. When she let me go, her eyebrows went all the way down and now creased her forehead.

"What happened to your face? What's with all the pimples?" she asked. She was now holding me at arm's length.

Tears welled up in my eyes and filled my throat. My nose started prickling.

"I don't know; it just happened," I blurted, refusing to let the tears fall.

We walked out of the airport, and I went back into her arms. She squeezed again. I had missed her so much. I had been in the U.S. for less than a year, yet it felt like I hadn't seen her in a decade. We took a ton of pictures, then headed home.

———————— ⊂═══⊃ ————————

My mom spent two weeks in the U.S. The first with me in Chicago and the second with Naomi in New York City. I showed her around the places I knew, and we had a great time. We went shopping downtown and took pictures at the Bean. We walked along Michigan Avenue and the Chicago River, looking at and taking pictures of the dazzling lights. We also took pictures everywhere we saw a Christmas tree. We went to the movies and ate a lot of good and not-so-good things. Whether we cooked at my apartment or ate out, we sent pictures in our WhatsApp family group chat to make everyone jealous, especially my little sister Emma. We spent almost an entire night at the Lincoln Park Zoo, watching the ZooLights Christmas show.

While my mom was in New York City, I stayed in Chicago to take my final exams at Berlitz. They marked the end of the program, thus the expiration of my I-20. It'd been issued until the end of December, which was still three weeks out, but the program end date on the I-20 is not really its expiration date. It is the day that the program *effectively* ends that represents the I-20 expiration date.

In my case, even though I still had three weeks left on my I-20, it expired the day I took my last exam, on December 12th. From there, I had the usual sixty-day grace period to either enroll in a new program, change immigration status, or leave the country.

So, there I was again, after my exams, unsure what was going to happen next. At that point, Roosevelt had gotten back to me with the great news of my admission to the two-year MBA program that would start in January 2018. I'd shared the news with my mom, but she wasn't sure she would be able to afford the $25,000 annual tuition fees. Combined with living and other expenses, we would have to show proof of at least $40,000 for the first year of the program for my new I-20 to be approved.

My mom's flight back home departed from Chicago, so I waited until she returned to talk about next steps for me.

I had looked for scholarships, loans, and other ways to subsidize the cost of attendance but found nothing I was eligible for. For scholarships, the application deadlines had either already passed, or I needed to already be enrolled in a program, or my ineligibility came from not being a U.S. citizen or Green Card holder. The same was true for loans. International students were not eligible for government loans at all, and private loans required guarantors who fulfilled almost the same financial requirements as those of the I-20.

Roosevelt University, like most universities, also had graduate assistantship programs. These programs allowed grad students to work with professors in exchange for a monthly stipend and money toward tuition. One requirement for the position was to have a grade point average, or GPA, of at least 3.5. GPA scales varied among institutions, but most universities—including Roosevelt—converted letter grades to a 4.0 GPA scale.

I had a 3.2 GPA but applied anyway. However, I was unsuccessful.

I looked everywhere, tried everything I found. I prayed. I hoped. I believed.

Nothing happened.

The day before my mom left, we went out to run a few errands, and I helped her pack once we got home. I went back and forth between the living room and my bedroom where she was, bringing her random stuff and looking for nothing other than the courage to bring up the topic. *Okay, ask her now.* I repeated that to myself eighteen million, four hundred and seventy-six thousand, nine hundred and thirty-two times. No kidding, I counted. I could never find the right moment, just like I couldn't find the right moment the whole week we were together. But that day was my last chance, so I eventually made the jump.

"So … about Roosevelt … will you still be able to help me with my I-20 paperwork?" My voice was a whisper, and I was surprised she heard it.

My mom raised her eyebrows and pressed her lips together, dimples digging holes into her cheeks. *I know that face.*

"Well … I don't think so." She shook her head slowly, then carried on. "Things are a bit complicated right now. I was going to suggest you try training schools; I know they're usually cheaper. Maybe you can do that for a while before going back to school for your master's?" She sounded optimistic.

"I looked into that before going to Berlitz but like I told you, these types of schools are not usually authorized to issue I-20s to international students."

"Yeah, you did tell me that. How about a job? Just something to do in the meantime?" she asked.

"Yeah … I tried that too, but I'm not yet eligible to work," I responded, feeling bad that she was going to feel the same frustration I felt from facing all these roadblocks.

She sighed and shrugged. "I don't know what to do."

My heart broke, and my nose started prickling. Not because there didn't seem to be a solution, but because I had never seen my mom this vulnerable. I had never heard her openly say she could not afford something. Sure, there were times when she didn't get me certain things because they were too expensive, but those things were not essential. There were other things she didn't buy or pay for, not so much because she couldn't afford them, but because she didn't think they were worth the money. And sure, she couldn't afford DePaul either, but I didn't hear it. I didn't *see* her say it. I just understood what she meant by "That's very expensive" or "Let's find something cheaper."

I didn't know what else to say, and I certainly wasn't going to let my tears fall.

"That's okay, no big deal. I'll keep looking." I smiled and changed subjects.

———— ⚬⚬⚬ ————

The next day, before her departure, I went out alone to buy Christmas gifts for my little sister Emma and my oldest niece Nora. On my way to Water Tower Place, I couldn't stop thinking about that conversation with my mom. Once more, I had no idea how I was going to get out of the situation I was in. *Oh, God, why is all this happening? What does all this mean?* I thought about my two older brothers and two older sisters, and how they were all able to get master's degrees, most of them abroad. I wondered if they had gone through difficult times as well. I thought about my friends and peers. Most were in school, or working, or both. *I just want to go to school like everyone.* I wondered how I was going to tell people I wasn't going to school anymore if they asked me. I wondered if God heard my prayers. I had been praying more and reading my Bible every morning; why wasn't He doing something? If not for me, at least for my mom? *What do I need to do to make You listen?*

------⊂⫸⊃------

My mom left a few days before Christmas. Father Andrew picked us up from my place and helped drop her off at the airport. I don't usually cry in public, or at least I try not to, but there's just something about airports and saying goodbye that always gets me.

On our way back, I couldn't help it either. As much as I tried holding them back, tears just kept spilling over my cheeks. I turned my face away to look through the window, quietly crying and hoping Father Andrew would not hear. But my sniffing was the only sound in the car. I was crying because I was going to miss my mom. I was crying because I felt guilty for putting her in a situation where she couldn't afford to send me to school, but still had to pay for my rent every month while Emma was also going to start university soon. I was crying because I was once more in my grace period with no visibility of what was ahead, and aware that doing another language program was no longer an option. I was crying because I was going to spend Christmas alone. I had gone to New York for Thanksgiving weekend in November and had to save money for the last few days of December until my mom sent me rent money again. Whenever she did, she always added a buffer as my allowance.

"Are you gonna be OK?" Father Andrew asked, as he pulled up across the street on South Peoria, after what seemed like a five-hour drive but really was a forty-minute one. I hadn't said a word the entire time.

"Yes! Don't worry. I am just not very good at goodbyes." I smiled. My eyes and cheeks had already dried. "Thank you so much for all your help, Father." I unfastened my seatbelt and grabbed my purse. "Have a great rest of your day and Happy Holidays! Bye!" I stepped out of the car and ran across the street.

The last week of December was when temperatures started dropping below 0°C, and I mean double digits below. The coldest I'd experienced thus far was -2°C in March when it snowed on my birthday. Back in August, three other girls had moved into the apartment. Unlike the previous three, who were all American, these were all international students: two from China and one from Russia. They all went to the University of Illinois at Chicago (UIC), just a few minutes walking distance from our apartment complex.

My roommates and I had been complaining to management about the defective heating system in our apartment, but they did nothing about it. Utilities were split evenly among the four of us every month and included electricity, heating, gas, trash removal, and Wi-Fi. For the month of November—when we turned on heating for the first time—we each had to pay more than $200 in utilities. That amount was about $100 higher than usual, which was outrageous on its own, but even more considering we'd barely felt any heat throughout that month.

From December forward, we decided to turn off the heat and keep it off because we didn't want to continue paying that much money for something that didn't work. But we were freezing. Literally. So much so that my roommates did not stay at our apartment anymore. On the coldest days and nights, they stayed at their friends' or boyfriends' places. I had neither, so I just bundled up in my warmest clothes and stayed in bed all day. If I had to get some water or cook something, I wrapped myself in a blanket and went to the kitchen.

That is exactly what I did on Christmas Day. After church, I went back home and decided to cook something nice for the occasion. I threw on a pair of leggings and a fleece sweater, then wrapped my warm gray blanket around my chest. I also put on the fuzzy socks my mom had gotten for me when she visited. I smiled at the thought of her pointing out that *all* the socks I had were too thin, and none were warm enough.

After eating, I stayed in the kitchen for about half an hour until the remaining air that was still warm from cooking completely diffused, then went back to my room.

I was the only one in the apartment because, you know, it was Christmas, and people celebrated with their families and friends. I called and texted mine, but that was about it. I spent the rest of the day looking at pictures my family sent in the group chat, watching other people's stories and pictures on WhatsApp, Snapchat, and Instagram, watching Vlogmas on YouTube, and wishing I had friends to celebrate with.

———⚬⟊⟊⟊⚬———

A week later, it was finally the end of the year. I had never wanted for a year to end as much as I did 2017. It'd been the hardest year of my life, each month bringing its troubles. Joyful moments were sprinkled here and there, and I was thankful for them, but I was ready to be *happy* more consistently.

Among the highlights of the year was the fact I was going to attend Roosevelt University. Yup! A few days after my mom left and before Christmas, my other older sister Sophie called me. She wanted to check on me, see how things were going and let me know she was planning to visit from China where she lived. She would come sometime in March during the Chinese New Year holiday.

Sophie and I texted but didn't call often. She didn't have all the details on my situation, either. I didn't hide them—I just didn't talk about them. She knew I had to change schools and study at Berlitz to buy myself some time; she knew I'd been admitted to Roosevelt, but she didn't know I couldn't afford to go and didn't know about my deadlines.

So, during our call, we talked, and we talked about everything. I told her about this payment plan that was available to international students at my school, but for which I did not qualify because I had no eligible guarantors. She volunteered to be added to my application in addition to my mom, and she herself was going to assist in paying for my first semester.

Classes were set to start on January 16, 2018, and the deadline to apply for an I-20 was a week before. With the holidays, that meant I only had a few days to put in my application for an I-20 and a SEVIS record transfer. Fortunately, after going through this process what felt like a million times, I already knew how it worked and already had most documents ready.

Once again, at the very last minute, something finally happened for me. I couldn't complain. This was my Christmas gift and my end-of-year miracle.

I felt good about the upcoming year. After what I'd been through in 2017, 2018 was bound to be my year. I was going to be a young graduate student. I was going to get a job and have enough money to pay for my rent and personal expenses, so my mom could breathe a little. I was going to get a membership at my favorite gym again. I was going to get facials every couple of weeks to get rid of my acne and dark spots. I was going to get my nails done every month with the friends I was going make in my program. I was going to explore Chicago and travel. I was going to celebrate my birthday and have a cake with candles. I was going to be *happy*.

About an hour before midnight on December 31st, I pulled out my planner to reflect on the year, write my goals for the new one ahead, and entrust them to God.

About 2017

<u>Low</u>: Probably the worst year of my life (I cried so much; I felt super lonely, had so many challenges; I doubted myself; I thought God did not hear my prayers, etc.).

<u>High</u>: But also the year I grew the most, became more aware of certain things, and matured. Number one thing I learned: TRUST GOD (wholeheartedly)! He does listen. "Do not mistake darkness for God's silence."

<u>High</u>: Some ups and the end (Sarah and Mom visited, got into Roosevelt, was able to extend my stay in the U.S., went to NYC to celebrate my first Thanksgiving).

<u>High</u>: I learned to be patient and thankful for what I have.

<u>Low</u>: Almost fell into depression (maybe I actually did...)

<u>Low</u>: Had skin issues.

<u>Low</u>: Wasn't able to save money.

<u>Low</u>: Broke up with Lucas.

<u>High</u>: Went to confession before Christmas for the first time in three years.

<u>High</u>: Started my journey to be closer to God.

<u>Low</u>: Wasn't able to move out.

<u>Low:</u> Was alone on my birthday and had no cake.

<u>Low:</u> Spent Christmas and New Year's alone.

<u>Low:</u> Didn't get a job.

<u>Low:</u> Didn't have friends.

2018 Goals and Wishes

- Get a summer internship at my dream firm (Deloitte).
- Move out and pay my own rent.
- Celebrate my birthday somewhere other than Chicago and have cake.
- Have Lenten goals and achieve them.
- Be an overall better person.
- Buy and customize an Erin Condren LifePlanner (once I get a job).
- Have a closer relationship with God.
- Exercise regularly and drink more water.
- Get a graduate assistantship for the fall semester.
- Go to Ed Sheeran's concert in October. 😊
- Get a job.
- Buy the Google Pixel 2 XL.

I finished writing everything a few minutes before midnight. I was sitting on the edge of my bed, facing the wooden cross I'd placed on the zenith of my bedroom—the gap between my closet wall and the ceiling. The priests at my middle school gifted these crosses to everyone for their first communion. I had done mine eight years earlier and kept my cross ever since.

My planner was open in my hands as I eagerly waited to cross over to 2018. As had been the case lately, I was alone in the apartment. Earlier that day, I'd gone down to the lobby to reload my laundry card. I didn't see or hear anyone, except for security, on my way down and back up. I thought I was alone in the building as well, until we were sixty seconds away from the New Year. People started counting down, and their voices seemed to be coming from the many bars around, but also from my building. They were all out of sync, but I could hear some more clearly than others.

"FIIIIVE...FOOOUUUR...THREEEE...TWOOOO... OOOOONE... HAPPY NEW YEAAAAARRR!!!"

As soon as I heard those last three words, unexpected streams of tears made their way down my cheeks; they came from the unknown depths of my soul. I slowly nodded, acknowledging all the painful moments I'd gone through. I closed my eyes, pressed my planner against my chest, and let the tears wash away the pain.

Now that I'd had my challenge, the one I'd been hoping and waiting for, things were finally going to get better.

I wiped my tears and prayed that God would help me achieve my goals. I prayed for my family, and I prayed for my friends. I texted everyone Happy New Year.

I was ready and excited for what 2018 had in store for me.

It is going to be my year.

CHAPTER 6:

THERAPY, MAYBE?

Earning an MBA degree from Roosevelt University entailed successfully completing twelve to sixteen courses, depending on whether the student had one or two concentrations. Considering I wanted to work in management consulting, I thought it only made sense to have a management concentration. Tuition fees depended on the total number of credits, so the higher the number of classes (and credits), the higher the fees. So, when I met with my academic advisor to register for my classes, I elected to do only one concentration. This was not only for financial reasons, but also because at the time, nothing else interested me. We also went over requirements to maintain good standing as a student in general, and an international student specifically.

With my one-concentration option, I was going to have to complete a total of twelve classes. I couldn't have more than two C grades throughout the program, could only repeat a course once, and could not repeat more than two courses. I wasn't planning on failing any of my classes or intentionally having bad grades, but that felt like I didn't have a lot of room for mistakes either.

Additionally, as was the case for all international students in every school, there were specific requirements related to my status and how to maintain it. I had to be enrolled full time every semester, which meant taking at least nine credits per semester. I couldn't take more than one online class during the spring (January to May) and fall (August to December) semesters. But in the summer (May to August), I could take as many online classes as I wished, because that semester was considered optional. I could not miss more than a certain number of days of classes, with or without a good reason, and my attendance could not drop below seventy percent.

I filled out the concentration declaration form to confirm management as my sole concentration and enrolled in four classes: three in-person core classes and one online class. As soon as my academic advisor told me it was an option, I let her know I wanted to take summer classes. My initial intention was to "catch up" on the time I thought I'd lost by doing additional language classes instead of going to "real" school.

I'd been feeling behind, struggling with the idea of graduating an entire year after everyone I knew. I thought starting a two-year (four-semester) program in January 2018 meant only graduating in December 2019. But as soon as I realized there was an opportunity to take summer classes and graduate in May 2019 instead, I jumped on it. As you will soon read, I later learned to let go of this idea of following a specific timeline to feel "on track."

⸺ ◦⧉◦ ⸺

My on-campus classes occurred every Tuesday, Wednesday, and Thursday, from 6:00 to 8:30 p.m. I was the only international student in two of them, which wasn't a bad thing but made me uncomfortable at times. I was going to turn twenty-two in March and was probably the youngest in all my classes. My classmates were all professionals who worked during the day and came to school at night. Especially at the beginning of the program, I used to think that I wouldn't do well because of my limited work experience, but I was wrong. The online class was self-paced with a deadline to complete it, which gave me some flexibility around when to take it and the amount of time to devote to it every day.

As my second Quantitative Analysis class was ending on the Wednesday of the second week of classes, I thought about my I-20 application and the fact that I'd still not received a response. Thinking about it had been keeping me up at night, and as much as I wanted to believe that everything was going to be fine, I was worried. It doesn't usually take longer than two weeks for an I-20 to be issued, so the fact that my application was still pending made me worry that something was wrong.

I packed my stuff and headed out of the classroom to go home. Walking down the hallway toward the elevator, I looked around, listening to people chat but not paying much attention to what they were saying. At the end of the hallway, there was a corner seating area with floor-to-ceiling windows. I walked all the way there and sat on the red chair against the light green wall. I was on the twelfth floor, looking out toward Lake Michigan, though the darkness of the night made it impossible to see, except for the glistening reflections of light on the waves. *I like this school. Please, don't let this go away like DePaul. I don't know what I'll do if I can't go here, especially since my grace period will be over soon. Please, make this work. Let me have my I-20.*

I don't know how long I stayed in the red chair.

———— ⚞⚟ ————

Just about a week later, I was home watching a movie when I got an email from the Office of International Students. My I-20 had been approved and was ready for pick up. "Yayyyy! Yayyyyy!! Yaayyyyy!!!" I jumped out of my bed with excitement and did a little *happy* dance in my room, jumping and going around in circles. I held up my phone to the cross. "Thank You, thank You, thank You so much!!" I couldn't stop smiling. I didn't immediately inform my family; I wanted to make sure everything looked good before saying anything. The email came a little bit after 4 p.m., which didn't give me enough time to get to the Office of International Students before it closed at 5 p.m. So, I decided to wait until the next day.

The next day, I got to school at around 4:30 p.m. and picked up my I-20 before class. When I got out of the office, I sat in the lobby and opened the envelope. *Name looks good; SEVIS ID number is there; designated school official's signature doesn't look great but it's fine; issue date looks good … Wait what?!* My mouth opened on its own when I looked at the expiration date. *December 2019?!* For some reason, I thought my I-20 would only be issued for my first year, and I would have to resubmit required documents to extend it for the second year.

My mouth closed into a smile, and I breathed a sigh of relief. I pulled out my blue pen and signed my new I-20 before taking a picture and sending it to my mom and sisters. *What a perfect cold day!* That was one of the most freeing experiences. I was no longer going to worry about finding ways to remain in the country. My lawful status was valid for two full years; I just needed to maintain it.

The euphoria eventually wore off after a few days, and I didn't feel happy as consistently as I was hoping to. In fact, I could barely go a week without crying. The financial struggles, the cold, the loneliness, the job search, the heartbreak … I cried for one of these reasons, or for all of them at once.

By February, I'd exhausted all my savings and wasn't even buying stuff for myself anymore. It got to a point where I had to return some of the things my mom had bought for me when she visited to use the money for the additional expenses that came with attending school; textbooks were one of them. I didn't think they were that important until I almost didn't get graded on my first accounting assignment. The textbook for that class cost more than $100, which I couldn't afford to spend on just one book.

I remember doing that assignment on the morning it was due with a classmate who shared her textbook with me. As I wrote on my paper and peeked into her textbook, it reminded me of the times I shared my textbooks with classmates who couldn't afford them. I shared, not thinking beyond the mere fact that I was helping someone out. I shared, but I didn't know how it felt to be on the other side; that day, I did. Growing up, I didn't have trouble going to school or buying supplies. I'm sure it was not always easy, but I never saw how hard it was. I just went to school and never really wondered how that was possible.

What I ended up doing was rent used books on Amazon, which worked out well. They were still in good condition, and I wasn't going to need them after the semester was over anyway, so I returned them at the end of the semester.

Asking my mom for more money was not an option. At least I didn't consider it as one. She was already paying a lot for my school and my rent and utilities every month. Speaking of utilities, I was officially the sole tenant of the apartment. My roommates had moved out to live with other people because the heating issue remained unresolved, despite our multiple complaints and maintenance requests. They came back to the apartment on rare occasions to drop off and/or pick up some stuff before heading right back out. The apartment was a freezer mirroring the outside temperatures that dropped to minus twenty degrees Celsius on some days. The only source of heat I had was the kitchen stove.

Now that I was attending "real school," I wanted to get a job to support myself, but that didn't happen. Finding a job was a laborious process, especially for international students. I attended many of the employment workshops hosted by the Office of International Students at my school, which made me realize how complicated my life was going to be in the U.S.

As an international student, I could legally work in the U.S. in one of three ways: off-campus through Optional Practical Training (OPT), off-campus through Curricular Practical Training (CPT), or on campus.

Students could work using OPT before graduation while enrolled in a program (pre-completion OPT), but they generally used it for full-time work after graduation (post-completion OPT). Both were limited to a combined twelve months, with no option to renew for most students. Science, technology, engineering, and mathematics (STEM) students were eligible for a two-year extension on post-completion OPT under certain conditions.

I was a business, not a STEM, student, so I was only eligible for a one-year post-completion OPT. I didn't want to apply for a pre-completion OPT because I wanted to have my full year of post-completion OPT after graduating from my program. I go deeper into my grueling process of applying for and obtaining OPT later in this book.

CPT, on the other hand, was used for jobs that were an integral part of an academic program, or for internships that were directly related to the field of study.

In my case, because my MBA did not require a work term, I could only use my CPT for an internship. That internship would have to be eligible for school credit and not surpass twenty hours per week when school was in session, with the ability to work up to forty hours during school breaks.

Full-time CPT was limited to twelve months, consecutive or not. If I worked full-time for more than twelve months using my CPT, I would no longer be eligible for OPT.

However, to be eligible for CPT, I would need to complete at least one academic year (two consecutive semesters, excluding summer and language classes). The only way I could use CPT in my first semester was if an internship was required as part of my program, which wasn't the case. Once eligible, and after receiving an employment offer letter specifying the job start and end dates, I would request a letter of support from the designated school official to apply for a social security number, without which I could not legally work.

With no support letter from the school, I could not apply for an SSN. With less than two semesters completed and no job offer, I could not request a support letter. I also go over my process of applying for CPT later.

So, my only option was on-campus employment. On-campus employment was limited to twelve hours per week at my school, and opportunities did not exactly abound. I'd applied for multiple on-campus jobs, but I either did not receive a response or my application was rejected.

My sleep and my skin hadn't gotten any better. I only went to school at night, meaning I spent plenty of time in my freezing room. Sure, assignments kept me busy, but they didn't take the whole day. It was cold in and outside of my apartment, and by 4 p.m., the sun had disappeared. A mix that isn't very conducive to a good night's sleep, and the hours I managed to get in were certainly not beauty sleep.

My heart hadn't completely recovered from the breakup with Lucas either. I wasn't receiving as many comments on my decision anymore, but Lucas was obviously still mad at me. We'd kept in touch, though we didn't talk about anything personal. I've always been an advocate for staying friends after a breakup (yeah … I know, I know), or at least not hating each other, so I didn't want to not talk to him anymore. Unfortunately, our conversations somehow almost always ended up in him reminding me what I had done to us. He would tell me things I didn't even know he could think of me.

That, in addition to everything else I was going through, made me realize I needed to start seeing someone. A therapist, that is.

Roosevelt had a health and wellness center where students could schedule appointments with medical counselors to get help with mental health issues. I walked by that center sometimes on my way to the library, without thinking I would ever need its services.

Seeing a counselor, a therapist, a psychologist, a psychiatrist, or any mental health professional isn't really in my culture; it's not something people do or talk about. When they do talk about it, most say it's "White people stuff." But at that point, simply watching YouTube videos of people going through similar breakup experiences was no longer enough to make me feel better. Though these videos helped me realize I wasn't alone and had a valid reason for wanting to be single, I was going through a lot more than just a breakup. The whole process of finding and working on myself wasn't going too well, and I needed to talk to someone. I needed help from someone who didn't know me.

So, one day, I went into the wellness center about an hour before class. I filled out a form with my personal information and a brief reason for my visit, then handed it back to the receptionist. He smiled and gestured to the chairs in the waiting area. I sat down and anxiously waited, unsure how it would all go.

"Danielle?" a woman asked, walking into the waiting area from across the hallway. She was blonde and probably in her thirties, and the smile on her face melted my anxiety.

"Yes!" I got up and followed her.

We walked into a dim-lit room with two chairs facing each other in the middle. "Take a seat wherever you want, and I'll be on the other side," she said, closing the door behind her. *Is this a psychological trick or something?* I sat on the chair facing the door.

"So, what brings you here today?" She asked, leaning back in her chair. Her smile had not faded. After a moment of silence, I started talking.

The experience was a bit different from what I had envisioned. I pictured myself lying on an oddly shaped sofa, staring at the ceiling and hardly being able to express my feelings, while she asked questions and took notes. You know, just like in the movies. She didn't have glasses either. Well … the hardly-able-to-express-my-feelings part was spot-on. She also nodded while I spoke, leaned forward, and had a sympathetic look on her face, so I guess it was a real therapy session.

We mostly talked about my relationship with Lucas and barely touched on other subjects because I had class afterward and only booked a thirty-minute session. To be quite honest, though, I'm not sure that given more time, I would've opened up more and talked about other things. I didn't want to be more vulnerable than I already was. I knew I would not manage to talk about the other stuff I was going through without crying, and I didn't want to cry in front of a stranger. I didn't want to be judged or pitied. So, we talked about Lucas and how my fear of losing people made me hold on to something she believed I should have already let go of.

Before ending the session, she gave me the assignment not to talk to or text Lucas for the following thirty days. My next appointment, if I came back, would be two weeks later. She would then check on how things had evolved and go deeper into the topics we had only briefly touched on.

The weight on my shoulder when I entered the wellness center was half gone when I exited, but the last part of my conversation with the counselor scared me off, so I never went back. I didn't immediately do my assignment either. It took another emotional blackmail, on Valentine's Day, to finally stop talking to Lucas. I waited until after his exams, at the end of the month, to tell him I would no longer force the friendship I so desperately wanted us to have. I'd forgiven myself, and I'd forgiven him. And more importantly, I no longer wanted to feel bad about myself because of what he or people thought about my decision. I was ready to completely let go and whether that meant never speaking to him again did not scare me anymore.

--- ⌘ ---

Sophie landed in Chicago the day before my birthday, on March 12th. I picked her up from the airport right after my class and, just like my mom, she wondered what had happened to my face. And just like I did with my mom, I just brushed it off. I was happy to see her. We hadn't seen each other in almost two years when she joined my mom, Emma, Nora, and I as we were visiting Naomi in New York City in the summer of 2016.

My birthday fell on a Tuesday, so I went home straight after class to get ready and wear the dress I'd prepared for the occasion. I leaned my mirror against the window to look at my full reflection. I turned around, then back around, and smiled. The low-cut, dark brown dress hugged my curvy figure just the way I liked it. I narrowed my eyes at the reflection of my chest, then walked two steps forward to have a better look at my acne and dark spots. It was almost like I was seeing them for the first time. My smile faded, and I sighed. I ran my right hand slowly across my face and chest to feel the bumps on my skin. The only makeup I had was eyeliner and lipstick, but my brows and nails were done.

I wish I could see past those imperfections. I loved the dress but couldn't go out in it anymore, not until my chest looked better. I quickly swapped it for a black turtleneck dress with shoulder cutouts, then Sophie and I sped out the door. We went out around 11 p.m. on a weekday, which meant we had about three hours before most bars and restaurants closed. We went to a few places, ate, and had drinks. I didn't have a cake, and I wasn't in another city, but I loved every second of that birthday night and was thankful I hadn't spent it alone.

The two weeks Sophie stayed were a lot of fun. We visited Naomi in New York, and all three of us spent Easter weekend in Washington, DC, before we each returned to our respective cities. It felt good to go out and to see people, to travel and to eat different things, to dance and to laugh, to sing and to play. It felt good to *feel alive*. My mom even commented on the pictures we sent to her, saying I was glowing. I still had acne and dark spots, but I guess not crying every day for two full weeks helped my overall appearance.

It was a much-needed break before what would turn out to be one of my worst experiences of the year, bringing me back to my dark childhood days.

CHAPTER 7:

OOPS

Back in January, I'd expressed to my mom my desire to take summer classes so I could graduate in May 2019 instead of December of the same year. She wasn't sure how that would play out financially, so she asked me to wait. I didn't want to pressure her; my even starting school was already a miracle, and I knew she was doing a lot so I waited. I waited and prayed; I hoped and believed.

Three months later, in early April, she texted to let me know I was good to register for my summer classes. The dozens of smiling and dancing emojis I sent her were an accurate representation of what was happening. She laughed and asked about the payment plan information for that semester.

I can't say just how much I thanked God for answering my prayers. More than a way to catch up on my classes, going to school in the summer was going to keep me busy. I didn't want to spend another summer alone in my room, watching the sun rise and set.

As we were nearing the end of the semester, it became apparent that I would not work on campus, since on-campus jobs only lasted for the duration of the semester. The frustration of looking for a job without finding one was growing by the day. On-campus jobs paid between \$10 and \$14 per hour for a maximum of twelve hours a week, so working on campus wouldn't even cover half of my rent. I just wanted something to at least buy groceries on my own or treat myself once in a while. And again, if not for me, why wouldn't God do it for my mom?

The many questions I asked myself were especially confusing now that I was reading the Bible every day (or at least tried to), still going to church every Sunday and trying my best to be and stay positive, even when I was feeling down. I thought I was doing what He wanted me to do. I thought He would make my paths straight.

Not being able to find a job didn't stop me from daydreaming about going to school in the summer, and I was thankful that was going to happen. *Maybe that's when He'll give me a job. Maybe that's when I'll have friends and go out and do my nails and take care of my skin and be happy. Or maybe I'm asking for too many things all at once? Maybe only one prayer can be answered at a time?*

I registered for my summer classes toward the end of April. Roosevelt University had two main campuses at the time: the Loop campus in downtown Chicago and the Schaumburg campus in the northwestern suburbs. The school offered most classes on both campuses in the fall and spring. Mine were downtown in the spring, but the ones I registered for the summer semester were only offered in Schaumburg. That campus was about an hour and a half away from home by train.

With the summer being an optional semester, I would no longer have access to certain student benefits, such as U-Pass, the transit card that allowed students to ride trains and buses for free during regular school terms. I didn't know exactly how I was going to get to campus and back three times a week with my limited resources, but it didn't matter. I was going to figure it out. Maybe I was going to get a job on campus.

On the afternoon of May 7th, two days after my semester ended and about a week before my U-Pass expired, I went to Schaumburg to visit the campus. Very different from the downtown campus, but each had its own beauty.

There wasn't much going on in Schaumburg, which I kind of expected because of its suburban location. No stores or restaurants or skyscrapers around campus. The downtown campus was a thirty-two-story building with views of the city's skyline and Lake Michigan, while the Schaumburg campus was a spread-out single-story building in a quiet area.

It was a beautiful day. The sun was beaming through the blossoming flowers on the trees surrounding the campus, and I took dozens of pictures of the beautiful scenery. I could see myself studying there, but good thing it would only be for a semester because it wouldn't be long before I needed my "city dose." People also seemed a lot nicer and more welcoming in Schaumburg. They weren't necessarily rude in Chicago, but not everyone greeted or smiled at me every single time I entered a building. The campus wasn't huge, but big enough that I got lost trying to find my way out.

I went back home that day glad I'd made the trip. I couldn't wait to start my classes. The following days were quite nice as well. Summer was there early, especially for a city where it's cold eight months out of the year. The beautiful weather and the anticipation of going to school made me feel better, so I started going out for walks again.

A few days later, I was texting with my mom, and we eventually got to talking about school. We'd already missed the first installment for my summer semester, and the second one was due a week later. When I asked if she could still afford the tuition fees for the semester, she said no. My heart broke before sinking into my stomach. The little joy I'd been feeling, the light I'd started to see… everything got sucked out to make way for pain.

I don't understand. What was the point of answering my prayer if You were going to revoke it later? Did You do this on purpose? What am I going to do for four full months, assuming I even go to school in the fall?

I sent my mom a single sad emoji and told her it wasn't a big deal, but streams of tears were flowing down my face.

I didn't know what to do. I was confused and needed to talk to someone, so I called the only person who'd heard me cry a dozen times.

"Hello?"

"Hey, Lucas, it's me." My voice was trembling. "I know we're not supposed to be talking to each other right now, but please listen to me; don't hang up. I promise I won't be long. I just don't know who else to talk to."

I gripped onto my phone, pressing my eyes full of tears and hoping he was not going to shut me out. This was our first call since the end of February. We had exchanged a few texts here and there, but just to say hi. He'd wished me a happy birthday, and I'd done the same on his birthday.

"Okay, I'm listening."

"So, I don't know what's wrong with me or with my life or if it was a mistake coming here. Ever since I stepped into this country, weird things have been happening to me. I try to stay positive; I try not to let negative thoughts get the best of me, but it seems like it's all for nothing. I just started school this semester and even that was a miracle. I asked my mom back in January if I could enroll in summer classes, that way I wouldn't be bored at home alone like I was last summer. She initially wasn't sure and told me to wait, and that's what I did. But I prayed so hard, you have no idea how much. Every time I went to church, every day when I woke up, every night before sleeping, in the middle of night when I couldn't sleep, I just prayed that I would go to school in the summer. She then told me a few weeks ago that I could enroll in my classes, and I was so happy! I enrolled in my classes, all of which are on another campus, in Schaumburg, kind of like another city. I went there the other day to see what it was like, and I loved it. It was so beautiful, and I was so excited.

"Then today, she told me she wasn't going to be able to pay for my classes anymore. I'm not mad at her; I just don't understand why all this is happening and what I'm supposed to do. This was the only thing that kept me sane these past few weeks. This semester has been so hard. Yes, Sophie visited, and we had fun, but you don't know what I was going through before and even after that. I don't have any income. All the money I have goes into either school stuff or random expenses that come up that I wasn't expecting. I've been paying my rent late these past months because my mom has so much to pay for at the same time, and now the extra money that she normally sends for me has to go into paying late fees. I cancelled all my subscriptions to save money: Netflix, Spotify, Amazon Prime, everything. I even canceled my gym membership. I try not to eat more than twice a day and only buy groceries every couple of weeks. I looked for jobs, but I am not eligible for work right now.

"What else am I supposed to do, Lucas? What else am I supposed to do? Why is all this happening to me? It's been a year, I don't understand. If I have to leave, then I will but I just need to know. I'm so tired, Lucas. I am so tired of everything that keeps happening."

I went on and on. I did not stop, not once.

"Wow … I'm really sorry. I had no idea you were going through all this," he started. "Uhm … I'm actually on my way to class right now. I have a presentation, and I'm already late. Can I call you back?"

"Yeah, of course, and thanks for listening." I wiped my nose with my already wet paper towel, still heavily sniffing.

I would be lying if I said I didn't want to hear more than what he'd said. I know he wasn't trying to be mean, and he did call back later, but at that moment, I needed more.

When he hung up, tears would not stop flowing so I didn't bother wiping them anymore. The throbs in my head intensified and everything around me was spinning; this lasted longer than I was used to. I had cried before, but this time felt different. I was standing in the middle of my room, between my bed and my desk. I bent my burning head down to hold it in my hands, then lifted it back up, in a motion that seemed abnormally slow. My breath was a heavy cloud wrapped around me. The chatter and laughter of my roommates in the living room had become muffled. The bed in front of me, the desk beside me, the bathroom door behind me, the carpet under my feet—everything looked like it was moving away, further isolating me in the center of this room that seemed larger and larger. My eyes slowly closed, and all I could hear was the sound of my breath and my heart beating in my ears. I was in quicksand drifting away, and I almost let myself go—until I sensed that *something* was going to happen. I immediately straightened and forced myself to stop crying. I wiped my tears and fixed my face as best as I could, then sped out the door for a walk.

I went out not because I wanted to, but because I feared what was going to happen if I'd continued to cry. When I went back to my room, I dropped the classes I'd registered for.

———— ⊂⊸⊸⊃ ————

After a few days, I decided to look for a job again, hoping to find something that did not require an SSN. I started looking on websites such as Craigslist, where people post all sorts of listings. Unfortunately, many are scams, inappropriate, or outright illegal. The jobs I found that didn't require an SSN did not align with my moral standards, and I wasn't willing to compromise them.

The money I needed was going to serve not only for everyday life, but also to repay George. During one of our conversations, I finally opened up about my financial situation. I never spoke to him—or to any other friend, for that matter—about money, because I'd never really had money issues before.

I lived a pretty comfortable life back home—my family wasn't the wealthiest, but we weren't broke either. I could afford most of the things I wanted, within reason. If I didn't run out of money, though, it wasn't because I was "loaded" or "rich," as some people often commented. I may have been more financially stable than some people, but I was also disciplined. Back then, I had budgets and separate funds for different parts of my life. I saved at least half of my allowance in an interest earning account, and although I liked treating myself to nice things, I lived like there *was* tomorrow. I was self-sufficient and rarely had to ask anyone for money. Whenever that happened, it was probably because I needed change, which I paid back as soon as possible. On the rare occasions that I did run out of money, I relied on my savings until my mom remembered (or until I nudged her to remember) she hadn't given me my allowance yet.

Losing that control over my finances and not being able to save anymore was a hard pill to swallow and one I didn't want to talk about. My conversation with George about my financial situation was very uncomfortable, and to be honest, I was also ashamed. My situation made me feel like I had gone all the way down to the bottom of Maslow's Pyramid, only now trying to cover basic needs when I knew there was a time I was closer to self-actualization.

George also lived a comfortable life and had never complained (at least not to me) about money, so I didn't think he would understand what I was going through. In fact, I feared he would look at me differently. I also knew he was going to try to help me, but the thing is, I didn't want it to look like I was only telling him about my situation so he could help me financially. And I certainly didn't want to feel like a burden, even if sending me money was going to have little to no impact on his life.

After insisting and later completely ignoring the fact that I told him his emotional support was more than enough, George sent me money. A few days after our conversation, I found $250 in my PayPal account that came from him. I was working on myself and on accepting help, so I didn't return the money right away like would have been the case if this had happened years earlier. This was especially hard to do because I did not accept money from men, except those in my family. I accepted George's money and thanked him, but I felt the need to pay him back as soon as possible, which I ended up not being able to do.

Another reason why I went on Craigslist is because it was that time of the year again—I needed to find a new place and move by July 31st. For real, this time. So, I looked on Craigslist for less-expensive options and this time, I wasn't looking at studios or one-bedroom apartments. I was looking to rent a room in a multi-bedroom apartment to share with other people. Many room listings on the website bypassed the credit check requirement, and some did not require or had lower application fees, which was great considering I still had no credit, no SSN, and no income.

My budget this time was about $900. I didn't want to move too far from downtown. I wanted to still be able to walk to my most frequently visited places without having to worry about transportation costs. Living in the West Loop definitely had that advantage and as much as possible, I wanted to keep it that way. I also wanted to have my own bathroom. I was fine sharing everything else, but I wanted to be the only person using my bathroom. All these criteria eventually changed later in the summer after realizing how hard it was to satisfy them with my budget.

Naomi called one day to see what I was up to for the summer. When I said I was no longer going to attend school and was looking for a job, she suggested I join her in New York where she was going to help me find something. She believed that once I found a job, I would be able to apply for an SSN with my offer letter. She later sent me the link to a job opening at ASM, an outsourced customer service center specialized in luxury brands in New York. She knew someone at the company who told her they were looking for a seasonal employee (just for the summer), so Naomi recommended me. She helped me tailor my resume for the job, insisting that I only keep two names on my header if I didn't want to face discrimination, as my five names were already an indication that I wasn't "local." I made the changes, then applied for the e-commerce brand ambassador position with Gucci.

A positive response came a couple of days later—the company wanted to interview me. The first step in the process was a phone screening and if successful, I would move on to the first, then second round of in-person interviews.

> **From:** HR *Specialist*
> **To:** *Me*
> **Subject:** *Phone Interview Invitation*
> **Date and Time:** *05/14/2018 at 3:06 p.m.*
> *Dear Danielle,*
>
> *Thank you for applying for the e-Commerce Brand Ambassador position with us.*
> *We are a customer service center specialized in luxury brands. We have counted over 250 collaborators worldwide with partnerships of over 77 luxury brands. The Brand Ambassador will play an essential role in delivering the customer services for high-end luxury brands.*
> *Would you be interested in hearing more about the position? Please let me know, and we can schedule a quick conversation over the phone this week.*
> *I look forward to hearing from you.*
>
> *Best regards,*
> *HR Specialist*

I felt a mixture of anxiety and excitement. That interview was going to be my first interview experience in the U.S., and I didn't know what to expect. I had an "interview notebook" where I kept a list of some of the most frequently asked behavioral interview questions and answers, in case I got invited to an interview on campus. That didn't happen, so I guess this was my chance to put my notebook to use.

I emailed the HR specialist back with my availability, and she called me two days later. The call was scheduled to last thirty minutes, but we spoke for less than fifteen, so I worried that I wouldn't be moving forward. And I'm sure she could tell I was nervous. To my (pleasant) surprise, she called me a few days later to confirm my availability to speak with the operations and HR managers at ASM's main office on May 22nd. I obviously said I could meet them.

Despite the joy of moving forward in the process, my anxiety skyrocketed. The thought of having full conversations with two strangers, completely in English and for longer than fifteen minutes, made my stomach cramp throughout the days leading up to my departure. However, I continued to practice interview questions during that time. I watched YouTube videos of customer service job interview questions, scoured the Internet for more common interview questions and responses, added them to my list, and wrote scripts in my interview notebook. I practiced those scripts until I memorized them.

The day before I left Chicago, I said a little prayer while I was packing. I wanted this trip to be worth it. I wanted it to be the reason God had taken my summer classes back.

Please help me get this job. You know how much I need money right now, and You know how helpful this is going to be for my mom and I. You also know I need to find a new place soon and will need to pay a deposit. I won't live in a furnished place anymore, so I'll need to buy at least a mattress, and You know how expensive that is. And there's also moving expenses. Please, help me get this job. I'm not mad at You that I'm not going to school anymore; maybe getting a job was the reason. I just ask that You please make it happen and if You know it's not going to happen, please don't let me go. Just cancel my flight or something; I'll understand. Please don't let me be heartbroken again. Please make this trip worth it.

CHAPTER 8:

UH-OH

I f selected for the job at ASM, I was going to get paid $17 per hour. As a 40-hour full-time job, that meant my monthly gross income would come to around $2,700. I didn't know what my tax and other deductions would amount to, but that didn't matter to me. The gross income from this job was already a lot more than would've been for an on-campus job, a lot more than I even thought I would earn.

I had my first-round interview as planned on Tuesday, May 22nd at the ASM office in Soho, which is what I thought would be my workplace if selected for the job. I met two managers simultaneously, and I don't remember having spoken to either for longer than twenty minutes. Still, I moved forward to the next round, which they told me was going to be at Gucci's headquarters; that is where I would potentially work.

The end of my interview coincided with Naomi's break at work, so I joined her at a coffee shop and filled her in. Afterward, I did a dry run to Gucci's corporate office to locate my next place to interview and a potential work location. It was on the twelfth floor of a skyscraper in Manhattan's Financial District. I took the train to 195 Broadway

Street and got off at the Fulton Center station. The sun was blazing hot on my skin, and its rays were flaming arrows, threatening my sight. I shielded my forehead with my right hand and squinted to look up at the buildings across the street.

I walked into Gucci's corporate office building but couldn't go past the lobby because I didn't have a badge, and my visit wasn't until the next day. After seeing the building and reminding myself I would interview at *Gucci*, I decided I needed a new outfit for my interview. So, I walked to the nearest H&M store to buy myself a new something. I got a straight, knee-length forest green dress. Its neckline ran along my collarbone, stopping at my shoulders, and the puffed sleeves tied into little bows at my elbows. *I can't wait till tomorrow.*

The next morning, I paired my new dress with black tights and black flats, then headed to my interview. My sister lived about thirty minutes away, so I left her apartment an hour before to be safe. I was not going to be late for my interview because the A line train randomly stopped in the middle of nowhere for like twenty minutes.

Luckily, that didn't happen. I was actually a few minutes early, so I waited for my interviewer to come get me in the waiting area. The office gave me real Fashion Week vibes, and I remember wondering if I would even fit in if I got the job. My interview notebook definitely came in handy, and I felt pretty confident when I left the building after meeting with my interviewers. They were looking for someone to start immediately—the next Monday—and it didn't seem like they had many more candidates to interview.

On my bus ride home, I prayed and hoped to get the job. I pictured myself working there, imagining the things I'd do during my breaks and outside of work with my coworkers, dreaming about my life during that summer in New York City. Plus, I was going to save money for when I'd go back to Chicago and move to my new place.

———————⊂▥▥▭————————

"Hello?" I picked up the phone without paying attention to the screen because I was too busy trying another key to unlock the door to my sister's apartment building. Naomi had given me a keychain with all the keys to her apartment and building, and I could never figure out which of the ones that looked the same opened the front door.

"Hi Danielle. This is the HR Specialist at ASM. I wanted to let you know we want to extend you the offer as the e-commerce brand ambassador at Gucci."

"Oh … Wow! Thank you … thank you very much! I … I look forward to starting!" She'd caught me off guard. I hadn't yet Googled how to accept a job offer over the phone, so I had no script.

She went on to explain that I would need to send her my SSN for the background check and for tax-withholding purposes. Before the day ended, she emailed me my offer letter and other administrative paperwork. *Thank You, God, thank You so much!* I could not stop smiling. I hoped Naomi was right that I could apply for an SSN with my offer letter, despite not having completed one academic year yet. When she came back from work, we talked about it, and she still seemed confident.

On Thursday, May 24th, I emailed my international student advisor at Roosevelt to inform her I'd received a job offer and to request a work authorization letter. She replied, asking if my request was regarding on-campus employment. I said no, and she responded the following Tuesday:

> **From:** *International Student Advisor*
>
> **To:** *Me*
>
> **Subject:** *RE: Employment authorization*
>
> **Date and Time:** *5/29/2018 at 12:12 p.m.*
>
> *Hello Danielle,*
>
> *You don't qualify for off-campus employment at this time. You must be a degree-seeking F-1student for at least one academic year before you are eligible for CPT or OPT. Since you began your program in January, you will not be eligible until January 2019. The time you spent in your previous English Language school is not counted toward this time.*
>
> *Since you do not have a work permit and do not qualify for CPT or OPT yet, I cannot write a letter to assist you with a social security number, and you should not be working. I'm sorry, I'm sure that the experience would be helpful.*
>
> *Best,*
>
> *International Student Advisor*

I did not respond, but to be honest, her email wasn't a surprise. I'd heard that information before; I just hoped I'd misunderstood it as Naomi suggested.

The job start date was May 28th, but ASM was willing to let me start the following Monday on June 4th, so long as I provided all the required documents. I couldn't and I didn't, so my offer was rescinded. My heart broke, but not for too long. Seeing that opportunity go was disappointing and painful, but I told myself it wasn't the end of the world. I kept hoping I would find something else. I was convinced I hadn't gone all the way to New York for no reason. There was something else out there for me.

I needed money. I needed a job, and it didn't matter what kind anymore. It was only going to be for a few months before I had to head back to Chicago. So, I started looking for jobs that paid cash to avoid taxes and keep whatever I earned for myself. In that case, there would be no need for an SSN. I wasn't comfortable doing things illegally, but I convinced myself it was necessary, wouldn't last long, and would only happen this one time. I looked on Indeed and Craigslist. I edited my resume and changed my current education to a bachelor's degree instead of an MBA to avoid looking overqualified.

I applied to be a waitress or a server at local restaurants and bars. The nicer ones required SSNs and even certifications to manipulate food or alcohol, which I didn't have. I applied to be a receptionist or a front desk agent. I applied for sales jobs at small shops and clothing stores. I got up every morning, applied for jobs online, then printed copies of my resume to apply for similar jobs in person. Some paid less than the $14 per hour minimum wage, but I didn't care. All that mattered was that I got paid something.

Looking for a job was draining, but I didn't let my first few rejections bring me down. I'd prayed for my trip to bear fruit, and I was going to find and pick that fruit. And whenever I did not hear back, I kept hoping the next job would be the one. I kept telling myself there was something better coming. Maybe I was going to find something that paid more. Maybe I was going to find something that wasn't too far from home; that way I wouldn't have to spend a lot on transportation. Maybe I was going to find something with a better work environment. I kept looking. I kept hoping. I kept praying. I kept believing. But my motivation eventually wore off when every door I knocked on stayed closed, literally and figuratively.

My frustration was now growing more intense with every new rejection. I was spending what little money I had on printing resumes and taking the train or the bus to places I was going to apply for a job but not get it. I lowered every possible standard I had for a job. I just wanted to do something and get paid for it, whatever the job or the compensation.

Meanwhile, my LinkedIn was buzzing every day with notifications telling me to congratulate people for starting a new job. I read about how excited people were to announce that they had accepted an offer, or that it was day 1 at their new jobs. I wasn't jealous that they were doing well for themselves, but I felt like I was missing out. Also, the types of jobs I was applying for weren't exactly my pride and joy.

Looking for a new place remotely also had its challenges. I couldn't meet with landlords or current tenants to tour apartments, and we didn't do virtual tours. I also came across multiple scams on Craigslist, but I luckily did not fall for them. Listings—the good ones—requesting roommates for an August 1st move-in date became rarer as days went by. And this time, I really needed to move out by the end of July.

Watching people on social media continued to have its detrimental effects on me. From wishing I had enough money to travel and do fun things, to wishing I had clear skin, to wondering what would've been if I'd gone to school in Europe instead where I knew more people and the cost of living wasn't as high, to wishing I had more interesting things to say about my life when people asked how I was doing ... it became harder and harder to remain positive. Almost every platform now had stories. Even when that wasn't my intention, I somehow ended up seeing what people were up to. I couldn't just chat on WhatsApp anymore—I felt compelled to swipe right to the status tab to watch new stories. So, even when I didn't go on Instagram or Snapchat, I still saw how much more fun people's lives were compared to mine.

I'd been thinking about leaving social media for weeks. I wasn't posting, but I didn't even want to open these apps anymore. I needed a break, but I didn't want to have to explain myself. I'd tried limiting my daily consumption of certain platforms, but my attempt was unsuccessful. I did not feel well. I wanted to leave social media. I *needed* to leave social media.

On June 5th, 2018, Kate Spade committed suicide. I didn't know her personally (shocker, I know!), but I always loved her bags. I didn't own any back then but was looking forward to when I'd make enough money to afford my first Kate Spade crossbody or satchel. On the day she died, I read a tweet that I sort of resonated with:

> *Kate Spade's tragic passing is a painful reminder that we never truly know another's pain or the burden they carry. If you are contemplating suicide, please, please seek help.*[2]

I wasn't contemplating suicide, at least not at that point. However, I'd started to understand why some people might not wish to be alive anymore.

I took a screenshot of the tweet and posted it on my WhatsApp stories. That was one of the few times I posted something there. In fact, I didn't even have a profile picture, well … not a real one. My profile picture was a black circle, and it'd been that way for months. I only changed it when I felt relatively happy—on my birthday and on Easter, for example.

---

2   Trump, Ivanka. *Twitter*, 5 June 2018, https://x.com/IvankaTrump/status/1004050868025503749.

My posting the tweet was not a signal that I was going to hurt myself; I just found the first sentence to be very relevant to my situation. I hid my emotions and didn't talk about what I was going through. Whether that was true or not, I said I was fine whenever someone asked how I was doing. Opening up about my feelings would mean opening up about my entire situation, which I didn't want to do. I wanted to be and feel strong, so I kept everything to myself. That said, I didn't expect people to guess that I wasn't well or dig into my answers to find out the truth.

———— ⊂▦▦▷ ————

Three days later, on June 8th, I hit rock bottom. I had my first interview since Gucci at 12:30 p.m. that day for an office assistant job. It paid $20 per hour, and the Craigslist post mentioned it paid cash. *Maybe this is it. Maybe this is what I've been looking for.* It all started making sense. All the rejections and disappointment I'd been through, all the frustration I had felt. *There was something better.*

My short conversation with the "office manager" didn't feel like an interview. I was so desperate I didn't see it as a red flag when he asked me to pay $60 for "training" and rushed me to sign an agreement he'd barely given me the time to read. In fact, the first red flag was being notified via text message that I had an interview. Not even a phone call. Certainly not an email either. I was "hired" on the spot and told to start the following Monday. The job was a scam.

After my "interview," I called Naomi all cheerful to tell her the "good" news, and that's when I learned that these scams were common practice. I got confirmation when I tried calling the number that texted me that morning to get my money back. No one picked up at first, then my second, third, and fourth calls didn't even go through.

You might think $60 is not the end of the world, but when there's not more where that came from, and when you have very inconsistent cash inflows, losing $60 is a big deal.

That same day, the owner of a listing for a room I was looking to rent in Chicago took it down from Craigslist. I couldn't pay the deposit, so they gave the room to someone else. And it still wasn't clear if I would go back to school for the fall semester, which started the last week of August. I didn't have the strength to continue looking and applying in person as I'd been doing that day, so I just headed back home with tears threatening to spill from my eyes.

I can't do this anymore. I was exhausted physically, emotionally, mentally. I sat at the dining table and released my tears. They poured out as if I'd held them captive for years.

Why are You putting me through this? Why did You let these people scam me when You know I am broke? Why aren't You helping me find something? Anything. Don't You know how much I need a job? Why do I even keep trying? All this hope I keep putting into finding the next best thing, all this positivity I try to maintain, what is that for? I keep telling myself it's just another challenge and I'll be fine, but clearly that's not the case. What was even the point of coming to New York? Didn't I ask You to cancel my flight if the trip wasn't going to be worth it? Or did You just want to watch me suffer? Haven't You seen me cry enough over the past year?

Trying to make sense of what was happening was disheartening. I especially did not understand God. I wasn't sure who to turn to with matters concerning God, so I texted the person I thought could help me best:

Danielle: Hello, Father.

Father Andrew: Hello Danielle. How are you?

Danielle: I'm good. Are you busy?

Father Andrew: Not really. What's up?

Danielle: I don't want to bother. If you're busy, maybe we can talk later.

Father Andrew: No, it's fine. Do you want me to call you?

Danielle: No, not really.

Father Andrew: Okay, tell me.

Danielle: I just have a quick question. So, I know God is good and everything, but why do you think He would give you something you have prayed for and later take it back?

Father Andrew: That's a great question. Sometimes it may be one's judgement on the sequence of events. I may not have an answer, but we can talk about the actual issue.

Danielle: So, you know I started school in January, and throughout the semester, I prayed to take summer classes to "catch up" and graduate next May. Also, immigration-wise, it makes more sense to graduate in May because of OPT, work visa application and stuff like that. I prayed so hard and sometimes worried that it would not happen because our financial situation has gotten really tight.

Just before my semester ended, my mom told me to go ahead and register for summer classes. I was so happy God had heard and answered my prayer, and I thanked Him with all my heart. Then a month or so later, my mom told me she wouldn't be able to pay for my classes anymore. (Please, never mention this to her.)

I was so down I started questioning everything. That's why I'm asking you. I don't want to get things wrong.

Father Andrew: I will not tell your mom. I am so sorry to hear about this. Must be quite a load to sit in with. In whatever we ask, we are told to ask, "Is it God's will or is it my will?" This opens us more to His divine leadership and helps us abandon ourselves to Him so that He may create ways and means to achieve our goals. It is difficult to discern His purpose, but there are a few ways to know when you are on the right track:

1. Have I prayed about it?

2. Have I declared that "His will be done vs. my will be done"?

3. Have I considered other people's welfare (question of charity and ecojustice)?

4. What is the end goal?

Danielle: On number 3, if you're talking about my mom, I wasn't mad at her because she couldn't pay for my school anymore. I understood and still understand that.

I'm just wondering if it was not His will, why did He let that still happen? Why did He let me be happy, knowing I would be sad later? I'd rather my mom had not told me to register in the first place because then I would have guessed it was not His will. Still would have been disappointed, but not as much.

Also, every time I pray, I pray that everything is done according to His will. I have learned to let go of my own desires. That's what makes everything more disappointing to me.

Father Andrew: Number 3 involves anything outside you: your mom, availability of funds, your school, any other factor that may surround you and the decision at hand. I know you love your mom, and you are not mad at her. It is OK to feel disappointed when such a deal doesn't go through, especially if it was already in place.

It is hard to actually know what happens in such situations. But one thing is for sure; it might have been your interpretation that God let you have it rather than that God had actually given it to you. See, He wants the best for you (Jer. 29:11).

God has the best plans for you; even this you will conquer.

Danielle: I know I will; I have no other choice. I just don't know what to ask for, or if I should even ask anymore. This was just one example; there are so many other similar things that have happened to me, and it's just tiring. I will not lose my faith; I know these are just trials. I just don't know how to pray anymore because I'm afraid of being disappointed again and again.

Father Andrew: The thing is, that's exactly where the devil wants you to be and to do. Lose hope. Be confused. Stop praying. Do not be tired of asking, but just ask the questions that I posed above.

It is also important to know that other people's decisions may affect our goals, and God is not a dictator. So, He may not wrestle with others, but He still works in the background. Just recall we had a similar conversation when DePaul frustrated you, but God opened a good way at Roosevelt. He opens doors.

He will continue to. He may not fulfill all our desires, but He will move us toward our goal.

Danielle: Okay, thank you, Father.

Father Andrew: I will keep you in my prayers. Especially for your peace and tranquility.

Danielle: Thank you very much.

I did not want to discuss my current employment situation, so I chose to talk about something similar. I can't say I was completely fine after our conversation. I still had many questions and wasn't entirely convinced, but that was a start.

I tried putting myself together over the weekend to find the strength to apply for jobs again. That was going to be the last time, not only because I was tired but also because I had to be in Chicago soon to look for an apartment, pack my stuff, and move. That meant if I found a job, I would work for a maximum of five weeks. I didn't even know what kind of job was going to hire me for just a month, but I decided to try again anyway. I contemplated leaving social media again, but at the same time, I wanted to stay for my friends, for my family.

———⌀———

On Monday, June 11th, I got back home exhausted. Again. I took my shoes off, and the cold floor under my sore feet felt like a massage. I'd spent the day walking and taking the train up and down to new places that all rejected my applications. When I got an update on my online application, it was always negative. My whole body was aching. Maybe it was from walking in the sun for hours, or maybe my mental exhaustion had radiated into my body. I poured a glass of water, sat on the couch, slowly winding down and coming to terms with the fact that I wasn't going to find a job. Right then, I decided to stop looking. *Maybe it's for the best.*

I came across another picture I resonated with. This time, it was from an Instagram account that usually posted funny quotes. Interestingly, that day, the quote was not funny:

Please look after your friends. Make sure they are well and okay. Sometimes they are going through things that are heavy. They may not say it, but they are. Please love them and take care of them.

This time, I one hundred percent related to the post.

I posted it on my WhatsApp stories, then stared at my apps menu, debating whether I should only mute my social media notifications or delete the apps altogether. I wanted to stay. If I left, I wasn't going to tell anyone. But I didn't want people to worry, especially after my recent posts.

I don't think I should leave. I want to, but I also want to stay. God, help me stay. Maybe this is just a phase and it'll end soon, and I just need to stick it out. Just give me a sign that I should stay, please. I want to stay.

Almost immediately after my mini-prayer, I got a text from Lucas. *Okay … that was fast. But thank You!*

We exchanged a few texts, then our conversation turned into yet another emotional blackmail. I was just too tired for that. I didn't have the energy to write long paragraphs explaining how much I hated what he was doing. I couldn't, so I did not entertain the conversation much longer.

"I won't be here anymore. Bye." I texted, when he said he wanted to call.

And I was gone.

I didn't know or plan how long I was going to be gone for; I just left. I uninstalled all my social media and chat applications, except for Facebook Messenger that my friends, family and I didn't really use anymore. I kept it just in case people *really* looked for me everywhere and couldn't find me and decided to try Messenger. I wasn't going to—and I didn't—initiate any conversation; it was just going to be my way of letting people know I was still alive.

Every time I went to New York, for some reason I had connectivity issues with the phone I was using at the time. So, when Naomi got home from work that evening, I told her these issues were now preventing me from logging into my social media apps. That's the best excuse I'd come up with to justify why we'd have to go back to texting or calling each other via the normal route instead of WhatsApp, as we'd been doing, and why I would not be active in our family group chat anymore. She let everyone else know.

———— ⌀⫘⊃ ————

Four days later, on June 15th, I started receiving texts on Messenger asking where I'd been. The excuse about my phone issues did not fly. My sudden departure was not very well-received by certain people, but that didn't come as a surprise. I knew leaving without warning was going to have its consequences. What I did not know was how harsh the comments would be.

Once more, I had made a very selfish decision.

"You could have at least said where to reach you instead of disappearing and expecting people to look everywhere." "Clearly, you didn't care about how your decision was going to affect the people in your life. So then, why should we care about you when you come back?" "Everyone has issues. Why did you need to drag others because you couldn't deal with yours? We didn't deserve that."

And it went on. The fact that I didn't regret leaving didn't make things better.

While I understand leaving without warning may have hurt people who cared about me, I truly needed a break. Each day was worse than the previous; I didn't leave so I could feel better. I left to stop the downward trend, to at least stagnate at a low point rather than go lower every single day.

I eventually reinstalled my apps at some point and when I came back, I didn't feel better. But I didn't feel worse. And as much as I knew that was nearly impossible, I didn't want people to look for me while I was gone. I truly hoped more days would go by before they found me on Messenger. Ironically again, I needed to be left alone. So no, I didn't regret leaving, but I regretted hurting people in the process.

Leaving without warning was also a way for me to avoid answering questions about why I was leaving. I knew people would ask. I knew that at least one person would come looking for me, then one would turn into two. I knew I would be expected to read and respond to messages. I knew I would have to force myself again to appear to be fine. I knew I would have to go look deep inside me for the strength to listen, text, speak, and laugh when I didn't want to. I knew in the end I would be doing exactly what I'd been doing for months, when the whole point of leaving was to stop.

How did I know that? Well, that's kind of what happened as more people realized my Messenger account was active. I started having conversations again, mostly to explain myself. Two days barely went by without someone texting me. I hadn't learned how to set boundaries yet, so I continued to reply to texts, to listen to voice messages, to take calls, until I was drained of all my energy. Again.

Not all was bad, though. I had some heartwarming calls and texts as well. Some of the regular ones were from George, who checked in to see how I was doing. I'd also lied to him at first and when I told him the truth, I apologized, thinking that he, too, was angry at me. He never fell for my lie; he wasn't angry and didn't need an explanation. George told me to take all the time I needed to feel better and that once I did, he would be there, ready to welcome me back. Some people reminded me they loved and cared about me. Others, like Cedric, who I'd known since middle school but only became friends with during college, regretted not being there for me enough to notice I wasn't well.

My goal wasn't to have them tell me all these things, but it sure felt good to read or hear those words.

CHAPTER 9:

THE PAIN

What is this? My eyebrows lowered into a puzzled frown as I reached for the white rectangular card taped to my bedroom door. I flipped it to reveal a $100 fine to be paid by all tenants of the apartment. I didn't think it was a love letter from a secret admirer, but I didn't expect a fine on my first day back in Chicago, either.

Building management did routine apartment and room inspections every quarter and gave fines to some or all residents when they judged the place was not clean enough. Who got a fine depended on whether the filthy area was common or individual. I'd never gotten an individual fine, but this was our second common fine since January. It was dated June 5th to be paid within a week to avoid additional fees, and it was now June 23rd. When I asked my roommates, they told me they'd already paid theirs. *Great!*

I tried disputing the fine, pointing out to management that I'd been away, but they'd already posted it to my online account and refused to remove it. My mom had access to my account, which is how she paid my rent, but I didn't want her to pay my portion of the fine, even though I knew she wouldn't mind. Again, $25 might not sound like a ton of money, but I had less than $30 left in my bank account to hold me up until at least the end of the month.

I definitely need a job. I started looking for a job again, thinking maybe the issue in New York was that I was too short on time. But now that I was back home, nothing would prevent me from getting a job. Once I found one, and if I went to school in the fall, I was going to continue to work during the day and go to school at night.

———————— ⌘ ————————

My days were split between looking for an apartment and looking for a job. I took the bus or the train every day, got off somewhere, and walked around looking for shops, restaurants, or any place where there was a "Help Wanted" sign on the front door. I continued to apply on Craigslist as well, careful to not get scammed again. I did another round of edits on my resume, which now indicated that I wasn't even pursuing a bachelor's degree, but only had a high school diploma.

I looked and applied online.

I looked and applied in person.

I walked.

I prayed.

I hoped.

I believed.

Nothing happened. I couldn't find one single job that would pay me cash, full or part-time.

My apartment search wasn't going too well either. What I found was either too expensive, too far from school, or was only available starting in September and later. When I found something available and within my budget, I met with the current tenants and toured the apartment but did not receive a call back. I followed up. Still nothing. I looked for rooms in places I wouldn't normally go to. I went to neighborhoods I didn't feel comfortable or safe living in, only because that's where the rent was cheaper. I lowered all my standards. I didn't care that I was going to share a bathroom with someone else anymore. I still preferred living with women rather than men, but I started looking at listings posted by men looking for roommates. I was running out of time, and I just wanted to live somewhere cheaper. Still, I found nothing.

I thought about renewing my current lease, though I had once more missed the renewal deadline. The thing is, it was going to be even more expensive with the usual annual rent increase, and I didn't want to spend another cold winter in my room either. Renewing my lease was my last resort. I was going to if I had to, but only at the very last minute.

⟶ ⌒⫘⌒ ⟵

Sometime in early July, I took out my planner to do my usual mid-year check-in to see what I had accomplished so far in the year. I opened my planner on the page where I'd written my 2018 goals and wishes. I inwardly sighed, confirming that I hadn't accomplished anything, not even getting an assistantship for the fall despite my 4.0 GPA. I crossed out everything I should've already done instead of putting a check mark next to it. I had little hope I would achieve the remaining goals for the year.

After a month away, I decided to reinstall my social media apps and slowly come back, monitoring how often I went on Instagram, Snapchat, and even LinkedIn. Again, I wasn't feeling better, but I was glad I had taken that break.

My mental exhaustion plummeted to another level after a while, but that was unrelated to social media. I can't pinpoint the day or the exact moment it began, but I remember starting to feel a continuous pain in my heart, as if a hole had been drilled in it. It felt like a tiny pea-sized hole at first, but then it grew overtime. It wasn't a void; it was a pain. And it wasn't in my chest either; I felt it in my *actual* heart. It was dull and deep and intense, intensifying when I cried or when I couldn't sleep at night. It didn't prevent me from getting up or walking around; it was just there, like a new part of me. I felt it all the time. My body also ached sometimes, with the pain seeping deep into my bones. That, on the other hand, made it harder to get out of bed.

By mid-July, I was back on my normal sleeping schedule, which was no sleep. I felt lonely. I felt sick. I felt *the pain*. My mind was tired. My body was, too. When I lay on my bed, all I could think about was jobs, apartments, and school. That's when my heart would start aching more intensely for hours. I couldn't keep my eyes closed for too long because I had nightmares. Some nights, I was scared to go to sleep because I dreaded this scenario of pain and nightmares that had been happening for days.

And then came the anxiety attacks. I went to bed one night at around 11 p.m., feeling as I described above. A few moments later, I jumped from my sleep, sat up right on my bed, and felt around for my phone. I pressed the middle button to check the time: 1:08 a.m. I'd just woken up from another nightmare. My heart was racing and hurting. My chest was tight, as if my sides had been pulled, folded, and sown together, and I couldn't pull them apart to catch my breath. The walls of my room were closing on me while tears made their way down my cheeks. I was scared. I pressed my eyes shut, rolled up my blanket and pressed it against my chest, slowly rocking back and forth, trying to calm myself. My breath was heavy. I squeezed my hands around the knot on the blanket and said a short prayer.

God, please just help me sleep through this night. I don't care about the pain; let it stay if You want, but please help me sleep. I'm begging You. It hurts, it hurts so bad, but I just want to sleep. Please, just tonight.

A few moments later, I released my grip on the knot, unfolded the blanket, and pulled it over my shoulder, sliding back into bed.

When I opened my eyes again, the sun had risen, as evidenced by its rays piercing through the window blinds. I swept my hand across the empty side of my bed to find my phone. I pressed the middle button: 7:35 a.m. For the first time in weeks, I'd slept more than three consecutive hours.

Thank You so much for helping me sleep, God.

I was glad but confused.

So, You do hear me, You do hear my prayers! You see me crying; You see everything I'm going through. So why won't You let me have a job? Why won't You let me go to school? Why won't You help me move out? Why do You let all these things happen to me? I don't understand.

I continued to have disturbed sleep and anxiety attacks here and there. I tried talking about them once, but people said since going to the U.S., I'd been having "White people issues." When I talked about my struggles finding a job or an apartment, they said I must've not looked hard enough, or that knowing me, I was probably too selective or aiming too high. People didn't understand me or what I was going through, so I decided not to bring up my issues anymore.

The time I spent on social media had decreased, but that didn't change how I felt inside. My negative thoughts actually got worse. I started wishing I could sleep and wake up months later. I pondered the possibility of finding pills that could alleviate the pain in my heart, or if there was a way to administer local anesthesia to my heart. I looked up hospitals that would only do that. I wanted to be numb to the pain.

I knew these were bad thoughts and, if presented with pills, I honestly would not have taken them. But that's also what frustrated me—I wasn't going to start drinking or doing drugs or getting high, and I wasn't shopping to feel better anymore either. So then, what was *my thing*? How was I supposed to cope with the pain or stop feeling it if all the things I could think of were bad for me?

I resisted thinking or saying I didn't want to be alive anymore, until I caved. What I did not think or say was that I wanted to die, though my thoughts pretty much meant the same thing. The reason I didn't go as far as to say I wanted to die or commit suicide is because of the promise I'd made to God and to myself, about ten years earlier, not to think or say those words ever again.

Younger, I struggled a lot with being and accepting myself. I struggled with who I was and how I looked, especially in comparison to my peers. I don't know if I qualified as overweight, but I sure was chubbier than my friends and classmates for the better part of my childhood. People already made fun of me and made nasty comments on my body in primary school, but I managed to either ignore them or cry about it, then move on with my life.

Middle school is when it got bad. I had the hardest time being myself and *fitting in*. For starters, the middle school I went to was exponentially larger than my primary school, so I could see at a larger scale how *not* skinny I was compared to everyone. At that point, I couldn't ignore people's comments anymore.

"You're too fat." "You need to exercise more." "Have you tried lemon juice?" "Boys only like skinny girls."

My cheeks and thighs were too big and my stomach not flat enough for people's liking, and now for mine either. Physical education class was, for sure, my least favorite. The comments were harsher and the laughter louder. My classmates laughed at every race I came out last and every time I couldn't jump as high as everyone else; they laughed louder at every forward or backward roll I didn't perform as well.

Every ounce I gained always seemed noticeable.

"Did you gain more weight?" "At this pace, you are going to explode." "Do you just eat all the food at your house?" "You're always eating; how are you not going to gain weight?"

There were times when I forced myself to only eat once a day or not at all, so I wouldn't gain more weight. I weighed myself more times than necessary—that is, every day. I snuck into my parents' bedroom every chance I got to climb on the scale and see how I was doing. Maintaining my weight, or better yet losing some of it, always brought a smile to my face. A smile that turned into tears when I couldn't sustain my eating habits and saw the repercussions on the scale.

Other times, I wished to get sick just so I could lose some weight. I wasn't a sickly child and though I knew that was a good thing, I thought maybe being ill was what I needed to finally go down a few sizes. Most of my close family members had gone through some type of surgery for various issues unrelated to their weight. However, seeing how much weight they were losing because of their surgery made me wish I had surgery too, or instead of them. Whenever Emma had a contagious disease, I tried my best to get contaminated so I, too, could be ill and lose some weight. From sleeping in the same bed when we had separate rooms to eating off the same plate and spending unusual amounts of time with her … I did everything I could, but something about my antibodies always made my schemes fail. I didn't like how I looked; I dreaded, then hated seeing my reflection in a mirror. Overtime, I also started hating and avoiding taking pictures. Pictures of myself.

Besides my problematic weight, there was the fact that I was "too emotional." I cried "too much" and "too easily." It didn't matter that they were tears of joy or sadness.

"You need to toughen up." "You're too sensitive." "You're such as a baby." "You need to have thicker skin."

I was also apparently "too kind," "too generous," and "too much of a good girl." People said I was either fake or too naïve.

"Okay, Mother Theresa, we get it." "Why do you always have to be the Good Samaritan?" "Why do you always have to act like you don't do anything bad?" "You act like you're perfect but you're not." "You follow the rules too much; you need to loosen up."

When I wasn't criticized for my generosity, I was taken advantage of because of it. Now, I will admit there were times when I did things hoping to be accepted, gaining a friend or finally belonging. But for the most part, I was just being kind. I was being myself.

My dad was quite strict, so I wasn't allowed to go out very much, and I barely participated in any extra-curricular activities. I only saw my friends at school or when they visited me at our house, which means I missed out on a lot of the things other people did on the weekends or during school breaks. I would see pictures on Facebook of how much fun they were having and wish I were there. I dreaded going back to school after the Christmas or Easter and summer breaks because of all the comments I knew I would get on the weight that I'd gained.

Coming into the world seven years after my parents had four children did not make me feel good about myself, either. All of them are only one to three years apart, which led me to think my parents were already done having children by the time they had my closest older brother. I thought they were already a perfect family, at least from a numbers' perspective: parents + two girls and two boys. I thought they did not want me. I used to think I was not planned, and that my parents made up for it by giving me the name Aimée, French for "Beloved." I would compare the age gap between my brother and me to the four years between Emma and me, wondering why I, too, hadn't been born four years or fewer after my brother instead of seven. Sometimes, people jokingly pointed out those age gaps and although I laughed, it wasn't funny to me. It was confirmation of what I was already thinking.

And now for what I've dreaded writing here the most: I was sexually assaulted by a person who worked at our house. I don't remember exactly how old I was when it happened, but I wasn't older than eleven; that all further degraded my self-esteem.

I used to calculate how much money my mom would save if I weren't born, all the things she wouldn't have to buy or pay for.

I used to feel like a burden.

I used to feel useless and out of place.

I used to wish I' never been born.

Back in middle school, I held a journal—or rather a diary. Of course, my classmates did not perceive it as "grown up" enough, but that was the only way I could get my thoughts and feelings out. I eventually stopped writing in that diary when I, too, felt like I was a little "too old" for that.

But while I had it, I wrote about my day every day after school. I wrote about how much I wanted to be "normal"; how much I wished I were like everyone else; how much I wanted to fit into smaller clothes so I could finally be pretty; how much I wished I could control my emotions and not cry so easily; how much I wished I could talk back when people attacked me; how much I wished I wasn't so naïve.

I am disgusted at myself. I am ugly. I am useless. I hate myself. I hate my body. I hate my life. I want to die. I want to commit suicide.

I wrote these words and their variations in my diary for two years—seventh and eighth grade. I used to think about ways I could die without hurting myself, without cutting or without hanging myself. When I realized there was nothing I had the courage to do to take my own life, I started praying that God would take me back because I was a mistake. Because *He had made a mistake.* I would go to bed praying and hoping that I wouldn't wake up in the morning. I would wake up every morning disappointed that God had not answered my prayer and hoping that maybe the following night was *the night.*

I starved myself.

I prayed to lose weight.

I prayed to get sick.

I prayed to die.

But I woke up unchanged day after day, and I eventually started thinking about taking my life away on my own again.

I didn't do it, and the main reason was my fear of going to hell. Someone once told me in sixth grade that everyone who commits suicide goes to hell. True or not, I believed them, and that stuck with me.

At my Catholic middle school, we had a weekly catechesis class during which we learned about God. Besides that, students who wanted to get baptized or do their first communion took specific catechesis classes to prepare for their sacrament. These were separate from the curriculum and occurred on Wednesday or Saturday afternoons throughout the academic year the sacrament was scheduled.

I got baptized as a child and did my first communion in eighth grade. As part of my preparation for the sacrament, I also had to go to confession; that was going to be my first time. So, a few weeks before the ceremony, my classmates, who were also preparing for a sacrament, and I headed to our school's chapel to confess our sins. When we got there, we found booklets on every seat to help guide our examination of conscience before entering the confessional. I picked mine up, sat, and read it. Right there, on the first page of the booklet, having suicidal thoughts was listed as a sin. It wasn't a surprise; it just looked more *real* written like that. While I was waiting for my turn to go into the confessional, and as I was trying to recall my (other) sins, one of the catechists advised and insisted that we confess our gravest sins first, as if he knew I was there and hesitating to even mention *that* sin.

"Everyone, don't forget, your gravest sins first." He said that eighteen million, four hundred and seventy-six thousand, nine hundred and thirty-two times. No kidding, I counted.

I went into the confessional and confessed my gravest sin last, because it wouldn't come out first.

When I got home, I wrote in my diary. Then, I tore a piece of paper and wrote:

I will never say that I want to die again. I will never say that I hate my life again. I will never say that I want to commit suicide again. I make this promise to God and to myself.

I folded the piece of paper into a small square, ran downstairs, and out into our backyard. I dug a hole in the ground with a small wooden stick, put my promise in it, then covered the hole back with my hands and feet. I'd already made that promise to God when I did my penance in the chapel a few hours earlier, but I guess I needed a symbol.

Things didn't magically get better. In fact, I still struggled with negative thoughts, and many of the things I previously mentioned continued to make me sad. But now that I had a promise to keep, I did everything in my power to not think about suicide or say that I hated my life. Over time, I developed self-confidence and in some areas of my life, people's opinion mattered less to me. I had negative thoughts here and there, but nothing too bad (I think). I never wished to be ill again, though I will admit that it made me happy to lose a few pounds whenever I was a little under the weather.

And at some point, suicide or anything related to death didn't cross my mind anymore … until that summer of 2018. Battling with these thoughts, trying to fend them off and hold on to life, was one of the hardest things I did that year.

———⌖———

A week before the end of my lease, I still hadn't found an apartment. By then, I'd decided to focus on finding a new place, so I put my job search on hold. What made it more difficult to find a room in a shared apartment was the fact that some tenants were looking for a "good fit" in a prospective roommate, which I understand. However, one way they went about it was to request social media handles to see what the potential roommate was into: their lifestyle, hobbies, activities, etc. They wanted "someone fun and down for anything." Well … let's just say that criterion alone was enough to disqualify me.

After yet another bad day, I texted Cedric—the middle school classmate who became my friend in college—and opened up for the first time in months about my struggles. I'd been feeling like a burden, calculating what my life was worth, adding up the costs of all my education and living expenses since I was born, and realizing it probably surpassed that of the people who came before me. And yet I couldn't find a job.

Danielle: Hey.

Cedric: Hey. What's up?

Danielle: I don't feel well.

Cedric: Tell me.

Danielle: I don't want to be alive anymore. Or at the very least, I'd like to get my heart anesthetized.

Cedric: Lol! Okay, chill out.

Danielle: You think I'm joking, but I'm actually very serious.

Cedric: Okay, I'm listening. What's wrong?

Danielle: I don't want to be dramatic and say everything is wrong. I know there are people in worse situations, but it really feels like everything is wrong.

Cedric: Do you want me to call you?

Danielle: No, not really. At least not now.

Cedric: Okay…

Danielle:

1. I still haven't found a new apartment, and my lease expires in a few days.

2. I had a bad day.

3. I've been having anxiety attacks. Yes, I know what you'll say: "White people stuff." And I'm serious when I say I am not well. I can't sleep at night. When I manage to close my eyes for a little bit, I wake up at least once in the middle of the night. And when I wake up, I have a terrible headache, and my heart is pounding.

   I also feel dizzy and nauseous at night. Not every night, but it happens often. The anxiety attacks, on the other hand, are more frequent.

   I've been thinking about taking sleeping pills, but I don't want to depend on them, and I read they can have bad side effects like depression. I'm already depressed enough. Even if I don't want to be alive anymore, I don't want to take away my own life.

4. I'm scared of going crazy. This is not a joke. I feel extremely lonely, and there's not much I can do about it. Add to that the move, the fact that I still might not go to school next semester, my financial situation … it's a lot to bear. Sometimes even during the day, I feel dizzy, and I feel like … I don't even know.

5. Crying is a disaster. Not only do I have a headache, but now it seems like I am allergic to my tears. Every time I cry, I wake

up with new pimples on my face. Last week, I only cried twice (yes, "only"), and right now my face is just...

It's so frustrating because even when I'm sad, I try not to cry. But sometimes I really want to let it out. And when I do, my face immediately reacts. And it's not like I'm not already spending a ton of money on skincare products.

6. Yeah ... I may not go to school in the fall unless another miracle happens.

7. I am physically and mentally exhausted. I don't want to feel anything anymore.

8. I feel weak. I can't control ANYTHING in my life anymore. I control absolutely nothing!

9. I hate feeling like this and having all these thoughts. I do everything I can to block them, but they always find their way back, and they consume me. I don't do it on purpose.

What bothers me most are my anxiety attacks. I try to stay positive, but if I manage to control my thoughts, I can't control my attacks. That's why I wanted to take pills. But then again, I don't want to depend on them and possibly overdose.

Last night (or rather, this morning, since I don't sleep before 2 a.m.), I got really scared. I woke up suddenly around 5 a.m., and I was in pain, and my heart was beating so fast! At least this time I didn't have a nightmare.

10. Have you ever been bored? Like you had absolutely nothing to do, and no one was there with you—no family, no friends—while you live in a tiny bedroom? Can you imagine living like this every single day? Well, that's exactly how it is for me. The sun

rises and sets before my eyes. I can't tell you what I did in July, and yet it's the end of the month.

Assuming I don't go to school next semester (which starts at the end of August), that is how I'll spend all my days until January 2019, if I do go to school then.

That is how I've been living since last year, and it's been really hard. I can't keep doing this. I feel like my head will explode. Even right now, my shoulder hurts. I just want to get a full body anesthesia.

Cedric: Wow … that's really tough, and I'm really sorry. But Danielle, have you considered coming back? To get a fresh start maybe?

Danielle: It's not as easy as it seems. You can't imagine the sacrifices and efforts that have been put into getting me to where I am now. Last year, I almost came back around September. I was ready to do it until the opportunity to stay presented itself. It's hard, very hard. But I don't want to lose all the effort I've put in so far and come back to start another master's all over again, when I've already done one semester of an MBA (not to brag). And if I do come back home, I'll feel like a failure.

I'm not complaining about my problems. I'm just talking about them and regretting the effects they have on me. All I want is to graduate and move on. And it may sound contradictory to what I said above, but I feel like I'm going to make it. I want to work for and earn my degree as well as everything that will come after. I'm not in the worst position. I'm just exhausted.

Cedric: See, you're even stronger than you think. Hold on to these values, and you will find more strength.

Danielle: For now, I just don't have any more of that.

Cedric: You just need some rest. Take a break and then get back up.

Danielle: Do you really think life gives me time to rest? Even when I'm down, it keeps hitting. That's why I say I don't want to feel anything anymore. It's like I have no limits, and I can take anything. My body, my head, my mind … all my tanks are empty, and yet challenges keep increasing. So, it's best to just get a full anesthesia; that way, I'll be able to take it all in without a problem.

Cedric: You know this is not different from a suicidal thought, right?

Danielle: Yes, and I also said I wasn't going to take away my own life.

Cedric: Yes, but you're still very close. And let me just say this right now: You'll hurt your family more than yourself.

Danielle: I don't think so. And I'm not saying this so you can make me feel better about myself but … think about it: You know how you calculate the net present value for a project to determine whether to invest in it? So, I'm I0, the initial investment, and my NPV is all the way negative. Let me explain. I'm alive, and I don't produce any cash flow, but people keep spending on me. I have to eat, live somewhere, and go to school in the U.S., where the cost of living is super high. In return, what do I bring? Stress to my mom, for example. And what else? Nothing. And when your project is not profitable, what do you do? I know you're smart.

Cedric: Lol. Well, yes, I am smart, and most projects don't pay off immediately. For now, your mom is investing in you. No one is asking you to earn anything right now.

You think you're stressing her out? She's been stressing out since you were born because she wants the best for you. She's stressed out about Emma because she wants the best for her. Just keep fighting. Danielle, life is a battle. You are strong; don't let these challenges bring you down.

Danielle: Thank you. 😊 🖤

CHAPTER 10:

EVEN CLOSER

O n the afternoon of July 29th, two days before I needed to move out of my apartment, I still hadn't found a new place. I came back home from touring a three-bedroom, one-bathroom apartment in Lincoln Square, a forty-minute train ride from home. I didn't love that I was going to share the bathroom with two other people, but at that point, it didn't matter anymore. I felt safe in the neighborhood and the rent was within my budget, and that's all that mattered.

I waited for one of the girls who lived there to call me back, as she said she would, but a few hours later, she still hadn't called. I gave up and decided to see if I could still renew my lease at the student complex. Before going down to the leasing office, I checked Craigslist one last time for no reason at all. I was casually looking, almost certain I wasn't going to find anything. But then I came across a listing of an available bedroom in a four-bedroom, two-bathroom apartment within ten minutes walking distance of my building. The room had been posted earlier in the day, and the landlord was looking to lease it out as soon as possible. I looked at the pictures, not really caring what the room looked like. Rent was $950 a month, slightly over my budget, but I was hoping that would be doable for my mom. The landlord also lived nearby, so we agreed to meet at 5 p.m. the same day.

The apartment was on the second floor of a three-story walk-up building, with no other amenities than the laundry room in the basement. I didn't realize from the listing that the available room was the master bedroom, meaning it had its own in-suite bathroom. Three other girls would share the other bathroom, who, like my soon-to-be ex-roommates, all went to UIC right across the street. I didn't see them; in fact, one had not even moved in yet, according to the landlord.

The available room was big enough to accommodate a queen-size bed and a desk comfortably. It was bigger than my current room. The rays that came through the single window shed squares and rectangles of light on the wooden floor, making the step marks more noticeable. They were probably from the other tours the landlord had done during the day. When I walked into the bathroom, I noticed the streaks on the mirror and the stains on the shower glass door that made it hard to see through it. *That's fine; I can fix all this.*

The bedroom wasn't furnished, but the kitchen had two medium-size refrigerators—one for two tenants—a microwave, and an oven and a dishwasher, both of which did not work. I didn't care. The living area did not have a TV, but I didn't care either because I didn't watch TV at my current place, anyway. Not so much because I didn't want to, but because it had an issue that never got fixed, despite mine and my roommates' complaints to management. So, I eventually got used to not watching any TV at all. The amenities were minimal compared to where I lived, but I didn't look at amenities anymore when I toured apartments. I just needed a place to rest my head.

The application fee was $70 and if approved, I would have to pay a one-month deposit in addition to August's rent, due on the

1st. That was going to be a squeeze, but at least the landlord wasn't going to do a background check. After he told me the other girls were all international students, I told him I was, too. He understood why I didn't have credit, unlike some of the other landlords or tenants I'd met before.

"So, how do you support yourself?" he asked to find out how I was going to pay rent.

"I … so uhm … my … my mom? She'll help me pay," I started, but felt like that wasn't enough, so I continued: "B … but I also have a job. I work full-time as a waitress at a restaurant nearby, and I'll continue part-time when I go back to school next month," I blurted, as fast as my heart was beating. He'd caught me off guard. I crossed my fingers behind my back and hoped he wasn't going to seek confirmation.

"Okay. I just emailed you the application form. Just fill it out and send it back to me tomorrow morning at the latest with your fees," he responded.

Oh my God, thank You!

"Yeah sure! Will do it as soon as I get home."

I went home and did exactly that. The landlord also needed references. He wanted my current leasing office's phone number to confirm I always paid rent on time, as well as one of my roommates' phone numbers to enquire about the type of roommate I was. I asked Flora, who I was closest to, if I could give her phone number. She agreed. I sent the application and paid the fees. With the leftover money I had, I bought an inexpensive mattress on Amazon and had it delivered to the new place, hoping my application would be approved.

Shortly after, I texted my mom to let her know I had potentially found an apartment. She knew I was looking to move out and was already prepared to pay for August's rent, but I needed help to buy moving boxes, pay the deposit, and hire movers. All of that needed to happen the next day, because I had to move out no later than 10 a.m. on July 31st, or else I would get a fine.

The next day, I woke up to the approval email from my new landlord. That was great, but only half the battle. Later in the day, my mom sent me a text with the information related to the money she had just sent me. She'd sent enough to pay for my deposit and moving expenses and was going to send the rest the next day, on August 1st.

I walked to the nearest Western Union to pick up the money, but they had trouble disbursing the funds. I tried another location and faced the same issue. I tried a third and was told I wouldn't be able to pick up that money because it seemed I had received *too* many payments. *Are you serious right now? What do you mean, "too many payments"?!* That didn't make any sense. When I called customer service, they said the same thing, informing me they'd already sent the money back to my mom. I needed to wait another *thirty days* if I wanted to receive "more" money. We would have tried MoneyGram, but it was already past normal business hours back home. We'd tried PayPal in the past and had no luck. We tried again, and it didn't work.

I burst into tears. *Why is everything always so complicated? Why can't this one thing go smoothly?* Now my mom was going to have to send all the money at once the next day. I know this wasn't my fault, but I felt like a burden putting her through all this. *If I weren't born, this would've never happened. She wouldn't have to go through this.* That voice was loud in my head as I reached out to Sophie for help. She was able to send me enough money to buy moving supplies. I went to U-Haul, bought moving boxes and tape, then headed home to start packing.

———— ⊂▥⊃ ————

Everyone in my apartment was moving out, and it looked like many people in the building were too when I went down to the leasing office on July 31st to pick up my move-out form. I'd found movers on Craigslist and told them to be there by 9:30 a.m. They called around nine to let me know they were going to be *a little bit* late. I watched my roommates leave and couldn't help but wish I too had friends to help me move out, so I wouldn't have to spend $150 on movers to get out of that place.

At 11:30 a.m., the movers were still not there, and I was the only one left in the apartment when management came in to do the inspection. I got a $50 fine for not moving out on time. Additionally, they charged my now former roommates and I a combined $250 for the cleaning they said they would have to do in our suite.

I only paid the late move fine because it was due immediately. I didn't have another $62 laying around, waiting to be spent on fines. I didn't have a good experience living at that place anyway and had paid enough fines and given them enough money as is. The other fine was posted to my online account; I was moving out, so I just never logged back in. They called several times afterward, and I just didn't pick up.

———— ⊂▥⊃ ————

The movers arrived at noon, and I finally caught my breath when I got to my new place with all my stuff around 1 p.m. I'd walked about twenty minutes to 820 South Morgan Street, taking longer because I was carrying a few bags. My mattress had been delivered earlier that day, which the movers helped bring into my room. I still had the bedframe I'd bought a year earlier when I wanted to move to the

Rogers Park studio apartment, but it needed to be assembled. One of the movers had volunteered to do it but bailed out last minute after I gave him his money for the move.

I spent the rest of the day trying but failing to finish deep cleaning, unpacking, and putting everything where it needed to be. Who knew you couldn't do it all in one day?

From what I had seen and heard from taskers on Craigslist when I called them, assembling my bedframe was going to cost me anywhere from $100 to $200. I didn't have that kind of money.

My mattress was still in its box by the time I finished unpacking the rest of my stuff, but I was too tired to open it. So, for my first night, I slept on the floor. I laid a pair of sheets somewhere in the middle of the room and rolled up an old T-shirt to rest my head on it because I didn't have pillows yet. It was a summer night, so the floor wasn't too cold. I can't sleep without a blanket, no matter the season of the year, so I covered myself with the light soft grey blanket I got when I moved into the previous apartment. I can't sleep in the dark either, so I left the bathroom light on before arranging my sleeping station for the night.

My hands and my back and my feet and my bones and my heart were aching. But despite all the stress and craziness I'd been through that day and the days before, I was thankful to finally be where I was. Before closing my eyes, I looked around the room, partially lit by the warm light shining through the open bathroom door. I had found a new place; and that place had a private bathroom. In that private bathroom, there was a mirror cabinet—something I'd never had before but always wanted. It wasn't something I was looking for when I toured apartments; it was more like a would-be-nice-to-have. The closet in my room also had mirror doors, something else I wish I'd had when my $10 full-length mirror from Target broke in my last apartment. I'd gotten another one, but it would've been nice not to have to. Plus, I loved how mirror doors looked, the illusion of additional space they give to a room. There was also a windowsill in the room, deep and large enough to sit on it. Something else I didn't look or wish for but always thought looked cute and would be nice to have one day. I smiled, thinking about how often I would go sit in that little nook and look out to the street or watch the sky while listening to music.

My room wasn't perfect, but it was everything I needed and more. The apartment wasn't perfect and not as aesthetically pleasing as the previous one, but it had everything I needed.

Thank You, God, for helping me find this apartment and helping me move in. Please protect my family, my friends, and me throughout the night, as well as those who don't have a shelter. Also, please give me the strength to assemble my bedframe tomorrow. Good night. I love You.

I closed my eyes just before two a.m. and opened them again around eight.

———⟨▦⟩———

After more hours of unpacking, organizing, and cleaning, I took a break before getting started on assembling my bedframe. I was hungry but didn't have groceries yet. I checked my bank account balance to see how much I had left after all the expenses I'd made. *Four dollars and eighty cents.* Taco Bell had a two-dollar burrito deal that summer. With tax, I was still going to be under four dollars, so I decided to get one later in the day at a nearby location.

All these pieces… I was staring at the small and large parts of my bedframe scattered on the floor. It was a metal frame with wooden slats. It came with a manual, but still, I had no idea how I was going to put that together—I'd never had to do something like that before.

Some of the assembly required the use of a hammer, and I luckily already had a toolbox. I took a "before" picture for my own records, then started screwing and hammering away.

Hours of struggle later, I was finally done. I took an "after" picture of the assembled frame and opened the mattress box. I crumbled under its weight trying to put it on the frame, and when I finally succeeded, I took another picture, then a final one when I put the sheets and blanket. I stared and smiled at my masterpiece for a few seconds, ignoring my burning back, my tingling hands, and my bruised knees. I was proud of myself. I liked my new room. I was still missing a few things, but fortunately, there was a table and a chair that the landlord said I could use at no extra cost. I put my wooden **DREAMS come TRUE** sign on the left corner of the table and organized the rest of it with my other desk stuff.

I cleaned up, showered, then headed out to Taco Bell. On my way, I got a Venmo notification—Naomi had just sent me $50 for no reason. I still wanted my burrito, so I stayed on my way to Taco Bell. Plus, I was going to use that money to buy groceries for later. Once I got to Taco Bell and was ready to order, the lady at the counter said there wasn't any more of the $2 burritos. That's when I realized Who the $50 had *really* come from. I ordered a more expensive item that my initial account balance wouldn't be able to cover. I ate my food, then went to Mariano's to buy groceries before heading back to my new home.

The package with my new devotional and prayer journal was delivered on August 6th. I'd stopped reading the Bible sometime in April because it'd become a bit boring, and I'd gotten scared of what was happening in the Old Testament. I hadn't finished reading the New

Testament just yet, but after a few weeks of reading almost the same thing in the Gospels, I felt like trying something new. But reading the Old Testament made me afraid of God. I didn't know how to interpret all the destruction and violence and the books. I wanted to know Him better, but I needed guidance. I'd looked for devotionals, done some research, watched YouTube videos, but nothing really spoke to me.

While I was battling with my negative thoughts a few weeks earlier on July 19th, I came across an interesting post on my WhatsApp stories. An old classmate used to post daily pages of the devotional he read: *Jesus Calling* by Sarah Young. That day, the devotional was about anxiety and fear. It recommended bringing all our feelings to God, including those we wished we never had; it emphasized that the feelings themselves were not sinful, but could lead to sin.

The entire text of that day spoke to me, so I decided to buy the book, hoping to find some semblance of peace and read the Bible through a new lens. I saw a prayer journal on the site that looked cute, so I bought it as well. The devotional and prayer journal both came on a Monday, which was perfect considering I didn't like starting new things mid-week. I read the devotional, then wrote in my new journal.

CHAPTER 11:

BACK TO BASICS—PART I

My prayer journal wasn't dated, but each entry was broken up into eight sections, starting with a field for entering the date. For the entries I share, I'll include some or all sections depending on the information it contains. If a section is missing, it may contain sensitive information, or it may involve other people whose privacy I want to protect. Sometimes, I also crossed out certain sections while writing because I needed more space to freely express my feelings. I didn't intend, through writing in my prayer journal or any other journal, to make my thoughts public; that being the case, everything I share is an accurate representation of my feelings at the time of writing.

What I've written in this book so far was based on memories, text messages, pictures, and emails. Though this will not change, starting this chapter and for the following three, I'll let the thoughts and feelings in my journals speak for themselves, while providing context and commentary where necessary. The regular narrative will resume in Chapter 15, with a few journal entries here and there.

I didn't write in my prayer journal every single day, nor did I write solely in the morning or at night. I wrote whenever I felt the need to, whenever I wanted to talk to God somewhere other than in my heart.

Date: 08/06/2018

Dear Heavenly Father... I love You, and I thank You for all Your blessings. Please also use me as a tool to bring Your light to the people in my life. I want to be a blessing for them as well.

Thank You for... Allowing me to move into a new place, with my own bathroom. 😊

I am worried about... Not being able to go to school this semester. Not FEELING happy again. My professional life. My future.

Here's what's happening in my life... I am lost, in so many ways. I know nothing about what's going to happen next for me. Not that I should know or control everything, I just feel powerless.

I need... You to always guide me through the right path. I want to become the woman You created me to be.

Other things on my heart that I need to share with You, God... I feel lonely and deep inside, I'm not happy. 😖

Date: 08/16/2018

Dear Heavenly Father... You know me, my heart and my thoughts. You know I try to be positive and to remain thankful for what I have, but I've been feeling so lonely. Please help me deal with my feelings.

Thank You for... My life, my family and friends, everything I have, material or not. My health, my new place, and all the things I unintentionally take for granted.

I am worried about... What's next for me, this year and beyond. Not being able to go to school, not finding an internship, not having a social life.

People I am praying for today... My mom. 🖤 🖤

Here's what's happening in my life... I am scared of life, my future, the plans You have for me that I don't know about, how I am going to make it ... I know I have You, but fear keeps coming at me. ☹️

I need... Strength and, most importantly, peace. I need You to always be with me and help me get rid of my fear of everything. I need help in enjoying what I have now and trusting You through the process.

Other things on my heart that I need to share with You, God... Do You think I'm going to FEEL happy again? Have an internship? Graduate next year? Please help me not forget about Your blessings; help me keep a grateful heart; help me get rid of negative thoughts.

Later in August, my sister Sophie got a loan she'd applied for to continue helping my mom pay for my school. About three days before the fall semester started, she paid the first installment of my tuition fees, and I started classes on time. This time, I hadn't met with my academic advisor before enrolling in my classes.

Had I done the summer semester, I would have taken three classes to graduate in May 2019. By taking one additional class in the fall (three + one = four total), the remaining two would be moved to the spring semester if I wanted to graduate that term. I enrolled in that additional class in the fall, hoping to find an internship in the spring and get credit for it, instead of taking an actual class. That way, in the spring of 2019, I would have five classes (three core courses, plus the internship, which was technically not a class, and the remaining class I hadn't taken in the summer).

The goal wasn't to "catch up" anymore. With everything I'd been through and was still going through, graduating "on time" was no longer something I cared about. In fact, I no longer felt "behind" for graduating after May 2019, because going to school was already a blessing.

My experiences made me realize and understand that everyone truly does have their own timeline. I also came to terms with the fact that my graduation year didn't matter, so long as I graduated. And if for some reason I had to go back home, sure, I would've been sad, but I no longer cared about what I would tell people or what they would think. What was going to bother me, however, was them seeing my face. That said, I still had a strong preference for graduating in May 2019, for OPT purposes and because I was getting tired of being in the U.S.

OPT, as mentioned earlier, is what would allow me to remain and work in the U.S. for a year after graduation. However, because of the many rules around it, it made more sense to apply for it when graduating in the spring rather than in the winter. Again, I'll go into more detail once we get to the point where I needed to apply for my OPT.

Summer 2018 is also when I started looking into going to Canada, though it wasn't anything too serious at first. I'd enjoyed my marketing class so much during my first semester at Roosevelt that I wanted to learn more and get some sort of credential in marketing. I'd been exploring the idea of getting a certification in digital marketing specifically, but I wanted to work first and save enough money to pay for that myself.

One night, as I was having trouble sleeping, I continued my research into marketing certifications and programs in North America. I didn't want to stay in the U.S., but if I had to, I was going to. That is when I came across an ad for the newly created Master of Marketing program at the Schulich School of Business in Toronto. I immediately fell in love with it. For starters, the school was in Toronto; that's where I wanted to live if I moved to Canada. Then, I thought the program itself was perfect—a one-year specialized master's program with a focus on modern marketing. But the tuition cost … CAD75,000. That was for international students, who pay three times as much as domestic and permanent resident students. On top of tuition, I would need to consider living expenses and other school- and non-school-related fees.

I decided to keep that school in the back of my mind. I was going to apply for it in the fall of 2022 or later, once I'd worked a few years and accumulated enough savings. I kept the school in the back of my mind, but it came back to the front on its own.

Date: 09/09/2018

Dear Heavenly Father... You know I'm thankful for what I have, and I try not to compare my life to other people's lives, but it's so hard when it seems like I am stagnating and don't have much going on.

Thank You for... Allowing me to start my second semester. My life, my family, and friends. My hair growth. 😊

I am worried about... Not getting an internship next semester. Not finding a job for my OPT. Struggling for everything.

Here's what's happening in my life... I am so scared that even for the most basic things in my life, I'm always going to struggle and suffer before I finally get them. I've been looking for a job for a year now, Lord, please help!

I need... "Hope deferred makes the heart sick." It's in the Bible ... Please Lord, make something happen for me too.

Other things on my heart that I need to share with You, God... I know Your time is the right time, but if everything that even happens comes at the last minute, why do I have to try so hard before that last minute? Why don't I just wait till the "end" to make a move?

I'd started classes and would begin looking for an internship soon. After an unsuccessful summer trying to find a job, I decided to only start looking again around October for my spring 2019 internship. At least by then, I would've already been a student for two consecutive mandatory semesters (spring and fall 2018), so I would be eligible for an SSN and for CPT. Making that decision reminded me of the prayer I'd made on Easter Sunday that year.

Back in April, I still wanted to stay and live in the U.S. for as long as possible, but I wanted to do it the right way, according to my *personal* values. I didn't want to break the rules too much. I didn't want to do anything illegal or have to marry someone to get a Green Card. It became harder to only pursue legal job opportunities when I was broke and needed money just to eat. But what I still would not compromise on was marriage. I told God I would rather leave the U.S. than marry someone to stay, even, and especially, if it was a fake marriage.

So, in August, when I decided to wait until I was legally able to work in the U.S., I thought maybe that was God doing me a favor and answering my prayer by not allowing me to get any of the jobs I so desperately wanted during the summer.

As for things happening last minute, you can tell, if you've read this far, that whenever something I wanted or prayed for ended up happening, it did so right at the deadline. I wasn't less thankful, but looking, walking up and down, doing research for months only for something to happen at the very last minute is exhausting and frustrating.

Date: 11/12/2018

Dear Heavenly Father... Am I supposed to not be frustrated if I trust You? What kind of strength do I have that I can withstand this type of frustration? I don't want You to think that I don't trust You or am being impatient; I am just overwhelmed!

~~Thank You for...~~ It's mid-November and I haven't found an internship for January. Yes, I have to be patient, but I have deadlines! Please don't be mad at me. I'm trying so hard to be positive, and You know I keep telling myself that You got me, but then am I supposed to not feel the pressure?

~~I am worried about...~~ I am extremely thankful for what I already have, but God, You know I am not comfortable and haven't been for a while. Why do You keep me in this place for such a long time? Almost everyone around me has a job or at least an internship, and I still can't eat without my sister's help.

~~People I am praying for today...~~ I know it's bad and it's probably the devil murmuring in my ears, but I've been feeling like there's something wrong with me. I feel like You're mad at me and every time I cry, I feel like it makes You angry and You further block my blessings.

Here's what's happening in my life... Please don't punish me. I'm begging You, please release my blessings. Or just show me what else I need to learn so I can FINALLY move on with my life. Please, please Lord, listen to my cry.

~~I need...~~ My job search is so overwhelming, I honestly feel like giving up. I won't, but I just don't know how and where to look anymore. I am so scared 2019 is also going to be filled with struggles in addition to my loneliness. Please make something happen.

At that point in my story, I'd been looking for an internship for over a month. I know today that it's not a very long time in Job Search Land; however, my frustration was factoring in the entire year during which I'd already been looking for a job. My loneliness and the fact that I had virtually no one to talk to did not help either.

I had class four times a week that semester, still at night. I came home around 9:30 p.m., depending on how quickly I could catch a Blue Line train at the Jackson station. I spent my days in my room looking for internships. During the day, my roommates would be at school, leaving the house mostly empty. By the time I got back from school, they'd already finished dinner and retired to their rooms. They rarely spent the weekends at the apartment, especially Saturdays.

One roommate, Charlotte, either spent the weekends at her boyfriend's, or he was at our place, so I didn't see her much. Not sure what Zoe's and Alice's relationship statuses were, but I didn't see them much either. When I did, it was probably on Sundays, on my way to or from church, or when I was cooking.

To be honest, I didn't spend a ton of time in the living room either, even when I heard them chat all together. Especially in the beginning, I was shy and unsure whether I'd be able to hold a conversation. Spending more than a year on my own made me forget how to interact with people. I didn't think my life was very interesting, and I always wondered what we would even talk about if I joined them. So, I stayed in my room and only listened to the sound of their voices and laughter.

I was still struggling financially and had no savings at all. I'd never gone this long with no money aside. In fact, I'd never *not* had savings. I could barely keep $50 in my savings account without having to transfer it all back to the checking account within a week, because something had come up that I needed to pay for. My money went into school-related expenses or into saving to buy my next Clinique Acne Solutions kit. I could not do my nails or my hair or take care of myself as I used to.

Sophie had been ordering groceries for me for almost two months at that point. She'd called me one day to see how I was doing, and somewhere in the conversation, I mentioned not having enough money to buy groceries and not wanting to bother Mom. She volunteered to buy them for me. Every two weeks or so, I would put my Mariano's groceries in my Instacart, show it to her, and she would check out for me and have the groceries delivered to my apartment.

I still remember the first time my groceries arrived. After putting them all away, I stood there, alone in the kitchen, looking at the cabinets and freezer full of food. I hadn't bought jasmine rice in a long time. If I bought meat, I would only eat it on Sunday, but not every Sunday. This time, I had meat and chicken to eat throughout the week. I was so grateful.

Overtime, though, this situation made me uncomfortable. My sister was already doing a lot for me, and I didn't want to ask for more. I wanted to take care of myself. Sometimes when she forgot to buy me groceries, I didn't remind her.

———— ⊂▦⊃ ————

I cried every day. I'm not kidding. I cried every single day of every single week, either because I wasn't getting interviews and my only updates were rejections; or because I felt extremely lonely and had no friends; or because of the way my skin looked; or because I wasn't financially stable and had too many bills and things to pay for; or because sometimes I couldn't find the strength to keep going but had no other choice; or because I wanted to experience happiness again and stop pretending I was fine; or because I felt like God wasn't listening to me; or because I felt like a burden; or because of the pain in my heart; or because of everything all at once.

Some days I wondered if the well of tears inside of me would ever dry out, and I would get the answer the following days when I cried even more.

It got to a point where I had to put a limit on the number of times I allowed myself to cry every week, because I didn't like the look of swollen eyes and tired skin every morning. I would give myself exercises, such as waiting until the weekend to cry and release the frustration of the week. When that wasn't possible, I would have to try to at least make it to Wednesday without crying.

Some weeks, I made a conscious effort to be positive and stay that way for as long as possible, but that wasn't easy. There was always going to be that *one* thing that was going to try to ruin my efforts. Sometimes it worked; sometimes it didn't. Some days I tried to convince myself that I was okay and that whatever was bothering me was not a big deal. *I am happy. I am fine. Life is good.* I wasn't being sarcastic. I repeated those words to myself, hoping that the more I said them, the better I would feel. Some days it worked; most days, it didn't.

I had another journal where I kept motivational quotes and the Bible verses I liked, those that made me feel a little less alone, those that gave me a little hope. One day, I wrote a few of them on colored pieces of paper that I glued to my wall, right above my desk. They served as motivation; as reminders to hope and continue holding on.

"The pain that you've been feeling cannot compare to the joy that is coming" (Romans 8:18).

This is one verse that I repeated to myself every time I cried and every time my heart was aching with *that* pain. Well ... maybe not *every* time, but like, most times.

Date: 11/17/2018

Dear Heavenly Father... Hey God, I just came here to tell You I love and trust You. For once, I don't come to complain about the current state of my life. Things are still all blurred and confused, but I just wanted to say I trust You.

Thank You for... The fact that You have been soothing my heart and spirit. I am still stressed out and overwhelmed, but I don't know ... I also feel some type of security and confidence that things will be fine, that my time will come, and it's all thanks to You.

I am worried about... I DO NOT WANT TO BE WORRIED ANYMORE. Yes, I've still got my struggles, but You will help me!

People I am praying for today... People going through hard times. Anyone looking for a job. The homeless and helpless.

Here's what's happening in my life... I am not yet where I would like to be. Nothing has changed substantially between last time I wrote in this journal and today, but I am feeling a little more ... at peace. I love You.

I need... You to continue to guide me and be with me along this journey of life. I 🖤 You. I trust You. 😊 🖤

Other things on my heart that I need to share with You, God... My job search is still overwhelming. The semester is coming to an end so that means more work and all assignments due soon. I still have no clue what I'm going to do next year after graduation, my skin has been breaking out, etc. BUT I trust You, God, I know You are with me. 🖤

I quite honestly can't remember exactly what put me in such a good mood that day. I know I was still reading my devotional every morning, and that did help. I'd also bought a job search book a few days earlier, but besides that, nothing major had happened. Unfortunately, that mood did not last very long.

Date: 12/17/2018

Dear Heavenly Father... So today is December 17th, and I still haven't gotten one single in-person interview for an internship that's supposed to start in January. I'm not coming here to complain; I'm just wondering if I shouldn't just give up and understand I won't get an internship.

Thank You for... The recent great experiences with Zoe. Really, from the bottom of my heart, thank You for that.

I am worried about... My professional and financial life. I have all these dreams and goals, but they all depend on my being financially independent, which I can't seem to make ANY progress toward. It seems SO out of reach!

Here's what's happening in my life... I kind of feel like I didn't get the assistantship position. I mean ... it's been more than a month since I applied and still ... no response. Again, I'm not complaining, I'm just lost and can't seem to find the purpose of having all these good grades.

I need... strength and guidance. You know, it's been overwhelming looking for a job; I don't even know if You want me to have one.

Other things on my heart that I need to share with You, God... I recently read that it doesn't matter how long or how many times or how earnestly we pray for something that doesn't align with Your will, because You won't make it happen. It makes total sense, and I get that. But then, how do I know when to pray for something, and what is Your will?

I was starting to get along well with my roommates, especially Zoe. She knew I spoke French and had a friend who was taking a French class at the time, so she would sometimes invite her over so I could have quick conversations with her or help with assignments.

One afternoon, Zoe and I were both home at the same time. She didn't have class, and I was in my room looking for internships. She wanted to hang out.

"Hey Danielle?" Zoe knocked on my door, and I opened it. "Do you wanna go out for a walk? It's not too cold outside today."

"Hmm … I'm not sure I can right now," I started. "I have a lot of work to do for my class tonight." I finished my lie.

I wanted to go out for a walk, but I was worried I would be too boring, and we wouldn't have fun.

"Oh okay … Bummer." She made a sad face and walked away as I closed the door.

I sat back at my desk and spent the following ten minutes wondering why I had just turned down an opportunity to not walk alone for once.

"Hey, do you still wanna go out? I'll take my stuff and finish my work at school before class." I asked, meeting Zoe in the kitchen.

"Are you sure?" She asked, looking up from her bowl with her mouth half full.

"Yeah, don't worry about it. My assignment is not super hard, so I'll be able to finish it in no time."

"Cool! Okay, let's gooo!!"

Zoe was a bit (or a lot) more extroverted than me. I packed my stuff for school while she finished her meal, then we headed out.

We walked, we talked, we laughed, we took pictures, we had a good time.

Having little to no social interactions for such a long time had made me forget how and who I was. I couldn't remember if I was funny, if I was nice, or if I had interesting things to say. I didn't interact much with people at school either for the same reasons. On top of that, I was extremely self-conscious because of my skin. Every time someone came close to me, all I could think about was what they were seeing on my face. And because of my financial situation, I didn't think I could afford to have friends to hang out with.

That short walk with Zoe was my first outing with someone my age, and it felt good. Later in November, she invited me to the Friendsgiving dinner she hosted at the apartment with her friends on Thanksgiving. On another night, as a thank-you for helping her friend with her French assignments and exams, she wanted all three of us to have dinner somewhere nice. So, we went to an Italian restaurant right in the West Loop. I spent about $50 that night, which was a squeeze, and though that would not become a habit, I was thankful to have gone out to eat with them.

Regarding the assistantship position, I had once more applied to be a graduate assistant. This time, I even had reference letters from two of my professors. I got A's in all my classes and hoped that both elements would play in my favor to get the position for my last semester. They didn't.

Date: 12/29/2018

Dear Heavenly Father... Hey God. How are You? I'm good, I guess ... I just feel like there's something (or many things) wrong with me. You know I don't say that to sound cliché; I really feel that way. I mean ... I feel like there are so many things I don't do right or that I don't do at all, and that's why I am still at this point in my life.

Thank You for... My sister coming to visit for the holidays, my family and friends, my education, and my life overall.

I am worried about... You already know. It's almost January and no internship so far. I'm just afraid You've decided I won't have an internship. Maybe it's still not the right time for me to work?

Here's what's happening in my life... I am trying to find myself and know who I am. I want to be a good person, but sometimes I feel like it's "too much" or that I HAVE TO have a "bad side" to be successful. I don't know. I'm not saying I am the "best" person on earth or that I'm perfect, but I really want to be good and follow the rules as much as possible, but apparently at some point you have to break them?

I need... You to help me find myself and be the person You created me to be. You to fix me if there really is something wrong with me. I love You, God.

Other things on my heart that I need to share with You, God... I would like to get to a point where I live comfortably without breaking the rules or going around them so much, and I hope that's possible.

Naomi came to Chicago for the holidays and stayed from December 24, 2018, to January 1, 2019. From going to the Christmas market and to Christmas-themed bars, to visiting museums and eating out at nicer restaurants, we had a good time. I was grateful I hadn't spent the holidays alone that year.

My internship search still wasn't going well. I'd spoken to a few people, and it seemed like I wasn't going to find anything if I didn't lie on my resume. I'd done that before, when I changed my education level because I didn't want to seem overqualified for the jobs I was applying to during the summer of 2018. But this time was different. I was looking for an internship that had to be related to my degree and match my education level. And regardless of the CPT requirements, I just didn't want to have to lie on my resume to get a job. I didn't, but I was starting to feel like I was being too much of a "good girl" and needed to "loosen up." Maybe I needed to lie more. At least just to get an internship.

Now, I'm not saying I'm a saint and I do nothing wrong. I've often made and still make bad decisions; however, those are mine. They are not pushed on me, and I am not forced to make them. I either consciously or unconsciously make bad choices, but I own them. Being pressured to lie is different from lying on my own terms. Yes, the result is the same, but the feeling is not.

––––––––⌀––––––––

There were three main issues I faced in my internship search journey. The first one was my lack of experience as an MBA student. Most MBA internship postings I came across on LinkedIn or Indeed required at least two years of experience. I could apply for internships that only required a bachelor's degree, but I would be overqualified; and even if I got the position, it wouldn't qualify for CPT because it didn't match my education level. The best I could do was to find something that did not specify the education level in the job description, and rather said something like, "The candidate should be working toward *a degree* in XYZ." But then again, the degree had to be business-related, or else my CPT application would be denied for not being related to my field of study.

The second issue I faced, which was probably more important and certainly the most frustrating, was the very fact that I was an international student. International students in the U.S. have a great number of work restrictions and rules to comply with, and many employers don't want to deal with those. Some internships and job postings blatantly said they were not open to non-citizens or non-Green Card holders. Others said they did not accept students on CPT or OPT and that their applications would not be considered. And most postings had a variation of this statement: "Candidates should not now or in the future require sponsorship for employment." In fact, questions such as, "Will you now or in the future require sponsorship for employment?" or "Are you authorized to work for any employer without sponsorship now or in the future?" were part of almost every job application and were used to screen out international students.

OPT and CPT did not require sponsorship, but the work visa–H1-B visa–did. You could only apply for the H1-B visa once you'd graduated from a U.S school and had completed an OPT. So, as an international student on CPT or OPT, even if you did not require sponsorship "now," you probably would at some point "in the future" if the goal was to remain in the U.S. after graduation and apply for an H1-B.

The employer sponsorship requirement meant you could not apply on your own—you needed an employer to support your application. The application window was only open once a year for a few days. And applying, even with all the right documents and the best employer sponsorship in the world, did not guarantee a visa. It was a lottery-based system where applications were selected at random until the quota was reached, and all non-selected applications were obviously not considered. If approved, there was also the restriction of working only for the employer sponsoring (effectively paying for) the visa. Transferring records was possible, but was another process of its own. If rejected, you'd fall out of status and have the typical sixty-day grace period to either leave the country or change status before trying again the following year.

My third issue, especially in the beginning when I had high hopes for the type of internship I wanted to get, was the fact that I wasn't attending a "target school." Target schools were the ones that had partnerships with top banks, professional services firms, or tech companies, to name a few. These schools were the renowned Ivy League schools, such as Harvard, Yale, or Princeton, but also included regional schools such as Northwestern University or the University of Chicago in the state of Illinois where I lived. When I looked on LinkedIn, there was a higher percentage of Ivy League and other target schools' alumni at companies such as Deloitte, where I wanted to intern.

Top companies had a strong presence on campus and frequently hosted all sorts of recruiting and social events at those schools, specifically allocating spots for students attending them. Though attending these schools did not guarantee a job at a top firm, it certainly gave more exposure and opportunities to make connections, apply, and ultimately get interviews.

With consulting, I often heard about how important it was to have a "brand-name" school on your resume to be considered for a role. And if not a brand-name school, at least an internship or some experience at a brand-name company. In fact, some job postings from big firms specifically had the names of the university in the headline, indicating that only students from that school should apply for that specific posting. That was the case for top schools, then there was a "general application" for all other schools.

With all that in mind, in addition to other people's opinion, I decided to *loosen up* and write a new resume with more experience than I actually had. To be safe, I indicated that my fabricated experience was acquired back home as opposed to the U.S. It felt very uncomfortable, but I thought maybe that was part of growing up. In the same spirit, I lowered my cumulative GPA and put 3.5 instead of my 4.0. Now this was *my* decision and no one else's. I thought maybe 4.0 sounded too "perfect" and would deter employers from calling me for interviews, especially since I wasn't involved in extracurricular activities.

For some internship applications, I used my "good" resume, and for others, I used my "bad" resume, secretly hoping that any positive outcome would be because of who I truly was. I also promised myself that this would be the last time I would lie on my resume. Once I got that initial experience in the U.S., I wasn't going to fabricate anything anymore.

———— ⌇⌇⌇ ————

When Naomi left, I took out my planner to do my year in review. The only goals that I'd fully accomplished in 2018 were my Lenten goals. I had celebrated my birthday, but not outside of Chicago as I wanted to, though I was still grateful. I had moved out, but I was not paying rent myself as I'd hoped to do.

I crossed out all the other items on the list. I thought I'd cried in 2017; 2018 had been even worse. It was *definitely not* my year.

I hadn't bought a 2019 planner just yet, so I wrote my goals for the new year on the back of the last page of my 2018 planner. I only had two: graduate with a GPA of at least 3.8 and be outside of my comfort zone as much as possible, meaning being less shy. I'd been so broken throughout the year that I didn't even want to have goals for the new one. I didn't want to have to go back to my planner, only to cross things out because they had not happened. I didn't want to experience that kind of heartbreak again. I'd almost lost hope; and I was scared to hope again.

All I wanted, and all I asked God for the year, was that I may not be depressed again, that I may not cry as much as I did in 2018. I didn't care if I wasn't *happy*. In fact, I didn't think I was ever going to truly feel happy again.

The pain, that once pea-sized hole on my heart, had grown to the size of a coin. And it kept growing and hurting. I didn't think it was going to go away. I just didn't want to cry as much anymore.

I'd gone to confession again before Christmas and renewed my promise to God that I would not have suicidal thoughts anymore. This time, though, I asked for His help.

I wasn't ready or excited for what 2019 had in store for me.

It was just going to be *a* year.

CHAPTER 12:

CURRICULAR PRACTICAL TRAINING

Date: 01/01/2019

Dear Heavenly Father... Thank You for waking me up today on New Year's Day. Thank You for all You did in 2018, and thank You for Your blessings. I hate to come to You feeling sad because I seriously feel like I am doing too much, but I can't help it.

Thank You for... Another year, my life, my family and friends.

I am worried about... It's a new year, but I'm just afraid I'll have the same worries and issues throughout this year as well. Not making my dreams come true. Setting goals and not reaching them.

Here's what's happening in my life... So, about this new year ... Yes, I'm scared, I'm not going to lie. I am scared to have plans and goals only to watch them be crushed again. I am not asking for an easy life, but PLEASE don't let me cry this year as much as I did last year. Please!

I need... the strength to face the challenges that 2019 will send my way. Guidance throughout the year. I'm begging You, please, improve my finances this year.

Other things on my heart that I need to share with You, God... I feel like giving up on my internship search for this semester. I mean ... it's officially January, and my internship was supposed to start this month, and yet … still nothing. I'm not mad at You or anything like that; I'll just accept whatever You decide, though it may hurt.

I had two more weeks of winter break, during which I continued to look for internships. My prospects of getting one didn't look very promising: internships with a January start date had already been filled, and the internship postings I came across were now for the summer. Still, I applied—if successful, I'd use them for my OPT, since I would've already graduated by then. I also registered for all sorts of career fairs: at my school, at DePaul University–though I was no longer a student there–, and even career fairs hosted by the city of Chicago.

In addition to that, I revamped my LinkedIn profile and started sending more connection and coffee chat[3] requests. Out of the more than one hundred requests I sent, only a handful of people accepted to connect and only one person agreed to meet. I will say, though, I wasn't very skilled at networking back then, especially in person, and my connection requests weren't very compelling.

At some point, I started getting calls to interview. Not a ton, but enough to make me feel like things were going to get better. Unfortunately, I almost never got past the first round of interviews and when I did, I didn't get the offer.

The dean at my school had approved my request to take all my remaining classes during the spring semester and graduate in May. However, because I still hadn't found an internship, all five classes were

---

3 A coffee chat is an informal conversation through which someone learns about a desired career path (or other area of interest) from a person already pursuing it. Coffee chats are common practice in the U.S. and Canada and are usually done in person (over coffee) but also over the phone or online.

lecture-based. The deadline to add or drop classes was January 22nd, so by then, I would need to have already secured an internship to drop one of my current classes and replace it with the "internship class."

No internship, no offer letter. No offer letter, no SSN support letter from the school. No support letter, no SSN application. No SSN, no CPT. No CPT, no class swap and no U.S. work experience. No U.S. work experience = harder to find a job for OPT after graduation.

This perpetual interrelationship between the things I was dealing with, along with the constant deadline pressure, was very frustrating. On January 10th, during a conversation with Cedric, I expressed my frustration again, and I *kind of* blew up.

Danielle: I don't think happiness is for me at this point. I don't know why I have dreams. All my efforts are vain.

Cedric: Some people aren't as lucky as you are, and I know you're not them, but Danielle, you are in the U.S., your dream country. You have a great educational background. You're just having some issues. Or maybe you're not fighting the right fight.

Danielle: You think I don't realize how lucky I am? You think I'm ungrateful and don't realize that there are people starving in the world or suffering all kinds of injustice? That is not the case! I am grateful for what I have and thank God every day for it, but that doesn't take away the fact that there are also many things I don't have that other people do. Yes, there is worse, but there is also better. I'm in the U.S … oh, how amazing! The U.S. hasn't been my dream country in a while.

Cedric: I know it's hard, but it's just for a moment.

Danielle: A moment that lasts forever. Apparently, my tunnels are very special ones because they don't seem to have the same dimensions as everyone else's. Everyone has an end to their story when they can say, "But I made it to the end, and I succeeded." Someone may be facing the same challenge as me today, but after a while, it gets better for them while I'm still struggling with that same issue. I am and will always be happy to know that people around me are evolving. In fact, I always pray for this to be the case, but it seems that my prayers are only heard when they're not about me.

I've been looking for a job for over a year now. I've looked from the "smallest" to the "biggest" (based on my education level), but nothing so far. You still think I'm joking when I say prostitution and drug-dealing are the only things I did not try, because according to you and many other people, you can't look that hard and not find anything. "There has to be something you could have done." And it's tiring and hurtful to hear that because no one knows how much or how long I've been looking and how many times I've been rejected, even by the "smaller" jobs. I've been looking in other cities as well, but the outcome is the same.

I've been looking for an internship relentlessly every day since October. I don't care about the type of company anymore. I don't care about the pay. I don't care if the company said it's an accounting internship, but I'll be ordering coffee and making photocopies. Every day I send out resumes and cover letters, I call companies, reach out and try to meet the people who work there … But no response unless it's negative.

Do you have any idea what it's like to not know what you're good at? Not a waitress, not an accountant, not a financial analyst, not anything. I don't know where to put myself anymore. I don't know what I'm worth. As master's students, people have at least two internships on their resume, but I'm carrying around my one and only internship to try and prove I don't even know what. Some internships require previous experience. Even when I fabricate that experience, it doesn't work. But I'm supposed to be strong, right? All these are small difficulties. Life is good, I am where I always wanted to be.

Anyway, back to the internship … I have a January 22nd deadline and knowing that right now all the internship postings are for the summer, I think I can give up.

I even applied for an assistantship position again, which required a GPA of at least 3.8 and guess what? I have a 4.0 GPA and still didn't get the position, despite having been recommended by two professors. But life is good, I have a dream educational background and perfect grades that so far are useless.

Do you think I want to give up at the first challenge? Do you think I don't try to motivate myself every day? Do you think I don't try to push myself? But don't I run out of strength? Even when I take a break to recharge, I run into the same issues or worse. What am I supposed to do? I pray. I'm grateful for what I have. I work well in school. I try to do things by the rules. I break them. I don't give up. I fall and get back up. But what's the point of all this if I can't see the results? When does my moment end and I can also say, "But I did it"? Who am I stronger than?

And it's not like I don't have other issues. I am still struggling financially. Yes, I'm grateful for the food on my table and the roof over my head. But even that is a struggle. My sister still has to order groceries for me, and I was hoping to find an internship so she wouldn't have to do that anymore. And I know not everyone has that chance, but there are also people who can eat on their own.

I've been feeling sad for weeks and didn't want to let it all out, just so it wouldn't look like I'm ungrateful. But I am human too. I have weaknesses too.

Anyway, good night, and sorry my text was so long.

Date: 1/22/2019

Dear Heavenly Father... Of course, I didn't get an internship. What was I thinking? I don't know why You do this to me, God. Is there something wrong with me? Do You not love me? Or do You just love Your other children more? Yes, I've been happy before, but was that it? Now I can suffer for the rest of my life?

~~Thank You for...~~ The one thing I asked You for 2019 was not even happiness. I begged You that I may not cry as much as I did in 2018 and 2017, and here I am, drowning in my tears, feeling the same pain as before. Does this make You happy? I'm serious, do You enjoy seeing me sad? If so, then okay.

~~I am worried about...~~ I just want to give up. Maybe You've decided I won't work, and I'll just remain broke. I'm just going to have to accept it if that's Your will.

~~People I am praying for today...~~ I am so tired of crying. I am so tired of feeling this pain. I am so tired of trying to be strong. I am so tired of being frustrated. I am so tired of not getting answers to my prayers when they are about me. What is even the point of trying?

~~Here's what's happening in my life...~~ What's the point of all the effort I put into trying to be a good person, in finding a job or an internship? No calls. No job. No money. But when I pray for other people to get these things, then You answer my prayer.

~~I need...~~ Do You not want me to also FEEL happy? Not just pretend. Not just being content. FEELING happy. Have a social life, a professional life...

~~Other things on my heart that I need to share with You, God...~~ I just want to give up. I don't know how I'm supposed to keep doing this. My heart is so broken, but my problems are still there. I still have to smile every day, talk to people like everything is fine, convince myself that it'll be fine when it doesn't seem like it. I just need a breather.

This is one of the times I snapped during the year. I'd been trying so hard to push through the pain and to keep motivating myself when I felt like giving up. Every call or email for an interview brought back hope to my heart, but the rejections stripped it away. The light would appear every time I had an interview, and it seemed like I was almost at the end of my tunnel. But every rejection would move the light further and further away. It felt like I was running a race with no finish line.

I had an interview scheduled at 9:30 a.m. on January 22nd with a French accounting firm, for a bilingual accounting internship position. I'd applied on Indeed and reached out on LinkedIn to the HR manager and to an employee who looked like he would be my supervisor, letting them both know I was interested in the role and wanted to be given the opportunity to interview. The HR manager got back to me and agreed to schedule an interview. She wasn't in the city, so we were going to meet over Skype.

That day, I woke up earlier than usual, got ready, and turned on my computer. I checked my settings to make sure everything looked good. I sat in front of my computer around 8:30 a.m. (pretty early, but I didn't want to take any chances). The HR manager emailed me at 9:20 a.m. to let me know someone else had been selected for the role, and she cancelled our meeting. Ten minutes before. *Great.*

I couldn't cry for too long because I had a coffee chat downtown at 11:30 a.m. with that one LinkedIn contact who had agreed to meet with me. I wanted to cancel, but then I thought maybe it was going to be worth it. And it was, kind of. It was a nerve-wracking experience because it was my first-ever coffee chat with a complete stranger, but I learned from it. Plus, she was nice.

We chatted for about thirty minutes, during which she answered all the questions I'd prepared for her. At the end, she agreed to look at my resume and recommended I apply for an internship position that was open at her firm. She worked at Mazars, a boutique accounting firm.

I left the coffee shop feeling better than when I walked in. I took the train home but decided to stop at Mariano's first to get something to eat. I was sitting in the eating area of the grocery store, munching on my spring rolls, when I got a LinkedIn message from my connection who I had just met. She was informing me that the position I was going to apply for was no longer available.

The hole in my heart expanded, and the pain deepened. I try my hardest not to cry in public, but at that moment, I couldn't help it. I didn't even realize I was crying until I heard tears land on the hard plastic food container.

Just like I'd done with the HR manager earlier that day, I thanked my LinkedIn connection for letting me know. I then opened WhatsApp and replaced my New Year's Eve profile picture with a black circle and changed my About section from "It gets better" to just a period. *It doesn't get better. I am tired, and I can't do this anymore.*

I decided to stop looking and deactivated all my job search alerts. I still had a few applications pending, but I did not have much hope anymore. I used to record my applications in a notebook then lost track, but at that point, I'd already sent hundreds of applications.

A few days passed, and I got two phone interviews; one for a tax assistant internship at Octagon, a large sports and entertainment company, and the other for a marketing and business development internship at CIVC Partners, a middle market private equity firm. I advanced to the final round of interviews at both companies, but on February 4th, Octagon let me know they would not offer me the position. I was already numb to rejection at that point. I didn't expect anything good to come out of that interview anyway, so the email did not affect me.

I didn't write in my prayer journal anymore. I was tired of writing about the same things all the time and didn't see the point of continuing to do so. What I kept doing was praying and reading my devotional. I didn't pray for a job or myself anymore; I simply made generic prayers or prayed for other people. I didn't want to admit it to myself, but I was mad at God.

On February 7th, I had yet another meltdown after reading the day's devotional. It was about going to God for rest and refreshment; it said not to give up despite feeling bone-weary and exhausted, acknowledging that the journey had been too much. It said to continue to hope because we would once more praise God.

The first two sentences of that text could not have been more accurate. I was *bone-weary*, and that wasn't the first time.

"So, You know I'm tired," I said out loud, covering my runny eyes. "You know the journey has been too much! I can't come to You for rest anymore, if that means You're going to strike me again afterward. Just keep doing what You're doing, but don't ask me to come to You for rest." Tears kept rolling down my cheeks. I was sitting on the edge of my bed, facing my desk. My eyes looked up on their own to see the wall of motivational quotes and Bible verses. And the first thing I read was this:

"For I know the plans I have for you. [...] Plans to prosper you and not to harm you, plans to give you hope and a future" (Jeremiah 29:11).

"This is not true," I said. "I don't want to believe this anymore. How could You let me suffer like this if You truly don't want to harm me? What kinds of plans involve keeping me in pain? I know You have other people to take care of, and if that's why You're not answering my prayers, that's fine. You probably have a lot to do, but don't tell me to rest when I know there's worse pain ahead of me."

The pain was a vise on my heart. *The pain that you've been feeling cannot compare to the joy that is coming.* "This is not true. Just let me suffer and be in pain."

At that very moment, I wanted to delete my social media apps again. I wanted to leave. Again. I'd been comparing myself to people on LinkedIn. To people I didn't know who went to prestigious schools and were working at the companies I wanted to work at. To those I knew from high school or college who were already working full time in France or were at least in a co-op program while I was struggling to get an internship.

Everyone seemed to be working either at one of the Big Four (Deloitte, PwC, KPMG, EY) or at a nice boutique firm, or at banks, insurance companies, or other financial services firms. I kept wondering if I'd made the wrong choice by going the U.S., considering I had the opportunity to go to France after high school but did not want to. To be honest, I knew deep inside I hadn't made the wrong choice and wouldn't have changed anything if taken back in time. But I was very confused.

I was exhausted and needed another break from everything. I wanted to leave and not tell anyone. Again. But I didn't. I stayed because I didn't want to miss the birth of my niece. My oldest brother and his partner were expecting a baby, and I would have hated not being able to see the baby's pictures and congratulate my brother at least through chat. Luna was born eight days later, and I was glad I'd stayed.

Date: 3/08/2019

Dear Heavenly Father... It is with a grateful heart that I come writing to You here. Thank You for giving me the opportunity to have an internship, finally. I really thank You for that.

Thank You for... My internship, first and foremost. My education. All Your blessings in my life.

I am worried about... Not being good enough at this internship. Not performing up to expectations. Failing?

People I am praying for today... All those who are looking for jobs or internships, especially international students here. My family and friends.

Here's what's happening in my life... You know it's been a journey to finally get this internship that, by the way, I didn't think I would get. Again, thank You, I am really ... happy about that. Happiness is such a strong word; I just don't want to use it carelessly. But I am definitely relieved.

I need... Your strength and Your guidance throughout this internship and for what's next after graduation. I love You. 🩶

After weeks of not hearing back, I got an email from the director at the private equity firm on February 21st, with the offer letter attached. I was in the living room with Zoe when the email came, and I'd left my phone plugged in my bedroom. I'd been teaching French to Zoe for a few weeks, so whenever we both had time, we would meet and do some exercises. When we finished that day, I went back to my room and turned on my phone to read the good news.

> **From:** *Director*
> **To:** *Me*
> **Subject:** *Offer Letter*
> **Date and Time:** *2/21/2019 at 1:55 p.m.*
> *Danielle,*
> *Thank you again for your patience as we were held up internally. We'd love to offer you the internship position here at CIVC Partners. Please review the attached offer letter and let me know if you have any questions. I'm available via phone today if needed.*
> *Director*

I honestly didn't think I was going to get the job. Not only because of the previous rejections, but also because I didn't exactly look like or have the educational background of the people who worked at the firm.

Prior to my interviews, I'd done my research on the company and the people who worked there. Mostly men. White men. White men who attended Ivy League and other prestigious business schools. White men who attended Ivy League and other prestigious business schools and previously worked at top-tier investment banks like Goldman Sachs, or at top-tier consulting firms like MBB (McKinsey

& Company, Bain & Company, and the Boston Consulting Group). The only Black woman at the time was at the reception desk the day of my in-person interview. Nothing wrong with being a receptionist, of course. But you get the picture.

Additionally, the office was located on the eleventh floor of a glass skyscraper right downtown on Wacker Drive, overlooking and giving a splendid view of the Chicago River. Considering how much I'd lowered my expectations for the type of internship I was going to get, if any, I crossed my fingers but would not be surprised if I didn't walk into that building again after my interview.

In any case, I was glad to have gotten the offer. Even more so because the resume that got me the job was my "good" resume. I can't express just how relieved I was about that. It gave me the confirmation that I didn't need to lie to get a job and that it was possible to get one by staying completely true to myself.

I was going to work twenty hours per week (to comply with the CPT requirement of working no more than twenty hours) and be paid $12 per hour, Chicago's minimum wage at the time. I knew I could be paid more, but I honestly didn't care. I even tried to negotiate, but I had terrible negotiation skills and that didn't work out. But at least I had a job offer for my CPT. I was finally going to work and earn some money.

Speaking of CPT, the day I got the offer, I immediately emailed it to my international student advisor (and designated school official) with all the other necessary documents so I could get my support letter for a social security number application.

To obtain CPT approval, a student had to be issued a new I-20 that contained job-related information on the employment authorization section on the second page of the form. Without the new I-20, I could not begin work, since that new form would now serve as proof of work authorization.

As for registering for the "internship class" after the January 22nd deadline, a weird thing happened with one of my classes. I'd registered for a class that apparently had a prerequisite, but I had no idea, and the school's registration platform had not prevented me from registering. I'd been feeling super lost in that class and barely understood anything.

One day, before I got my internship, the professor gave us an assignment that I absolutely did not understand. I went to him after class to let him know, and he confirmed that the class was building on a previous one. I couldn't stay in that class, so I dropped it.

I registered for another one that was going to start in the second half of the semester; however, a few days after registering for that class, I got my internship. So, I was still in the window to drop that specific class with no penalty, since it hadn't started yet. I dropped it and replaced it with my "internship class." Talk about a plan!

―――――――⚎―――――――

My CPT started on March 8th and luckily for me, my new I-20 was issued before then. I applied for my SSN and received it a few days after starting the internship, which was fine because I already had my new I-20.

In the context of employment, the SSN is mainly used for background check and tax purposes and does not serve as proof of employment authorization. The I-20 with CPT authorization on page 2, however, does. In fact, on international students' SSN cards, the following statement is written at the top in all caps:

VALID FOR WORK ONLY WITH
DHS AUTHORIZATION.

DHS stands for Department of Homeland Security. So, in theory, without authorization, you couldn't *legally* work as an international student in the U.S., even if you had an SSN. In theory.

CHAPTER 13:

OPTIONAL PRACTICAL TRAINING

I will now share my experience applying for OPT. Post-completion OPT started after graduation, but you had to apply early, and you'll understand why in a minute.

Before I begin, I'd like to remind you that the information here is not complete, is valid to the best of my knowledge at the time of writing, and is not intended to serve as legal advice. If you're an international student in the U.S., or are considering becoming one in the future, do your own research, check your school's resources for international students, speak to your designated school official, and make sure you're using the most up-to-date and accurate information.

———— ⊂⫘⊃ ————

My CPT application was free, which was great because I had just spent $410 in OPT application fees. Processing time for OPT applications was at least ninety days, so the school recommended applying up to three months before the expected program completion date.

The application window was no earlier than ninety days before the program completion date and no later than sixty days after. A new I-20 needed to be requested that included the International Students Office's recommendation for OPT application on page 2, and, if applicable, it should also reflect the new program completion date. Once that was done, the new I-20, together with all other relevant documents and application fees, had to be mailed to the U.S. Citizenship and Immigration Services (USCIS) within thirty days of the new I-20's issuance.

OPT application was done through, and approved only by, USCIS, unlike CPT that was done through, and approved by, the school.

OPT typically required full-time work, although part-time work of twenty or more hours per week could also qualify. That said, students could cumulate two or more jobs. The jobs could be paid or unpaid, as long as they were related to the student's field of study.

Now, one of the tricky parts of applying for OPT was that you were expected to choose a date in the future when you wanted your OPT to start and specify that date on your application. A job offer was not required to apply for OPT; however, whether you had secured one or not, you had to choose a future date at which your OPT would effectively start, and ideally, that was also when your employment would start.

If approved, an Employment Authorization Document (EAD) card was mailed to you that contains basic identity and OPT information, like the approved start and end dates. The projected start date (the one you chose) and approved start date (the one USCIS approves) could be different depending on when you applied or how long it took to process your application. The EAD card was valid for one year, with the countdown beginning on the approved start date whether employment had started or not. And, similar to some procedures I've discussed so far, there was a sixty-day grace period at the end of OPT to either leave the U.S. or change immigration status.

Another tricky thing was that your desired start date could not be earlier than your program completion date or later than sixty days after, and you couldn't start working before receiving your EAD card or before the approved start date printed on it, even if you'd found a job that unfortunately started before. Also, while on OPT, you were not allowed to be unemployed for longer than ninety days total, consecutive or not, and work that was fewer than twenty hours per week was considered unemployment. The unemployment countdown also began on the approved start date on the EAD card.

I know that's a lot of information, and that's not even all of it. It was a lot to process for me too, and as you can imagine, it created a lot of stress and anxiety. Let's walk through my situation as an example, and hopefully you'll understand better.

I was going to graduate on May 10, 2019, so I could not apply for my OPT before February 9th or after July 9th (application window). Knowing the average processing time of at least ninety days, I had planned back in 2018 to apply for OPT in February or March 2019 at the latest.

On February 11, 2019, I filled out my OPT recommendation request on my school's website. Processing times for CPT and OPT I-20s were usually shorter since they were not first-time issuances. So, on February 14th, my international student advisor informed me that my I-20 was ready for pick up.

From: *International Student Advisor*

To: *Me*

Subject: *OPT Recommendation*

Date and Time: *2/14/2019 at 7:50 p.m.*

Your recommendation for OPT has been completed. You have been issued 2 form I-20s. You should keep 1 for your records and send 1 to USCIS with your application. Additional instructions will be provided with your I-20 forms.

USCIS must receive your application no more than 30 days from the date the I-20 recommendation is issued. If USCIS does not receive the documents by this time, your request for OPT will be denied. If you do not send the application on time (and are near the end of this 30-day period), it is possible to cancel your current request and issue a new OPT recommendation; however, you must do this before you mail the application to USCIS.

You are still considered an F1 student at Roosevelt while you are on OPT. Please be sure to update us if you move, so this information can be updated in your SEVIS record. Please be sure to notify SEVIS when you find a job; you will be invited to create an SEVP Portal where you can report your employment start and end dates. You are only permitted 90 days of unemployment while on OPT; this information is tracked in the SEVIS system. Therefore, it is very important that you report all employment.

If you have any questions, please let me know.

International Student Advisor

My new I-20s showed the updated program end date, which was now May 10, 2019, instead of the initial December 2019 date. From an immigration standpoint, my initial I-20 was no longer valid, as my SEVIS record had also been updated with the appropriate program end date.

At that point, I had no idea when I was going to get a job. I certainly wished to have one soon enough after graduating; however, nothing was guaranteed. I couldn't pick a date later than July 9th as my projected start date (sixty days after my program completion date). However, I didn't want to risk choosing a date in early July, then get a job with a June start date that I wouldn't be able to accept if USCIS had approved my July start date (because you can't start working before the date on your EAD). Similarly, I didn't want to pick something like May 13th because that would have only given me a weekend to relax if I found a job that started that day, provided I had received my EAD card. My family was going to be at my graduation, and I wanted to be with them as much as possible.

I did a lot of thinking (and I mean *a lot* of thinking, staying-up-at-night type of thinking) and went with May 27th as my projected OPT start date, hoping to get a job that would start around that time. All my other required documents were ready, so I mailed my application with a $410 money order to USCIS on February 16th. This was two days after receiving my new I-20 with OPT recommendation, so that it would get to USCIS within the following twenty-eight days.

My application was approved, and my card effectively came in the mail three months later, sometime in May. It had my projected date as the approved start date. So, both my OPT and unemployment countdowns began on May 27, 2019. The expiration date was May 26, 2020, but I could stay in the U.S. until July 25, 2020 (end of sixty-day grace period). I could only stay until then if I had found a job before August 25, 2019 (ninety days after the OPT start date, the maximum unemployment time allowed) and had not accumulated more than ninety days of unemployment in-between multiple jobs. If I hadn't found a job by August 25, 2019, I would need to either leave the U.S. or change my status to something other than F-1.

Is this making more sense? Yeah, I know, same.

———— ⌒▥⌒ ————

I had absolutely no desire to remain in the U.S. after my OPT and didn't see myself there beyond that point. That had more to do with the fact that I didn't think my dream of working in consulting was going to come true in that country. Also, I didn't want to live the stress of trying to get an employer to sponsor me for the H1-B visa. Consulting firms had a *very* limited number of spots for international students, if any, and those were usually reserved for STEM students.

On top of that, I continued to think about going to Canada and studying at Schulich. Since I was going to leave the U.S. in the summer of 2020 anyway, I thought why not join the program in the fall of that same year? I didn't want to wait until 2022 anymore to apply to the Master of Marketing program. All I wanted was to find a job for my OPT, save as much money as possible, and leave. I was hoping to not look for a job for longer than three months, so I wouldn't exceed my unemployment quota. Cute. Let's revisit this later.

Date: 3/30/2019

Dear Heavenly Father... Hey God, how are You? I hope You're doing well despite all the craziness going on in the world. I just wanted to come here and tell You how grateful I am for the blessings You've been showering me with.

Thank You for... My life, who I am and will become, my education, my family and friends, my internship, and all the things I unconsciously take for granted.

I am worried about... I don't want to talk about my worries today, for once. I just want to be thankful for and enjoy what I currently have. Tomorrow will take care of itself. 😊

People I am praying for today... Anyone looking for a job and/or going through hard times.

I need... Your help so I stay grateful for what I have and where I am, even if it's not yet where I want to be. Help me "trust the process" and trust Your plan. Help me not rush, but rather appreciate every moment.

Other things on my heart that I need to share with You, God... So ... I've been wanting to say this but I'm wondering if it's really the case and if it's not too soon to say it. But ... I think I am happy? I don't know ... I'm scared to say it and then something messes it up and I go back to being ... depressed. Anyway, I love You. 😊

My mood had lightened up, as you can tell. The pain, that once pea-sized hole on my heart that then grew to the size of a coin, that pain had shrunk a little.

Back in January, I attended a career fair at DePaul where I met Christie, another girl from Cameroon. She'd heard me on the phone with Sophie at some point. It wasn't very common to hear people speak French in Chicago, so I guess she was intrigued when she heard me. She approached me and introduced herself. I did the same thing, and we exchanged numbers. We went out for the first time with two of her friends shortly after I got my internship. Then we went out again. And again. Each time I came home from one of my outings, I thanked God for it, almost incredulous it had happened. Above all, I was grateful.

I was finally working and able to buy groceries on my own. I went back to the gym twice a week again, and I loved it. As with most jobs, my paycheck came twice a month, on the 15th and on the 30th. I wasn't making a ton of money, but I started putting a few dollars in my savings account again. I was saving to buy myself a nice dress and nice shoes for my graduation, as well as the Google Pixel 3 XL as a graduation gift. I was starting to have issues with my Samsung at the time and had been wanting a Pixel for a while (#AndroidForLife).

I'd hoped to celebrate my birthday and have a cake, but that unfortunately did not happen. I was a bit sad, but I considered my internship to be my birthday gift. I'd also gotten some money for my birthday, and I saved most of it for my goals and got my nails done with the rest. I liked having that control back over my finances.

Date: 5/02/2019

Dear Heavenly Father... Today I cried for the first time in over two months. And for the first time in over two years, they were not tears of pain. I've been reminiscing, thinking about the past two years, what I've been through and comparing that to now. I am SO thankful, Lord.

~~Thank You for...~~ Although I am not (yet) where I want to be, I am so thankful that I am not where I used to be. I am graduating in one week, will hopefully get a return offer from my internship; I've met friends; I am healthy; my skin hasn't been breaking out as much, etc.

~~I am worried about...~~ Please help me find a way to thank You and give back to You, not as payback, but as a thank-you gift. And please know that I do not take anything for granted, not after what I've been through. If I ever do, it's unintentional.

~~People I am praying for today...~~ Wow! Now that I put it in writing, I realize even more how blessed I am and how You've been blessing me lately. I will NEVER thank You enough, Lord, but just know that I am thankful.

~~Here's what's happening in my life...~~ I love You so much, and I am really thankful. I had no idea I would be writing such things, so much I thought I would be sad for the rest of my life. I may not be as comfortable as I'd like to be, but I am thankful for what I already have.

~~I need...~~ Forgive me for comparing myself to others again and help me live in this moment, and appreciate and enjoy it before the next storm comes around, because I know life is not smooth sailing.

Other things on my heart that I need to share with You, God... I'm sad that Mom can't make it to my graduation and I lowkey feel like she didn't try hard enough, but oh well ... I love You. 😊 🖤

Something had come up, and my mom could no longer attend my graduation as initially planned. Before the last section of this journal entry gets misinterpreted, I want to clarify that the issue this time wasn't money. I was disappointed and quite frankly, a bit mad at my mom for some time; this degree was as much hers as it was mine, and I wanted her to see where all her efforts and sacrifices had gone. That said, I could never blame her for not being financially able to do something.

Graduation day finally rolled around. My last day at the office and in school was the day before, on May 9th. I did not get a return offer from my internship as I had hoped, which was unfortunate, but I tried not to focus on that. I was finally graduating. I got my hair and nails done a few days earlier and had been practicing doing a full face of makeup.

The ceremony started at 10:30 a.m. on May 10th, but the butterflies in my stomach woke me up around 3 a.m. I could not wait to walk across the stage. When I checked the time three hours later, it was only 3:45 a.m. Time couldn't possibly go by slower.

I had gone to bed shortly before midnight but felt like I had slept ten hours. I stayed in bed for another hour, staring at the ceiling and thinking about what was going to happen a few hours later. I was going to graduate. In May, not in December. I thought about when I held on to the idea of "catching up" to other people and when that was my motivation to graduate that semester. I thought about the frustration I'd gone through a year earlier and throughout the summer when I couldn't go to school or find a job. I thought about what happened in June of that year and the months that followed.

The journey. The sweat. The pain. The blood. The tears. The exhaustion. *The pain.*

And there I was, about to do something I'd felt was too distant in the future. Sophie and Naomi were sleeping next to me, and I wished my mom were there, too.

It was a good thing I was up early because it took me a good three hours to do a very simple makeup. I was watching YouTube videos, doing and redoing my foundation, trying and failing to do a cut-crease eyeshadow before realizing that was probably too ambitious.

I had a black bandage dress and leopard heels on. I took some (more like tons of) pictures, then put on my black graduation gown and its green, white, and gold hood. Gold decorative tape lined the sides of my cap and the gold sticky letters in the middle read: *Be still and know that I am God.* I'd decorated my cap in that way to remind myself of my journey to graduation.

Sophie helped me take another thousand pictures and videos while Naomi was getting ready. I headed out of the apartment around 9 a.m., walking on the tips of my toes, carefully avoiding all the balloons on the floor. Zoe was also graduating, and her friends and family had brought home tons of balloons. My sisters were guests, so they didn't have to be at Roosevelt's Auditorium as early as I did.

The 10:30 a.m. ceremony was dedicated to students from the College of Education, the College of Pharmacy, and the College of Business. My fellow graduating classmates and I gathered in an assembly room at the Roosevelt Auditorium before being ushered to our respective sections of the theater. Everyone looked their best. We were all smiles that Friday morning, and it seemed like nothing could dampen our mood, not even the six-degree temperatures we'd hoped would be at least ten degrees higher.

My feet started to hurt in my high heels after forty minutes of standing in line, waiting to enter the theater. But it was graduation day. Some girls and I exchanged knowing looks and smiles, encouraging each other to persevere through the pain until we could finally take our seats.

I was graduating. The day had finally come.

As I looked around at every smiling face and jittery hand, I wondered if this day had the same meaning for everyone, and if not, what the differences were. I wondered if someone else was there who hadn't thought they would be. I was now fully aware that you couldn't tell what people were going through just by looking at them.

After what seemed like forever, we finally entered the auditorium theater. I'd only been there once, for another school-sponsored event, but the theater was a popular venue for music and performance events in Chicago.

After the Colleges of Education and Pharmacy, it was now our turn. They finally called my names, all five of them. I walked across the stage for the very first time to the resounding cheers of my classmates and sisters who I confirmed were already there. The school hadn't printed the diplomas yet, so there was nothing inside the dark green cover the dean gave to me after shaking my hand. My smile did not fade as I continued to the other side of the stage to take the steps back down, careful not to trip.

―――――⟡―――――

Once the ceremony was over, my sisters, friends, and I took other sets of pictures, then headed to the cocktail party my school hosted on the twelfth floor in honor of the graduates. Some of us went to Z Bar—a hotel rooftop lounge—afterward to get some drinks. We didn't stay outside very long; the temperature was still around six degrees Celsius, but you couldn't tell from our pictures and the way we were dressed.

Later in the evening, we all went out for my official graduation dinner. I'd made a reservation at Cité, an upscale restaurant on the seventieth floor of Lake Point Tower in Streeterville. We dined with a 360°-view of the city, looking out the floor-to-ceiling windows. We watched the trailing blue, red, and orange hues of the setting sun and its perfect, sparkling reflection on Lake Michigan. We watched it disappear and give way to the spectacle of lights of the surrounding buildings, together with the stars that joined the party, watching us from the velvet blue sky. All were singing: *Congratulations, Danielle!*

Date: 5/16/2019

Dear Heavenly Father... Here I am again ... I'm not going to say back to square one because that wouldn't be fair or true, but as You know, I'm back to being unemployed. I don't feel as bad as I did last week but still...

Thank You for... My graduation and all the fun moments with my family and friends.

I am worried about... Not finding a job (again). To be honest, I know You'll help me; I just don't know when that will happen, and I'm afraid I'll spend all summer looking for a job.

Here's what's happening in my life... I don't know how to feel about the fact that they didn't extend me a job offer. I don't know if that's You having other plans for me or if I failed like I initially thought I would.

I need... Guidance. I don't know what You've planned for me after my graduation, especially now that I don't have a job, but please don't forget about me. I'm begging You, don't let me feel tired and/or depressed again, PLEASE! I don't want to go to that dark place again. Please don't let me.

Other things on my heart that I need to share with You, God... I feel like I wasn't good enough for that job. I feel like I let You and myself down by not getting an offer. Yes, I did the tasks well, but I was also very quiet, and I feel like that's one of the reasons they didn't make an offer. But as always, I trust You. Hear me, please.

I had hoped to be retained as a full-time employee at my internship so I wouldn't have to worry about finding a job again. It would have worked out perfectly for my OPT as well, but that didn't happen. It wasn't my favorite job in the world, both in terms of the content and the environment, but I was willing to stick it out for the duration of my OPT. Most importantly, I didn't want to relive the frustration of looking for a job, especially with my new deadlines and constraints.

I didn't stop looking for jobs when I was doing my internship, but I wasn't very consistent either. A few days after graduating, I updated my LinkedIn profile again and began looking for jobs more aggressively.

———— ⌀ ————

My countdowns began on May 27th as expected and by then, I'd already received my EAD card. It was now a matter of finding a job. Even though the graduation euphoria was beginning to wear off, I wasn't stressed out just yet. I was actually quite optimistic. I mean ... life seemed to have been smiling at me since March, and I had just graduated with an MBA, so I was hoping to find something (and not just anything) by July. I just didn't want to have to go back to a dark place, and I kept asking God not to let me.

I was also planning to go back home that summer to take a much-needed break, but I definitely needed to find a job first. And a new place. The day my EAD card came in the mail, I got confused about what was written in all caps on the front of the card:

NOT VALID FOR REENTRY TO THE U.S.

So, I emailed my international student advisor about it.

From: Me
To: International Student Advisor
Subject: Travel/immigration concern
Date and Time: 5/21/2019 at 4:15 p.m.
Hi International Student Advisor,
I just received my EAD card, but it says on the front that it is not valid for reentry to the U.S. I was planning to go back home this summer, so I'm just wondering what other documents I will need to be able to come back to the U.S.
Thank you,
Danielle

She replied a few minutes later.

> **From:** *International Student Advisor*
>
> **To:** *Me*
>
> **Subject:** RE: *Travel/immigration concern*
>
> **Date and Time:** *5/21/2019 at 4:30 p.m.*
>
> *Hi Danielle,*
>
> *It means that you cannot return with just the EAD. You also need your I-20 with a travel signature, a valid F-1 visa, a valid passport, and ideally proof of employment in your field for OPT.*
>
> *Best,*
>
> *International Student Advisor*

My passport was still valid, but my visa had expired a long time ago, since I was only issued a six-month single entry F-1 visa back in 2017. If I went home to Cameroon, I would need to apply for a student visa again, which would probably not be feasible considering I wanted to stay just a few weeks. And as an international student, it was not possible to apply for a student visa inside the U.S.

Summer 2019 was also that time of the year again—I needed to move. I couldn't (and honestly didn't want to) stay at my current place because I was no longer a student. I also really wanted to live on my own. I wanted to have a kitchen to myself but, most importantly, I wanted control of my apartment's temperature.

I get cold easily, and something my roommates and I always disagreed on was the right temperature for our apartment. Heat and AC were controlled centrally so that we couldn't have different temperature settings for each room. Winter temperatures in 2019 were worse than those of the year before (we had a polar vortex), but thankfully the heating system in our apartment worked. Still, I got very cold, but my roommates would not turn on the heat past a certain temperature because of the impact on our bills. That made sense, but the heat was never high enough for me, and I ended up buying myself a personal heater.

And now that it was summer, my roomates put the AC so high I sometimes needed to go out just to get some sun and warm up a little before going back into the apartment. I didn't have a choice—it was three against one. Now that I had graduated, it was the perfect time to get my own place.

On June 11th, I had an in-person interview with Fitch Ratings, a leading credit rating agency. After the initial phone screening, I reached out to a few current employees on LinkedIn to learn more about the role and the application process in case I moved to the next round. Only one person agreed to meet with me, but that didn't bother me because we had an excellent conversation. I remember calling George after my coffee chat with that employee, because I was so proud of myself for finally being able to hold a thirty-minute conversation with a stranger without feeling awkward.

The chat had gone so well that she even gave me a hug at the end. Now, granted, she was a bit younger. She was an operations associate at the firm and had graduated with a bachelor's degree a year earlier, so she was probably around my age. Regardless, I was proud of myself for getting outside of my comfort zone. She gave me useful tips that I later used during my in-person interview and even texted me good luck the day of.

The panel interview was scheduled for one and a half hour. As I was preparing for it a few days earlier, I kept wondering if I could go that long. I wondered what I would talk about for *ninety minutes* with people I'd never met before. All my previous interviews had lasted anywhere from thirty to forty minutes, and even that was a stretch for me. Well, I did my best, and they seemed to like me.

The recruiter called me the next day to see if I had any questions and to enquire about my salary expectations and work authorization.

"Hi, this is Danielle," I said when I picked up the phone call.

"Hi Danielle, this is John from Fitch Ratings, how are you?" He sounded so cheerful, it put me in a good mood.

"Doing well, thanks for asking! How are you?"

"I am doing fantastic! I know you had your interview yesterday, so I wanted to touch base to see if you had any questions for me."

"No … uhm … I think I'm good. I'm just looking forward to good news. So, I guess my only question would be to know when I can expect to hear back." I wasn't prepared for this call.

"Sure! We're still interviewing other candidates, and we hope to have a decision by the end of next week."

"Oh okay, great!"

"Yeah. So just following protocol here, I'd like to ask about your status in the U.S.—are you going to need sponsorship at any point?"

"I'm on OPT but I will not need sponsorship before next year." *I hate this question.*

"Oh okay. Just jotting that down … And what are your salary expectations?"

"Based on my research and considering the description of the role and my background, I expect to make around sixty thousand a year."

"Fifty thous–."

"Sixty," I clarified.

"Oh, sixty thousand dollars!" He sounded surprised.

Did I price myself too high?

"Okay, well thanks for taking the time," he carried on, "and like I said earlier, you should hear back from us by next week. Take care!"

"Perfect! Thank you, take care, bye!"

I did not specifically ask my contact at the firm for salary information during our coffee chat, but she did mention that the salary range for the position was fifty to fifty-five thousand dollars a year. This was in line with what I had seen on Glassdoor.

My response to the recruiter factored in my education, what I believed I deserved as a recent MBA grad, even with limited work experience. Now, I just needed to wait.

———————

Two weeks later, on June 26th, I still hadn't gotten a response, despite having followed up with the recruiter. I was beginning to go down a spiral of sad and anxious emotions, fearing to go back *to that place*. That night, I turned to God in my prayer journal to share how I was feeling and to ask Him to help me move on if that job wasn't for me, even though I liked it a lot.

CHAPTER 14:

BACK TO BASICS—PART II

I truly wasn't feeling well on June 26th when I wrote in my prayer journal. And as is the case when I don't feel well, I couldn't sleep either. My mind was overflowing with thoughts and my heart with feelings that begged to come out, but I didn't know who to turn to. So, I turned to myself.

A few hours later, around 1 a.m. on June 27th, I took out the journal where I keep quotes and verses, and for the first time since middle school, I wrote to myself. My prayer journal was fine, but it was dedicated to writing to God, and the pages were structured that way. Well … that and I was also a bit ashamed of my thoughts. Though I knew God is omniscient, writing somewhere else still felt a bit more "private." I had other journals, but I never wrote to myself anymore.

I didn't write in my "quotes and verses journal" every day either, but I began to reach for it more frequently than my prayer journal. Again, my intention was never to share my thoughts, so what you read is how I truly felt.

Date: 6/27/2019

I am so lost and confused. I am disappointed in myself, and I feel like God is, too. I don't feel strong; I don't know if I am truly resilient. I feel like I lack faith and I am ashamed of it. I've been questioning life, I've been questioning prayers, and I really don't feel good about it, but I am so lost. I'm just wondering if prayers really do affect outcomes. I mean ... God knows and plans everything ahead. Before we rise in the morning, He has everything all figured out. So, what if I don't pray for something, won't it still happen if it was meant to, and not happen if it wasn't? The Bible says to ask and we'll receive. What about the times we ask and DON'T receive? Yes, it may not be the right time, but why not wait until that time to ask? And more importantly, how do we figure out THAT time?

There have been so many instances these past few years when I asked and did not receive, when I prayed and believed my prayers would be answered but they were not. SO many things I've prayed for that did not happen, so much trust and confidence I've put in certain actions that ended up being pointless. I do realize that God is good, and He has done AMAZING things for me and in no way am I ignoring that, but I'm just so confused.

I don't even know if I'm strong, if I'm truly resilient. Are you really strong if that's the only option you have, given a set of circumstances? Are you really strong if you push through the pain not because you want to or you know it's going to be worth it, but because you have no other choice? Essentially, are you really strong if the only reason you swim is so you won't drown?

I feel like I don't know myself anymore. They say, "What doesn't kill you makes you stronger," and although I've learned a lot from my previous experiences, they seem to have made me weaker and more afraid of life. I'm scared to hope with all my heart. I'm scared to allow myself to believe something will happen, only to be disappointed in the end. All this doesn't mean I don't trust God. I do, I guess I don't trust myself and … life? I'm not sure what I am truly capable of.

I still haven't fully recovered from my past experiences, and it makes me feel bad. I feel like a bad Christian. I really wish I were a Proverbs 31 woman, who literally laughs at the future because she knows God's got her. I do know that God got me, but it's hard to just sit and do nothing while He works. (Is that what I'm supposed to do?) I also watch these people on YouTube who seem to have more faith than me, and I wish I could think as they do. I've been bottling up my feelings because I don't want God to be mad. At this very moment, I feel like He is because of all this confusion going on in my head. I wish I knew Him better.

Another thing is how do you differentiate between setbacks and signs you shouldn't keep going? How do you know God wants you to do this or that? I read one day that no matter how long you pray for something or how many times, or if you believe it'll happen, if it's not for you, it won't happen. It makes total sense. Now, how do I know what's for me? How do I know what to pray and hope for? I have an interview later today, and I am desperate for a job. Should I pray to get this job when I know I've prayed for jobs before and didn't get them? What if it's not the job for me; should I still pray to get it, even though I won't but I don't know? Will prayer really affect the outcome?

Life is just so weird, and it's hurt me so much that I feel like I'm always going to suffer or be frustrated. In two years, I've only had two months of peace, and I feel like that's the way life (or at least mine) is meant to be. I lowkey hope I'm wrong.

Days and weeks went by, during which I kept looking for a job and a new apartment. Neither search yielded positive results. I'd been looking for jobs on my own and working with staffing agencies as well. Sometimes Sophie sent me job postings, but nothing worked.

She probably heard me cry that summer on the phone more than she had when I was a baby.

One of my recent job applications included a personality test, which sparked a lot of confusion for me. One question asked whether I considered myself resilient and to what extent. They gave me a short scenario, and I couldn't tell if my response was motivated by a resilient mindset or a survival one.

Once more, I lowered my standards for the types of jobs I wanted to get. Of course, it would've been nice to get a job that I actually liked, but as an international student whose employment and unemployment countdowns had begun a month earlier, I didn't have the luxury to choose. As of June 27th, I could only be unemployed for two more months and now had eleven months left on my OPT.

A recruiter at the first staffing agency I worked with had told me it would be nearly impossible to get a job that paid me $60,000 a year with my limited work experience, regardless of my education level. Most of the entry-level roles these staffing agencies recruited for were contract positions; they paid an hourly wage ranging from $18 to $22. Annually, that was roughly $37,000 to $45,000 before taxes. After trying and failing to find jobs that would pay more (even if not necessarily $60,000), it started mattering less what I was going to get paid, as long as I got paid. I also completely scratched my desire to have a nice studio or one-bedroom apartment downtown. I just wanted something, especially since I didn't have all the time in the world to look.

Date: 07/02/2019

I guess a takeaway from my current situation is that "better," as in "God has something better for you," doesn't necessarily mean "bigger" or, in my case, "more lucrative" than what was taken away or didn't happen.

I don't want it to look like I'm ungrateful or will not be thankful for any job I get, but now that I've applied to the jobs I really liked and was turned down by all of them, I realize better is not bigger. I can't stop thinking about Fitch Ratings. I mean ... I did EVERYTHING I could to get the job, from an informational interview to studying and practicing for an entire day. And to be honest, I felt confident I'd get an offer. Here we are, three weeks later, nothing! No, they didn't specifically say "no," but the job starts on Monday (six days from today), and they were supposed to have all their candidates picked out by last week, but guess what? They didn't call or email me. Financial services company, good culture, people my age, corporate environment, sponsors the CFA exam... I even made a "friend." I just thought that was the job for me, but clearly it wasn't. I put so much effort into it and now ... so why did I even do all of that? Or where did I go wrong? Or is it just because they don't sponsor international students? They didn't even give me feedback when I asked.

Anyway, here I am applying to any and every job. The job I am interviewing for tomorrow pays half what I would have made at Fitch. It's not going to be enough to live on my own, not even sure I'll be able to pay for my CFA exam myself or save for my other goals. I know a job is better than none, but again, I'm realizing better is not always bigger.

I'm an international student in the U.S. (and we know what that means). I did not go to these top schools where the companies I'd like to work for recruit (don't even know why I aim that high). My lease is up at the end of the month, and I need a job that pays me at least three times the rent ASAP. Haven't heard back from Fitch, it takes at least two to three weeks to get interviews if any ... do you see where I'm going with this?

I may have to live paycheck to paycheck and probably won't be as comfortable as I'd hoped, but I'll adjust. This leads me to my second (pain)point: Who gets to have their dream job after college? Working in the finance industry isn't even my dream; it's just something I've grown to like (a lot). But who gets to make their dream come true in a snap and who has to wait for years or decades? And why these differences? If you can't tell already, I've been very confused lately. Since when do I even journal?

Anyway … we'll see how my whole job situation goes. I'll take whatever comes my way; I don't really have a choice. I just hope (?) my dream comes true one of these days.

My internship and the finance class I was taking during my last semester got me so interested in the field that I thought about embarking on a journey to become a chartered financial analyst (CFA). Although I was intimidated by the people at CIVC Partners (because of their degrees and previous work experience, and not because of their race or gender), they opened my eyes to world I didn't know existed—I knew very little about private equity. Going on meetings with senior employees at the firm and not understanding what they were talking about made me feel like I wasn't all that smart. But at the same time, it made me want to learn more about finance.

Part of my job involved doing some research; not seeing many women, and even fewer *Black* women, also sparked a desire in my heart to work in finance. However, anyone breaking into investment banking or private equity or venture capital is hard, even with the "right" pedigree.

I mainly wanted to pursue the CFA for myself, but having a job in finance wouldn't hurt, especially since one of the requirements to become a CFA charterholder was to get a minimum of three years of investment-related work experience.

The CFA is an expensive exam whose registration fees depend on the enrollment date. I was thinking to enroll sometime in August or September for the December 2019 exam, but I wanted to save up some money first. It was going to cost me around $2,000 to register.

And as much as I hate to admit it, at some point, I became ashamed of my school, or at least I wasn't proud to have it on my resume. Most of the companies I was targeting specifically asked for graduates from certain schools. Whenever I wanted to register for an event hosted by one of these companies or applied for a job there, I never saw my school on the list; I had to type it separately or check the "Other" category. I never got accepted into these events, and I certainly did not get the jobs either. This, along with the other rejections I'd faced, made me temporarily forget the sacrifices that got me into the school in the first place.

Date: 07/07/2019

Hey, me again. So today I'm confused about something (yeah, I know). I don't know why I've been thinking so much about life lately. What's on my mind right now is dreams. I'm scared of my own dreams. I feel like they're too big and TOO SPECIFIC! That scares me because people usually have vague or broad dreams, and then maybe they figure things out as they go. I, on the other hand, have the exact title of my dream job, the exact industry, practice, and, guess what, the exact companies too. I have these two huge companies I want to work for, the second one being even larger. I recently added that company as a dream company and turns out most people who end up there come from my first dream company. Awesome, you say, but not really. To me, it's just weird that it aligns so perfectly, because some things are too good to be true, and just because they look all nice and aligned doesn't mean they'll happen in that order, or ever.

Can you tell I've been hurt by life before? Can you tell I'm scared to hope? Can you tell I'm scared of my future? Well, it's all very true, even though I'm not proud of it. Deep inside, I kind of have this wish that my dreams will come true, but they scare me because they're just so big. I'm just like, "Who am I to make it to Deloitte, then McKinsey?" like, seriously, these two companies are giants in management consulting, and I don't know if I should pursue them. I know for sure that right now, I'm not McKinsey material (AT ALL!), but I don't know if I'll ever be. I'm scared to try and try again without ever making it, but still having that fire burning in my heart...

That was the "I'm scared" part. I will say though (or rather, write) that while I've been thinking about life and dreams, and how some people get to make theirs come true and others don't, I realized I could/should have a different approach when it comes to my life and my dreams. Rather than just feeling sorry for other people all my life and thinking about how unfair it is, I should be thankful for the position I'm in, for every blessing and opportunity that comes my way. I want to realize how blessed I am to be able to do certain things, and I want to go after my dreams as long as they align with God's plan.

If He wants me to be a consultant, I will do everything in my power (with His help of course) to achieve that. At the end of the day, what's the point of living if you do not accomplish God's purpose for you? So, I want to do that and help people around me (and even those who are not) to the best of my ability. If I am blessed enough to be in a good/comfortable position in my life, if God allowed for my dreams to come true, why not share the proceeds with the people I share the gift of life with? That's what I want. Yes, life is unfair, but I don't want to just sit around complaining about how unfair it is and not realize what I could be doing with what I personally have and try to make someone else's journey on earth a little more enjoyable.

I really hope (?), however, that my purpose is to become a management consultant. I hope my older self looks back at this journal and cries because she has accomplished/is accomplishing her purpose. I hope she cries as she remembers this day and can't believe she's now working her dream job, all while helping anyone that needs a little push in their life. I hope I become what I was ultimately created to be. 🖤 🖤

Well ... I think this speaks for itself. A few days later, though, things got a little grim.

Date: 07/17/2019

Dear Heavenly Father... I'm trying as hard as I can to stay close to You and not let my circumstances drive me away. I don't know how to feel; I don't know what to do anymore. I've looked everywhere, and yet, no job. Again, I have deadlines, I have other stuff that depend on my getting a job, and yet here we are.

~~Thank You for...~~ I was afraid I'd have to look for a job all summer, and that's exactly what's happening. I didn't want to spend days crying but again, I'm back at it. Why are You always so silent? I don't even know if I'm doing the right things or not; I don't know if I'm on the right path. Nothing feels like it, nothing works.

~~I am worried about...~~ Why do I always have to go through that much frustration?! It's not like I don't try to be positive; it's not like I don't try to find a job. At this point, maybe I just have to go back home.

~~People I am praying for today...~~ Again, am I not supposed to FEEL external pressure because I trust You? I tried to be positive, even when I applied for the jobs I didn't like. I didn't get them. Those that I liked, I didn't get either.

Here's what's happening in my life... What does all this mean? None of the jobs I applied for were for me? Then what is? Neither the small nor the big ones! Do I just have to be unemployed at this time?

I need... I am tempted to just watch my life happen before me again and not do anything because even when I do take action, things don't budge.

Other things on my heart that I need to share with You, God... I know You know what You're doing. I just don't want to do anything anymore. I don't have the feeling I've been doing what I was supposed to do. Just do Your thing. I'm tired.

I didn't write in that journal again until January 2020.

People around me were making moves, literally. Christie—the Cameroonian friend I'd met at an event at DePaul—graduated a month after me and was getting ready to start her new job in August. I'd been helping my roommate Zoe with her interview prep for a job in New York City, so some nights, we practiced common interview questions. Alice, my other roommate, had graduated in December 2018; she'd stayed a few more months with us, then had to move closer to her job. Charlotte was going into the last year of her PhD, but once her lease was up, she was going to move in with her boyfriend. I, on the other hand, hadn't been to a single interview in weeks. For almost every job I applied for, I reached out to recruiters on LinkedIn to let them know I'd applied for the position. I also tried to have coffee chats with current employees, but I kept getting rejections after rejections.

I had less than two weeks to find a new apartment. Because I was looking to rent a place on my own with no roommates, it was a lot more complicated. I couldn't live in student residences anymore and needed to show proof of employment. I also needed to have good credit, which takes months to build. Though I already had an SSN, a full-time job is what would make me eligible for credit cards to start building my credit. And one way I'd be able to build credit was to pay rent with a credit card, then pay it off later. But I couldn't because I didn't have a job. Once more, my problems were interdependent.

Unsurprisingly, I wasn't feeling well on July 17th and couldn't sleep at night. I pulled out my other journal again and, with teary eyes, I poured my heart onto the paper.

That's the only journal I wrote in for the rest of the year.

Date: 07/17/2019

I feel so lame. I seriously feel like I'm not good enough, or at least not for the things I desire. Not only do I feel like my dreams are too big and I don't measure up, but I also feel like the things I need to do to get there are well above me and are out of reach, which means I can't reach my dreams either.

I am so sad. Haven't found a job yet, don't even know if I will. I feel like I'll just go back home, that's it for me here. That makes me so sad, not because it's a bad thing but because I just didn't expect it to happen this soon, not after all the effort I've put into trying to make something out of my stay here. It's like I don't even know why I came here. Now, I'm extremely grateful for my degree, but everything has been SO HARD. There have been obstacles EVERY step of the way. The only time I felt at peace was from March to May this year and while I'm thankful for that, I don't want a life where I can literally count peaceful moments. I hate to say/write such things because it sounds like I'm ungrateful, which I'm totally not. I've just been through a lot, and it doesn't get easier. I understand life is not easy, and I'm not asking for an easy one, but my frustrations and challenges have the opposite effect of what they're supposed to do: I feel weaker; I'm not hopeful for the future; I doubt myself; I don't know what I'm capable of, etc.

I didn't get any of the jobs I applied for, big or small. What can I do? OK, I'm not good enough for the big guys, but what about smaller jobs? Full time? No. Contract? No. What I like? Certainly not. What I don't like? No luck either. What should I understand? I'm just going through the motions right now and don't feel like wasting my energy anymore because that's what it feels like. A question remains: Can I still allow myself to dream big and hope for big things? Am I worthy of a corporate job at this time? Will I ever be ready and get where I want? Yeah, I know that's more than one question, but they're all relevant.

I'm back to being desperate for just any job. Tired of feeling like a bottomless well into which people pour their money into without ever seeing a return on their investment.

No, I didn't have suicidal thoughts, but I constantly felt like a burden.

About a week after that journal entry, I was offered an unpaid sales position that I didn't plan on taking. On July 26th, I still didn't have a job, and it didn't look like I was going to find one anytime soon. I'd officially been unemployed for two months and only had one month left to find a job, so I decided to use the unpaid position to pause my unemployment countdown.

I logged into my SEVP portal to report that employment. I filled out the required fields—employer name and address, job title, job type (full or part-time), start date, description, and relationship to my field of study. I didn't actually go to work; I'd run out of savings and wasn't going to use whatever I had on hand to pay for transportation to a job that didn't pay me.

That day, I also emailed my landlord to ask if I could stay for an additional month since I hadn't yet found a new place. I wasn't sure he was going to agree—he only did annual contracts, and I couldn't sign one because I was no longer a student. He emailed me back, and it turned out the new tenant for my bedroom was only going to move in on August 31st, so I could stay until the day before. That worked out well, but also meant I *really* needed to find something by then. I sighed after reading his email; it was both a sigh of relief and exhaustion, realizing that if I didn't find a *paid* job soon, my mom would have to continue paying my rent.

August rolled around, and I decided to put more emphasis on my apartment search. I was still applying for jobs but spent more hours in front of the computer looking for apartments, on the phone speaking with leasing agents, and outside touring apartments. I wasn't getting interviews, anyway.

Zoe was already gone; she'd been offered the job in New York City. I was happy for her. I knew how hard she'd looked for a job and how hard we practiced for her interviews. She was also an international student trying to get a job for her OPT before her deadlines, so I knew how she felt. I also knew how badly she wanted to work in New York before going back to South Korea. I saw her get discouraged whenever she got rejected or didn't hear back from certain jobs, and I cheered her up as best as I could.

I was happy for her, but I would be lying if I said I didn't wonder why I too couldn't find something. Anything. Why was I the only one left without a job? Without a new place? Why weren't things moving for me, too? Hadn't I cried enough? Hadn't I gotten discouraged enough? Hadn't I practiced enough during my interviews that turned into rejections? Hadn't I done enough? How much longer did I need to wait?

A few days before Zoe left, we were in the kitchen talking about her job and how excited she was to start. After a moment of silence, a frown creased her forehead, and she looked straight at me for a few seconds. She seemed to wonder why I was still unemployed.

"I will pray to your God that you find a job," she said at last, with an unusual calm and not-very-Zoe kind of tone.

"Thank you." I smiled. *I hope He hears you.*

She was referring to Who I'd told her I prayed to every Sunday at church. I still went to Old St. Pats, which was now about twenty minutes on foot from our apartment on South Morgan Street. Zoe saw me go out every Sunday at approximately the same time, and one time she stopped me to ask where I was going.

"Why do you always go out on Sunday at this time?" she asked, as I was walking down the hallway toward the door. Her curiosity was cute and made me smile.

"I go to church," I replied, still amused.

"Ooh…"

I sensed another question coming, so I stayed a little longer.

"And so, what do you do there; what is it like?"

I finally let out a laugh. "Well, I just pray to God. I thank Him for everything and ask Him for things I need, for me, my friends, my family, and everyone. Mass lasts about an hour, so it's not too long."

"Okay! See you in an hour!"

I didn't think this conversation was going to affect her in any way, let alone remain in her mind. So, when weeks later, Zoe said she was going to pray for me, knowing that was probably going to be a first for her, it really warmed my heart. Well … it surprised me at first, then it warmed my heart.

——— ⬦ ———

On August 7th, the pain, that once pea-sized hole on my heart that then grew to the size of a coin and shrank a little at some point, that pain was back and bigger than ever. *Deeper* than ever. My heart was aching every day, but that day, I was broken. I pulled out my journal again, ignoring how much my tears were wetting the paper.

Date: 8/07/2019

Two weeks away from my deadline, and I still haven't found a job. I feel like a failure. Maybe I shouldn't say that, but I really feel that way. I failed. I failed myself; I failed God; I let Him down. Maybe He made a mistake by giving me that internship. Maybe He really thought I would be able to get a return offer, but I didn't. I failed Him. He gave me something, and I wasn't able to keep it. I feel like even after that, there was another job for me that He put on my way during my job search, but I wasn't good enough to seize the opportunity. Out of all the jobs I interviewed for, there must have been at least ONE I could have gotten, but I didn't.

I just want to give up. I am so lame. Nothing makes sense. I'm starting to regret why I got an MBA in management. My degree is so broad. An MBA is already broad enough, so why did I choose to "focus" on another broad subject? What can you do with a management degree at an entry level? And why did I become interested in finance? I just feel like this situation that I'm in is my fault, and I don't know how to get out of it. I failed and I want to give up.

Sometimes I feel like I'm doing the most with my education and that it's not even going to be that useful. See, I want to get another master's degree, and I'm thinking about taking all levels of the CFA. I already have an MBA, and some people don't even go that far, and yet they have great jobs and great lives. But the thing is, I do feel in my heart the desire to do all these things, and it's not even about the money I could potentially get from having all that education. I am truly passionate about marketing, and more recently, finance too. But I literally have NO full-time work experience, and I feel stupid for wanting to further my education. But it's not like I'm not trying to find a job either...

All these good grades, 4.0 GPA. Wow ... but here I am. You know how people say grades don't matter and people with the highest grades are not the most successful? I am the perfect example! No, I don't regret having good grades, but sometimes I feel like they don't play in my favor. I am all shiny on the outside, but I have nothing inside. Someone asked me the other day if with all my degrees and good grades, I too was struggling to find a job. Well yes, that seems to happen to me too. I don't even know what I am capable of.

By the last week of the month of August, I had no job and no apartment. What I had was a new phone, the Google Pixel 3 XL I got for myself as a graduation gift. A brand-new phone that started acting up out of the blue that very week.

On Monday, August 26th, I called a leasing agent to schedule a tour of a studio apartment I'd just found, but he couldn't hear me. *Seriously, Google? Now is not a good time!* After trying a couple more times with no success, I switched back to my old Samsung. It no longer worked. *Wow ... so I just can never have a normal move?*

I got up from my desk to lie on my bed, trying and failing to suppress my rising panic. *I have to make appointments. I have to call the agents when I get to the apartments. What if I even get a call from a recruiter? People should be able to reach me. Is this a sign that I need to just leave? And if I do, what am I going to do with all my stuff? I'm not even prepared. Maybe I won't get a job, and it's best to just leave now instead of spending more money trying to stay here. All this money we spend on rent, utilities, food. All these taxes and fees. But what about reaping the benefits of my degree? I paid to apply for OPT, shouldn't I at least get a job that pays me too? And what about saving for Canada? What about the CFA? This is so confusing. Nothing makes sense.*

That same day is when the new tenant started bringing her stuff to the apartment. Her official move-in day wasn't until Saturday, but she wanted to bring heavier stuff to her new (my current) room first. Understandable. What that meant for me was that I needed to be out by Friday.

I calmed myself and went back to my desk to continue my apartment search. I wrote a list of available apartments with their addresses and contact information on a sheet of paper, hoping the next day, one of my phones would want to perform its most basic function.

In the meantime, I had to think about another way to approach apartment- hunting. Being a recent graduate with no job, no credit, no guarantor, and no savings was not going to get me an apartment. And clearly, I wasn't going to get a job by the end of the week. Even if I did get one, I wouldn't get paid until at least two weeks later. So, I had to find an alternative to what I'd been telling leasing agents.

I still had my initial I-20 with the December 2019 end date, but I initially didn't want to use it because I knew it was no longer valid. *I* knew, not the agents. My back was against the wall. I was going to pretend I was still a student and use that I-20 to apply for an apartment.

⌖

The following day, my Pixel still didn't work. The warranty was still valid, so I sent it back to Google for replacement. Luckily, my old Samsung agreed to help. I had an appointment that afternoon to tour a studio apartment in Wrigleyville, fifty minutes away from my place by bus.

The apartment was only available for eleven months, which was perfect considering I was planning to leave the U.S. in July 2020— exactly eleven months out. It was on the last floor of a five-story building, and I loved everything about it except having to pay for laundry again. The property management company had several partnerships with local businesses, so that if I lived there, I would get discounts at local restaurants and gyms.

After going over the eligibility requirements, I showed my I-20 to the leasing agent. He said it would be fine but needed to double-check with his manager first. So, he called him.

"Yeah … so he said it's not gonna work, I'm sorry," the agent said to me when he hung up.

I inwardly sighed. The amount for living expenses on my I-20 needed to be four times the annualized rent, which it wasn't.

"Alright, no worries. Thanks for checking anyway!" I was hoping my face wouldn't betray my rising disappointment, but I probably failed because the agent looked sorry for me.

I headed out and called another leasing agent for another available studio apartment in the same area. She was available the next day at 2 p.m.

———— ⬤〰️⬤ ————

On Wednesday, August 28th at 2 p.m., the second leasing agent gave me a tour of the studio apartment and showed me around the building. The available studio was on the fourth floor of a five-story building. It was unfurnished, but the kitchen had the usual appliances— refrigerator, microwave, stove, an oven and dishwasher, both of which worked. What I loved most about that studio was the ample sunlight it received. The rays poured through the single window, sketching patterns on the hardwood floor, illuminating the entire room. Wearing sunglasses in that studio would not be a crime. There was a trash room on each floor and coin-operated washers and dryers on the first. Rent was $1,014, non-inclusive. Unlike my previous places, I would need to set up and pay for my own Wi-Fi and electricity, as well as buy and show proof of insurance before moving in if I were approved. Heat, water, and gas were set up but not included in the rent either.

The leasing agent went on to discuss the eligibility requirements and asked the usual background questions.

"Oh wow, congrats! You must be so excited!" she exclaimed when I told her I was a student graduating in December. She looked almost as excited as I was on my actual graduation day, a few months earlier.

"Thanks so much! And yeah, I *cannot* wait!" My smile matched hers.

I showed her my I-20 as proof that I was a non-citizen, which I also explained was the reason I had no credit. I said I'd been in the U.S. since January 2018–the program start date on my I-20–and hadn't had a chance to apply for a credit card yet.

"Oh okay. No worries! I think we can work with that," she started, scrutinizing the papers in her hand. "I'll have to double check with my manager first, but you can go ahead and apply and upload a copy of this document to your application," she continued. "And if you apply within twenty-four hours of this tour, we can waive the deposit requirement and application fees."

Girl, say no more. I'm applying as soon as I get home.

"Sounds great, thank you!"

I rushed home and applied. I texted my mom on my way to let her know I would need her help again with my moving expenses. The monthly rent wasn't significantly higher than what she was already paying and at least this time, it was for a studio and not a room in a shared apartment. I kept my fingers crossed that my background check would clear.

———— ⌾⫘⊃ ————

My application was approved on the morning of Friday, August 30th. This was great because I had no alternative and needed to move that same day. I'd kept looking but couldn't find anything else that was available within such tight deadlines. I'll let you imagine how much stress I was under before I got the approval email.

By noon, I was all packed and ready to head to my new apartment on West Sheridan Road. I just needed to clean my room, which I did after helping the mover load his truck later that afternoon. I could leave the apartment at any time of the day with no penalty, but I still wanted to leave early enough to get to my new place and finish unpacking before the end of the day.

The landlord was not available for the final inspection, so I put the keys on the windowsill as he requested. *I am going to miss sitting here.* My eyes scanned the room for the last time. I had a half-smile on my face, the kind of smile you have when you're going to miss a place and the memories you didn't know you were going to make there.

If there was anything wrong when the landlord came to inspect the room later that evening, he was going to take out the money from my deposit and send me the balance. I got my full deposit back.

Christie volunteered to help me move in, so she joined me at the new place, and we brought my stuff up to my studio together with the mover. I was grateful this time I wasn't doing it all on my own.

She stayed a couple hours, during which we talked about any and everything. About her job and how it was going. About my job search and how it was going.

"What's for you will not pass you by," she said at some point, probably because I'd failed again to not let the desolation show on my face.

I'd heard words like these before. I'd read quotes like these before. I just didn't believe them anymore.

"Yeah, we'll see." I smiled, then changed subjects.

———⬗———

I finished unpacking and organizing over the weekend. Turns out you really can't do it all in one day.

The afternoon of September 1st, I was sitting on the edge of my bed, looking around my new apartment. Empty, but nice and bright. I was once more grateful to have found a new place despite all the stress. But then it hit me: I had just signed a one-year lease, not knowing what was going to happen next. I wondered if this was a mistake. I wondered if this was a waste of time and money. I wondered what I was going to do for the rest of my time in the U.S. if I couldn't find a job for my OPT. I wondered what company would want to hire me for only eight months, assuming I could even start in October. I wondered what I was going to do with my days.

CHAPTER 15:

NOT ENOUGH

S tarting September 9th, my days were split between studying for the CFA exam and looking for jobs. Sophie had lent me the money to pay for the registration fees; even she no longer believed I would find a job for my OPT, but she was willing to help me keep myself busy until I went back home. Besides fulfilling the work experience requirement, to become a CFA chartherholder, I would to pass all three levels of the program (Level I, Level II, and Level III). Each exam level builds on the previous, so I started with Level I.

I now had three months to prepare for a difficult six-hour exam. I studied from 8 a.m. to 10 p.m. with a few breaks in-between.

I liked what I was studying, and some things I didn't understand at my internship at CIVC Partners were now making more sense. But after a while, the repetitiveness of my days started to wear on me. Sometimes I had to force myself to study because my job search had drained all the energy out of my body, and sitting at my desk for hours to study fixed income wasn't the best way to replenish. At least I now had a better answer for when interviewers asked what I'd been doing since graduation. Apparently, it wasn't a good look to be unemployed and simply look for a job with not much else going on.

September 9th is also the day a suspicious company offered me a job I couldn't recall applying for. It looked like a scam. It entailed collecting data from Facebook, doing some sorts of investment before converting the funds into cryptocurrency. The company was nowhere to be found on the Internet. I hadn't gone to a single interview; I just magically received a poorly written offer letter with no start date on it. It was definitely sketchy.

I didn't want to accept the job, but I also needed money. I didn't respond right away; instead, I set a deadline for myself for Friday to make a decision. As of that Monday, my decision was a hundred percent "no," but I wanted to see what it would be on Friday.

On Thursday morning, I got a call from a recruiter at one of the staffing firms I was working with. She was recruiting for an entry-level analyst position at a real estate investment firm looking for someone to join as soon as possible. The duties sounded interesting. Not that I had a choice, but it felt good to know I would actually like my job if I joined the firm. In addition, it paid $25 per hour, the highest hourly wage I'd been presented with.

An interview with the real estate firm was unnecessary because I'd already done two interviews with the staffing firm before we started working together. They told me for some positions, especially those that needed to be filled quickly, I wouldn't have to redo interviews. They basically just advocated for candidates they thought would best fit certain jobs based on the information they already had. They had all of my information: my work authorization, my resume, and the answers to commonly asked interview questions.

The recruiter asked if I was interested and if I gave her the authorization to share my information with the firm. Of course, I said yes. She was going to get back to me with the firm's decision later that day. I was *hopeful*. Maybe this was a sign that my answer for that weird job offer should remain a hard "no." The light began to take shape again.

The recruiter called me back mid-afternoon with some news.

"I'm so sorry, Danielle, but the firm doesn't sponsor international students," she said, "but we'll keep you posted if anything else comes up." She sounded less excited.

"Okay, no worries, thanks for letting me know." My throat was tight, but I didn't cry.

The light vanished.

The same recruiter called me again a few hours later. She'd come across another opportunity that she wanted to discuss with me. It was a temporary sales coordinator position at a hotel that would only last two weeks. The job description didn't sound very exciting, especially compared to that of the previous position. But then again, I didn't have much choice. Basically, I would answer the phone, take reservations, and help around with other tasks. The hourly wage was $14 to be paid weekly. The hotel was also looking for someone to start the next Monday, no interview required.

The recruiter tried to make the opportunity sound more exciting than it was, and though I appreciated her effort, I just wasn't thrilled, especially after that morning's call. I wasn't thrilled, but I was desperate and would have taken any job at that point.

"Because this is a two-week assignment, there's not going to be any issues with your work authorization if you accept the job," she told me after a few seconds of silence. "Should I go ahead and share your information with the manager?" she asked, a little too cheerful.

"Yeah, sure." My tone didn't match hers.

Another moment of silence passed before she finally said, "Perfect, congrats! You're gonna love it; the team is really great!"

Yeah, sure.

When she hung up, I dwelled on the thoughts that had made their way into my mind during our call. *I am not good enough. I don't deserve high-paying jobs. I will never make more than minimum wage. This is all I can get, and I should be content with it. I will never work at a corporate firm. It's too much for me; I don't deserve that. I would probably be too happy if I got that real estate investment job, and God doesn't want me to be that happy. Happiness is not for me.*

At least I didn't have to think about that shady job offer anymore. But this whole situation got me thinking. I wondered if I would've gotten the hotel job if I hadn't set myself a deadline to respond to the shady job, and if I would've gotten the hotel job at all if I hadn't been offered the shady job in the first place. I wondered why it had to happen that way, why I couldn't have gotten the hotel job earlier. I wondered what the deal was with me and deadlines that made everything happen at the *very* last minute. I felt like I couldn't get a job on my own, like it had to be handed to me. With my unsuccessful interviews, all I could think about was how much I had failed.

"Everyone, this is Danielle. She will be joining us for the next two weeks and help Gina and Chris on the sales side," the sales and marketing director announced, introducing me to the team during their weekly meeting on Monday, September 16th. I should've probably taken the dress code more seriously when the recruiter told me about it during our phone call. I didn't know what hotel it was until I got there that day. I had the address but didn't bother to check what hotel was located there. Either way, I should've known because Z Bar, the rooftop lounge where I had my graduation cocktail, was in that hotel—The Peninsula, one of Chicago's most luxurious hotels.

I had on a black blouse that I tucked into high-waisted black slack pants. I thought that was too much black, so I put on red ballerina flats. Bad idea. At least my hair was pulled back into a ponytail, which the recruiter recommended I do for my first day. I had no makeup on, but my brows were done. I didn't look bad; I just wished I could hide my feet. Put them out of sight. Put them out of *everyone's* sight. The employees, on the other hand, all looked as if they were coming straight out of a luxury fashion magazine. They smelt like it, too. And for a second, I wondered why I was only getting paid $14 an hour.

I spent the first half of that morning going over hotel policies and flipping through a dress code booklet that had too many pages in my opinion.

No patterns or bright colors.

Oh … so that's why people were staring! Okay, got it. I pressed my lips and nodded. There were specific nail color guidelines as well. *Okay, I'm doing my nails this weekend with my first paycheck.* I didn't have to; that was just my way of justifying getting my nails done. *Guys, I can do better than this, I promise. We just got off on the wrong foot.*

The office was freezing—the AC was too high for that time of the year in Chicago, so I made a mental note to always bring a scarf. I picked up the small square mirror on my desk to look at myself. *I feel so weird without my nose ring.*

The nose ring had fallen off while I was getting ready that morning, and after looking for it for less time than I usually did in the past, I let it go. That was partly because I thought it wouldn't look professional and partly because I was kind of ready to let it go.

Getting my nose pierced was a high school graduation gift from myself. I'd wanted to do that for about three years, but my parents and high school wouldn't let me. I went to a Catholic university that didn't allow piercings either, but I managed my way around security for the first few months of my freshman year until they eventually got used to seeing me with a nose ring. And it's not like I was the only student with a piercing, anyway.

My nose piercing was a stain on my image in college, especially during my first year. Having a piercing anywhere other than the earlobes was frowned upon, and people very much judged me for having one in my nose. That I went out to parties quite a bit and was more sociable did not make things better, as that didn't align with how people perceived me in high school and how they thought I should behave. I got called all sorts of names and heard crazy stories about the things I had allegedly done. These stories spread like a virus and muted into variants, and it seemed like I couldn't get rid of them no matter what I did.

These stories were not real. Though they sometimes got to me, they didn't deter me from keeping my nose ring. I *loved* my piercing. It looked good on me, so I was only going to remove it when *I* decided. Funny enough, throughout the years, more and more people got nose piercings. I am by no means implying that I set the trend, but some people who judged me for having a nose piercing now had one, too. How funny is that?

I was seventeen when I got my nose pierced and told myself I would stop wearing rings when I turned twenty-five. I always felt like that age had something special, not sure exactly what. I am twenty-five as I'm writing this chapter, and I still don't know what that special thing is.

I was twenty-three years and six months old when I lost my nose ring in my bathroom, but I thought that was close enough to twenty-five. Plus, I didn't want to have to force a ring into my nose every night because I couldn't wear it during the day at work.

Like every day, Gina came into the office one hour after Chris and me. I shadowed her for the rest of my first day, and she trained me on the tasks I would be doing. I was going to enjoy preparing gifts for guests and handwriting welcome notes, but answering the phone was going to be a challenge.

Talking to strangers on the phone, strangers who worked at prestigious companies and were used to a certain level of service when they called about their corporate events, or talking to some very rich and demanding strangers, was indeed the hardest part of my job.

I watched Gina answer the phone and have conversations with people she didn't know. *How do people even do that?* I wondered if I too would get to that point. I wondered if I would get past the stuttering when I picked up the phone and couldn't remember what I was supposed to say, and my mouth completely dried out. I wondered if I would get past losing my voice and not hearing myself speak, even when I did remember what to say, because my heart was beating too fast and too loud in my ears. I wondered if I would get past the overwhelming feeling that everyone in the office was listening to me while I was on the phone. I wondered if I would get past the shaky hands and my fear of not doing it right.

CHAPTER 16:

A GLIMMER OF HOPE

W hile working at The Peninsula, I continued to apply for jobs and study for the CFA exam. I got home around 6 p.m. and started studying an hour or two later until midnight. On Saturdays, I studied from 8 a.m. to 10 p.m., with breaks in between and on Sundays, I studied from 8 to 10 a.m. before church and from 2 to 8 p.m. after.

On Thursday, September 19th, I had a phone interview before work for an investment performance analyst role at Marquette Associates, an investment consulting firm. As usual, I didn't think they would call me. I'd applied without expecting much, so it was nice to see that my resume had sparked some interest.

At that point, I was already a lot more comfortable with phone interviews, which I credit to my multiple interview experiences and coffee chats, but also to the multiple networking events and career fairs I had gone to the past year and a half. Though my beginnings were very hard—doing small talk and talking about myself did not come naturally at all—pushing through the awkwardness and introducing myself to strangers multiple times over bore some fruits.

My conversation with the HR manager at Marquette Associates went well. My internship at a private equity firm and the fact that I was now studying for the CFA helped explain my interest in this finance-related position.

I felt good at the end of the forty-five-minute phone screening. I didn't know for sure I was going to move on to the next step, but I wasn't very surprised either when the HR manager emailed me later that day to invite me to the second round of interviews. What surprised me was how quickly that happened, especially because she was supposed to get back to me a week later, which was also what I was used to.

I emailed her my availability for the week that followed, and she responded with my interview schedule. I was going to meet with her for a few minutes, then with senior consultants and vice presidents for two one-hour panel interviews. Seven people total. My heart sank into my stomach. *That's many people, and a very long time...*

By now, I'd been to a total of four in-person interviews since May, and only one was a panel interview (the one at Fitch Ratings). One-hour interviews didn't scare me that much anymore; I'd gotten used to them. Though I was usually done before the sixty-minute mark, I at least tried to go longer than thirty minutes. I used to wonder how people were able to do two or more consecutive interviews in a single day. I was going to find out.

When I looked up my interviewers on LinkedIn, some of them had already checked my profile. I knew very well what it looked like, but I clicked on my profile anyway to see what they had seen before continuing my stalking. Unsurprisingly, almost all my interviewers were CFA charterholders. I checked the profiles of a few investment performance analysts as well. Most had graduated from a grad or undergrad program in the last two years. They came from a mix of renowned business schools and less-known universities, which made me feel like I had a chance. They seemed nice. I wanted to work with them.

On Wednesday, September 25th, I took the latter half of the workday off to go to my interview. Marquette Associates' office was located on the thirty-fifth floor of a skyscraper in the Loop. My first interview was scheduled for 2:15 p.m. but I got there an hour earlier, so I decided not to go into the building just yet. Instead, I went to Dunkin' Donuts at the Thompson Center across the street. I ordered myself an iced coffee to sip while I nervously reread interview questions and answers in my interview notebook. That notebook had become a gold mine. With each new interview I needed to prepare for, I added more questions and answers. I also added tips I found on YouTube or LinkedIn, plus any information I gathered from my visits to the career center at school.

My stomach was in knots under my black high-waisted crayon skirt, in which I had tucked a sleeveless turquoise blouse. I'd had that blouse for over a year but had never worn it—I kept it for a special occasion. For when I would go to an interview for a job I really wanted. A blazer that matched my skirt covered my arms and a pair of black tights covered my legs. That was probably a lot of black, but I had on black ballerina flats as well.

This job is too big and too good for you. You don't deserve it. You won't make it. The voice was loud in my ears as I prayed for everything to go well during my interview.

When I walked in, the entire office was doused in the 2 p.m. sunlight, beaming through the all-around floor-to-ceiling windows. I checked in at the reception, then waited for the HR manager to come get me.

My interview with her went well. It was more like a casual conversation—she already knew about my qualifications from my resume and our phone call. We spoke for a few minutes, shared some laughs, then I had to meet with my other interviewers. Those interviews were more stressful but went better than I had imagined. I even went overtime during the second panel interview. Turns out I had a lot to talk about. The people were also nice, and I was pleased to see that one of the vice presidents was an Asian pregnant woman.

With all the stressful talking and water drinking I had done for more than two hours, I had to use the ladies' room before my one-hour bus ride home. I met the HR manager in the main room afterward and thanked her for scheduling the interviews.

"I know it's almost 5 p.m., and you only had three interviews scheduled for today," she started, not letting me get to the end of my goodbye, "but I just spoke with our managing director, and I wanted to see if you had a few more minutes to speak with him. If not, that's completely fine; you can always come back next week."

Are you kidding me? Bring them all. The partner, the CEO, everyone!

"Sure! I'd be happy to discuss with him as well," I said, trying to contain my excitement.

Once more, I was fast-forwarded to the next step. I would have normally come back for the final round of interview within a few days or even weeks of that day, but apparently, they liked me.

The HR manager came to get me at the end of my twenty-minute interview with the managing director. She asked how I felt and sympathized with me spending my entire afternoon interviewing. Then she showed me around the office.

The sun was beginning to set, gradually permeating the office with gradient rays of amber. I marveled at its reflection on the surrounding glass buildings, brilliant red and warm orange with soft hints of blue. I saw myself sitting at the empty desk closest to the window, chatting with my new co-workers one minute and gazing at the scenery the next.

I refocused when the HR manager told me the salary range for this position was $50 to $55,000 annually. She explained career progression, saying analysts were typically promoted to consultants within two years; not that I would still be in the U.S., but I liked hearing that. We also discussed benefits, and she said I could take a day off before the CFA exam to study if I joined the firm. She asked when I would be done at the hotel and I said the following Friday, which apparently worked out well for the firm. She said she would get back to me a few days later. We shared a few more laughs, then I left.

I left feeling good. I left feeling proud of myself for interviewing for three hours. I left feeling grateful, though I didn't want to assume I had gotten the job. I left feeling confident. I left feeling *hopeful*. The light appeared again. This time, brighter, clearer. Maybe this was God's plan all along. He was preparing me for something better, something *bigger*. Something I was actually going to like.

When I got home, I thanked God for the experience, for helping me with the interviews and for making me realize there was something better. I liked this job even more than the one at Fitch Ratings. It was perfect for me. I wanted to get the job. I prayed to get the job. I hoped to get the job. I believed I would get the job.

The next day, the HR manager emailed me while I was working.

> **From:** *HR Manager*
> **To:** *Me*
> **Subject:** *Performance Analyst Role*
> **Date and Time:** *09/26/2019 at 9:58 a.m.*
> *Hi Danielle,*
>
> *It was so nice meeting you yesterday! I just wanted to let you know that we should have an answer for you by tomorrow or Monday. In the meantime, please let me know if you are legally authorized to work in the United States and if you require sponsorship for employment visa (H-1B visa)?*
>
> *Thank you!*
> *HR Manager*

I thought long and hard about how I wanted to answer her email. I thought about the time I lied during an interview and said I did not require sponsorship and wasn't on OPT, because I was tired of being discriminated against based on my immigration status. But then, they asked for my permanent residency documents, which I obviously did not have. I thought about how well my interviews had gone with Marquette and how I didn't want to ruin anything by lying. If they really liked me, maybe my status wouldn't matter.

I emailed her back during my break.

From: *Me*
To: *HR Manager*
Subject: RE: *Performance Analyst Role*
Date and Time: *09/26/2019 at 1:15 p.m.*

Hi HR Manager,

It was wonderful meeting you yesterday! I truly appreciate your time telling me more about the role, the company, and for showing me around.

I am authorized to work in the U.S. and will not require sponsorship until next June. I hope this is not an issue.

Looking forward to hearing back from you, and hopefully joining the team!

Regards,

Danielle

Her response reassured me.

From: *HR Manager*
To: *Me*
Subject: RE: *Performance Analyst Role*
Date and Time: *09/26/2019 at 3:45 p.m.*

Hi Danielle,

Thanks for letting me know! It shouldn't be a problem, just glad to be aware. Can you tell me what type of visa you're on right now? Thank you!

HR Manager

I told her I was on an F-1 visa and already had my EAD card. She didn't email me back until the following Monday.

———————⊂⊙⟩———————

On my last day at The Peninsula, Friday, September 27th, the sales and marketing director asked if I would be willing to work one additional week.

At that point, I was already more comfortable in my role. I wouldn't go as far as to say that it didn't bother me at all to speak with strangers on the phone, but I did it a lot better and a lot more naturally than on my first three days.

I didn't stutter when I answered the phone anymore. In fact, when the phone rang, I no longer pretended to be working on something else, so Gina or Chris would answer instead. I picked up the phone, and I knew what to say and what to ask and my mouth did not dry out anymore. I did not lose my voice and I heard myself speak, as well as the person on the other end of the line, because my heart was beating at normal speed in my chest. It didn't bother me as much that other people in the office heard me while I was on the phone. My hands weren't shaky anymore. I was doing a good job, and the fear was gone. One day, I even caught myself laughing with a customer on the phone! A complete stranger! Can you believe that?

I enjoyed the people I was working with, as well as the environment—I like luxury. And most people were nice.

As a sales coordinator, I worked in the sales and marketing department, which was split into two offices on the fourth floor. We collaborated a lot with other departments as well, mostly catering on the same floor, and room service down on the second floor. Gina, Chris, and I reported to one or two sales managers each, supporting their respective accounts and regions. There were several other employees in the department, but Gina and I were the only Black women. The only Black *employees*. Gina was good at her job, which managers and directors often recognized. I remember finding it unfortunate when she told me she'd been denied this position multiple times in the past because she did not have a bachelor's degree. She'd been at the hotel for several years but was first hired as a housekeeper. She worked her way up to the sales coordinator role, literally.

Gina had the craziest stories about celebrities who were staying at the hotel, having worked in different positions and departments over the years. She would tell me all about them during our breaks, while we were eating our complimentary chef-cooked lunch at the cafeteria, or toward the end of the day when there wasn't as much work anymore. Chris worked on NBA and other sports organizations' accounts and had some funny stories too. I worked on certain corporate and individual accounts, so I always knew when MBB or Big 4 consultants were in town and what for. I took their reservations and wrote their welcome cards, hoping one day I would be on the other side. The job was fun, and though I didn't see myself having it as a career (especially at that pay level), I was grateful I wasn't doing something I hated.

So, when the sales and marketing director asked if I wanted to come back, I said yes. Well … I would have said yes anyway, but I liked that it wasn't forcing myself. Also, I saw that as an opportunity to buy myself some time while I waited to hear back from Marquette, and it couldn't hurt to get one more paycheck. It was perfect timing, and I thought that was maybe God moving things around.

On Monday, September 30th, the HR manager at Marquette emailed me.

> **From:** HR Manager
> **To:** Me
> **Subject:** RE: *Performance Analyst Role*
> **Date and Time:** *09/30/2019 at 3:52 p.m.*
>
> *Hi Danielle,*
>
> *I hope you had a great weekend! Just wanted to reach out to say hello and let you know that I haven't forgotten about you! The feedback and approval process sometimes takes several days, so please bear with us. I hope to be back in touch with you very soon.*
>
> *Take care and talk to you soon!*
> *HR Manager*

Okay, this had *never* happened before. An HR manager emailing to say hello and reassuring me she was still working on my application? Never. I really appreciated her email, and for a second, I thought even if I didn't get the job, I would be thankful for the experience because of her. But I wasn't about to let negative thoughts get the best of me—I was going to hear back soon with good news. I thanked her for keeping me in the loop.

Then … nothing. Days went by, and I didn't hear back and had no other job interview. I must admit, I slacked off a little bit when I saw how great things were going with Marquette, but I quickly reminded myself of all the times I thought a job interview had gone well but didn't get an offer. So, I kept looking but had no call back.

CHAPTER 17:

BROKEN VESSEL

O n Thursday, October 3rd at work, on my third and last week at The Peninsula Hotel, I heard the sales and marketing director talk about my replacement. She was going to start the following Monday.

Did I do something wrong? Why don't they want to keep me? I don't understand what's wrong with me. Why didn't they tell me if I wasn't doing something right? Why did they keep telling me I was doing a good job? Why did he want me to come back this week if he'd already found someone else? Why hasn't Marquette gotten back to me? Why is all this happening? I am so tired of looking and I have only one month of unemployment left on my OPT. What am I going to do?

I didn't realize I hadn't said a word that morning until Gina messaged me on the hotel's private messaging platform, pulling me out of the pool of thoughts my mind was swimming in.

Gina: Are you okay? You're so quiet today.

Danielle: Am I? I'm so sorry! I'm totally fine, don't worry about it; just a lot to do this morning with all these contracts I have to turn over. How's everything with you?

Gina: Girl I know!! Work has been crazy these days. Reporting is killing me right now.

Danielle: Right?! Let me know if you need any help!

I lied. Of course, I lied.

Later that morning, I emailed the HR manager at Marquette to check on my application status. The wait was unbearable. I needed to know whatever the decision was.

> **From:** *Me*
> **To:** *HR Manager*
> **Subject:** *RE: Performance Analyst Role*
> **Date and Time:** *10/03/2019 at 11:32 a.m.*
> *Hi HR Manager,*
> *I hope all is well. I don't mean to rush you, but I wanted to check in and see if there are any updates on my application or if a decision has been made.*
> *Looking forward to hearing from you, hopefully with good news. Please let me know either way.*
> *Thank you and have a great day,*
> *Danielle*

She did not respond that day, or the day after. Now *that* is the experience I'd had with HR managers in the past. When I got home, I let out the tears I'd been holding throughout the day. Between moving and studying and starting a new job, I hadn't had a chance to write in a journal in what I considered a long time. Now was a good time. I needed to talk to myself. I still didn't want to write in my prayer journal, so I wrote in the other one. While I was writing and for no apparent reason, I thought about my little sister, Emma. Deep inside, I hoped she would never have to go through what I was going through and endure that much pain. I hoped I was feeling the pain for both of us.

Date: 10/03/2019

So ... I think that's it for me. I am honestly DONE looking for jobs. I am unsubscribing from every job board because my job search is pointless. I honestly feel like there's a certain level of happiness that God doesn't want me to reach. I feel like I just can't be fulfilled. My normal state is unhappiness, stress, depression. That's it. Even when I manage to get out of that dark place for a while, I always find my way back because that's where I have to be. I try as hard as I can to stay "unsad," but it's like being sad is how I'm supposed to live. I can't escape.

Here we are in October, and I still don't have a job. At this point, I don't think I will, and I am starting to be OK with that because it doesn't matter how hard I try, how many hours I look, how many prayers I make, how many tears I shed ... I still can't find a job. I did get a three-week temp job, which I am and will always be thankful for, but guess what? They've already found someone to replace me. Why? Why couldn't I just stay there? They said I helped them a lot. So, what is the issue? Why don't they want me to stay? I honestly feel like there's something wrong with me.

I am so done hoping to find a job. Hope is a trap, and it hurts. I interviewed for a perfect position (again) and felt like I could get the job. I felt like it was for me, I was hopeful ... but it always ends up the same. I feel so stupid for thinking I could ever get a job here. It's like, who do I think I am to get a full-time job with benefits and everything? Who am I to be fulfilled and happy? Happiness is elusive. I don't understand why God won't let me be happy for an extended period. Every time I think I've reached peace, it gets disturbed again shortly after. I CANNOT sustain a peaceful and happy state of mind.

Only a few months left on my OPT. Who will ever want to hire me? All these things I'm going through are pointless, I don't even try to make sense of my situation anymore. I'm tired, as I've said a million times. I have no self-confidence whatsoever, and I don't know if trials are supposed to help with that. Anyway, I'm out. Done hoping, done looking for jobs, done being positive, done trying to be happy. Happiness is not for me.

The next day was my last day at the hotel. It really bothered me not to know why they didn't want me to stay. I didn't ask for feedback at my previous internship, in part because I dreaded what they had to say. I wouldn't say I regretted it, but I didn't want to repeat the same thing at The Peninsula. So, I asked for feedback. Well … not to any of my managers or to the director, but to Gina. That's when I learned the role was never actually open. The person before me had transferred to another department; the team had already found her replacement, except she kept pushing back her start date. She could finally start the following Monday, which is why they didn't ask me to come back. So, it wasn't anything I had or had not done. Gina said they were actually happy with my work. What relieving news!

Before I left, Gina wanted to show me the most expensive suite in the hotel, so about an hour before the end of the workday, she asked one of our managers for the keys. She gave me a tour of the most luxurious hotel room I'd seen.

When we went back down to the office, it was about 4:30 p.m. That is usually when I would gather all the welcome cards for guests arriving in the next few days and take them down to room service. I would then go back up to the office and help Gina if she were still working on something. She would also let me know if anything needed to be done the next day before she got to the office. By 4:45 p.m., we were mostly done with our day and ready to leave. I wouldn't leave until 5 p.m. and Gina until 6, considering she started an hour later in the morning. We would spend my last few minutes in the office chatting and answering the dwindling phone calls.

When I got back to the office from room service around 4:40 p.m. on my last day, Gina told me to go over some contracts she was working on. There were only three folders, so I did that pretty quickly. She then asked me to prepare a gift bag for someone her manager was going to meet the following week. Done. Then she scrambled to find envelopes and blank cards so I could print welcome messages on the cards and handwrite guest names on the back of the envelopes, but it was Friday, and I'd prepared all the welcome cards for guests arriving over the weekend and until the following Monday. I checked the time, and it was almost 5 p.m.

"I am going to miss you too," I said with a half-smile on my face, realizing what she was doing. She made a sad face, the kind of face you make when you don't want to see someone go. *Oh no no no, don't do that, I can't cry. Not now, not here.*

"Girl, has it been three weeks yet?" she asked, fixing her face.

I smiled. "I know, where did time go?"

I checked the time again: 5:05 p.m. I got up and hung my bag on my shoulder. There was a lump in my throat, and my eyes and nose were tingling. Gina got up to give me a hug, and I refused to let those stubborn tears drop. I said my goodbyes to the team and thanked the director again for the opportunity. Something else I didn't do at my internship but rectified at The Peninsula was to send a thank-you and farewell email. Earlier in the day, I'd sent that email to the sales and marketing department and to people from other departments I'd worked with.

On Friday, October 4, 2019, at 5:10 p.m., I was officially unemployed. Again.

———⊂IIII⊃———

The Sunday that followed was a special one for me. That morning, I went to church at St. Mary of the Lake Parish like I'd been doing since moving to my apartment on West Sheridan Road. I missed going to Old St. Patrick's Church in the West Loop, but it was now too far from me, requiring multiple bus rides and more planning to get there on time. As much as I loved going there and tried to maintain attendance even after moving, I needed something more practical. St. Mary of the Lake was a fifteen-minute walk from my new apartment, and I discovered with delight that I could like another church as much as I did Old St. Pats.

During his homely on October 6th, the priest said something that resonated with me. In fact, the entire mass resonated with me. The first reading was about crying to God for help when it seems He doesn't answer, the second reading about withstanding hardships with the strength that comes from God, and the gospel about accomplishing things through faith. The priest said to go deeper into faith, to take a leap of faith in whatever we, in the attendance, were going through. He said to take a leap of faith eighteen million, four hundred and seventy-six thousand, nine hundred and thirty-two times. No kidding, I counted. So, I was like, *Okay, God, I get it.*

Right there and then, I decided I was going to take a leap of faith. I decided to hope one more time, one *last* time. I decided to have faith and believe one more time. To believe that He had something for me.

To believe that during the week or whenever I heard back from the HR manager at Marquette, it was going to be with good news.

It doesn't happen often, but I cried that Sunday in church. I knelt down, opening my heart wide open to God in a way I'd never done before. I told Him I was going to use the very last ounce of strength left in my body to hope with all my heart. I told Him that for once I wouldn't hold back, just as the priest suggested. I told Him I wouldn't let my fear of being disappointed prevent me from going all in. And I told Him that this was going to be the last time. That if it failed, I would expect Him to understand if I never wanted to hope again. I prayed with all my heart. I begged Him to listen to my cry. I asked Him to help me with my hardship. I surrendered.

The following Monday, October 7th, I went back to my pre-Peninsula study schedule for the CFA exam that was now two months away. It'd been hard to achieve my daily study goals while I was working, so I was eager to catch up. I was going to use that week and maybe the following to do all the catching up I needed before heading to Marquette Associates as the new investment performance analyst on the team. I looked forward to doing something related to what I was studying. The Peninsula was great, but it had nothing to do with finance.

I patiently waited for the HR manager's email that Monday, but it didn't come. *It's okay, no one said it was going to happen today.* On Tuesday, I wasn't a hundred percent at peace, but I was aware of the stress missiles coming at me. I did everything in my power to dodge them, and it worked. On Wednesday, I resisted the urge to check my phone every ten minutes to see if she'd emailed me. I remembered the promise I'd made to God—this was the week of taking a leap of faith, so I just waited and kept a hopeful heart.

On Thursday, October 10th, I was sitting at my desk, studying. Lunch break had just ended, and I was deep into the equity investments topic. My replacement phone vibrated next to me on the table and lit up. I saw the red Gmail envelope icon. It could've been any email; in fact, this wasn't my first email of the day, but I somehow knew it was the email I'd been waiting for. My heart skipped a beat. I picked up my phone and put my right index on the fingerprint reader at the back of my Pixel to unlock it. I opened the email.

From: HR Manager

To: Me

Subject: RE: Performance Analyst Role

Date and Time: 10/10/2019 at 2:50 p.m.

Hi Danielle,

I am so sorry for the delay in getting back to you. In the interest of time and so you can pursue other opportunities, I want to let you know that we are unable to make you an offer at this time.

Thank you for the opportunity to interview with you and to get to know you better. We appreciate the time you took to talk with us and your patience with the hiring process.

Thank you and best of luck!

HR Manager

Every word I read felt like a blade pressing onto my heart. One word made the blade go up, the next made it go down. I read the email as slow as one can possibly read an email, and the blade on my heart was moving at my reading speed. Tears of the deepest pain I've *ever* felt slowly and quietly ran down my cheeks. I was completely absorbed into the email. Everything around me evaporated. The light, for sure, had vanished. And this time, it was never coming back.

I don't know how long it took me to read the entire email. When I finished, I put my right arm on my desk to rest my burning head on it and face the already wet wood floor. I cried quietly for a moment, then louder, when I felt the pain tear my heart and explode through my body. I burst through crying with pain, *so much* pain. It hurt like it'd never hurt before. I removed my hand from the desk after a few minutes and turned around in my swivel chair to face my bed. My heart was bleeding. Streams of blood were flowing down my chest. The pain was unbearable. I bent down and continued to cry, holding the left side of my chest with both hands, pressing down to stop the bleeding and salvage what was left of my heart.

The pain, that once pea-sized hole on my heart that then grew to the size of a coin, the pain that shrank a little at some point then came back deeper, that pain tore my heart wide open. Almost as open as when I cried out to God four days earlier, except this time my heart was shattered, and I couldn't find all the pieces to stitch them back together.

If you've read this far, you know how much I've cried. Maybe you have an idea how many times it happened. Maybe you can even imagine how much it hurt sometimes. This time was like none before. I cried that day like I never want to cry again in my life.

It wasn't so much about not getting the job as much as it was feeling like God had let me down. For the very first time in my life, I had trusted someone with all my heart. For the very first time in my life, I did not hold back. For the very first time in my life, I took a leap of faith.

I'd heard the expression before. *Take a leap of faith.* I'd heard people talk about how life-transforming it can be. I'd even heard it a year earlier at Old St. Patrick's Church when I still lived in the West Loop. But I never fully let myself *fall*. I was too scared to come crashing down.

So, when I surrendered, what's more, to God, when I let myself fall into a deep void, trusting that He would catch me, when I finally abandoned myself and completely let go of my grip on fear, but then felt like He let me crash, I snapped. I fell and broke everywhere. My heart and my body were shattered, my heart more than my body.

My body was aching, and my head was on fire. I wailed. I sobbed. I choked on my tears. When I sensed that *something* was going to happen, I tried to calm myself. This time, going out for a walk wasn't an option because I couldn't. My heart was too broken, and tears wouldn't stop flowing. I couldn't even walk properly.

Right there and then, I ended my relationship with God. It was over. I'd never been hurt like this before, and I couldn't keep letting Him break me every time He had a chance.

I got up from my chair and headed toward my bed, bent over and hands still holding the left side of my chest, unable to stop the streams of blood flowing from my heart. As I walked past the nightstand on which I'd placed my wooden cross, I talked to God for what I thought would to be the last time. I told Him to leave me alone. And though He never spoke to me directly, I told Him not to ever talk to me again. As for me, I would never pray to Him again.

"You break people; that's what You do, and I am so tired of You. I can't believe anything You say anymore, and I never will. What kind of loving father does this to their child? You are so mean. Since You enjoy seeing me at my lowest, since that's where You want me to be so I can come running to You, I hope You are happy now. But don't You think I will ever run to You again. Forget about me, though I know You already have. I will continue to try to be a good person, but don't You think it has anything to do with You. I never want to hear about You again."

Even writing this now, and after multiple edits of this book, it still brings tears to my eyes.

That Thursday afternoon, the words came out of my mouth; I didn't just think them. I didn't expect to break like this and decide not to believe in God anymore. I thought I'd just lose hope like I said I would on Sunday. But then again, I hoped with all my heart it wouldn't happen. I didn't deny God's existence, but I was now certain He had favorites. To me, He was a mean and coercive God. He was a tyrant who didn't like to see me happy because making me sad was His way of keeping me close to Him, ensuring I always depended on Him.

I wanted to remove the cross from my nightstand and put it away somewhere, but I didn't. Not sure why.

I lay on my bed and dove deeper into my negative thoughts, agreeing with the voice that had been warning me something like this was going to happen, agreeing and coming to terms with the fact that some things were definitely too good for me, agreeing with the fact that I would never hope or be happy again. As usual, my apartment was bathed in sunlight. Yet I was in the dark.

I don't think it was already 5 p.m. when I got in my bed, but I only got out of it the next day. I didn't sleep the whole time; I just couldn't do anything—not even put away the books I'd left open on my desk or pick up the highlighters that had fallen to the floor. I had no strength left. No hope. No light.

Consistent with my new perception of God, I wondered if that was the day I was going to die, so He could judge me based on what I had just told Him and send me to hell. I'm not going to lie; that scared me. A lot. But I was more broken and hurt than scared.

The pain that you've been feeling cannot compare to the joy that is coming. "What a lie!"

———— ⊂▥⊃ ————

I didn't pray in the morning anymore. The next day, out of habit, I sat on the edge of my bed for a moment but then I remembered.

"Do what You want," I said, standing up to get ready for the day.

The following days, I did not forget. I didn't pray before eating. I didn't pray before going to bed. I didn't go to church on Sundays. I didn't want to hear about God anymore.

Despite my brokenness, I decided to start looking for a job again after a few days. As paradoxical as it may sound, my experience with Marquette gave me a little bit of confidence. For the first time, I felt like the only reason I'd not gotten an offer was because I was on a student visa, and not so much because I wasn't a good fit for the role. I'd asked the HR manager for feedback, but she never replied to my email, so I drew my own conclusion.

At the same time, I had absolutely no hope. I'd already accepted in my heart that I wouldn't get a job. Still, I set up LinkedIn and Indeed job alerts again and this time, I only applied to "nicer jobs." I paused my unemployment countdown on my SEVP portal again, using the unpaid sales job I'd previously used for that purpose before my stint at The Peninsula. I could only be unemployed for three more weeks.

I decided to ignore the recent suggestions I'd been receiving about getting married and applying for a Green Card that way; that was not going to happen. Every time someone suggested it to me, it reminded me of how badly I wanted to leave the U.S. It didn't seem like I could be myself in that country. It didn't seem like I could reach my goals without doing something illegal, immoral, or in opposition with my *personal* values and principles. I didn't hate the country; in fact, I made a promise to myself not to become bitter toward it, to never discourage anyone from going because of my experience. But at the same time, I wasn't going to try everything to stay, just for the sake of living in the United States of America.

October 2019 is also when applications for the 2020 Master of Marketing program at the Schulich School of Business in Canada opened. I'd started preparing my application months earlier and had everything ready by the end of September. I only needed to review my essays and update my resume. Admission requirements included two online videos, essays, and one interview after the preliminary screening.

I remember being anxious about all these steps, especially back in April and May when I hadn't done as many interviews yet. I used to wonder if I could handle *two* consecutive video essays, what I would say, how long they would be, what types of questions I would get, and how to even prepare. I'd reached out to two current Master of Marketing (MMKG) students on LinkedIn and though they provided more clarity, I was still anxious.

I found out through my research that Schulich was one of Canada's top business schools. One reason I became obsessed with it was that Deloitte—my dream firm—recruited heavily on campus. From what I'd seen on LinkedIn, hundreds of Schulich's alumni worked there, and I couldn't wait to join the program to stop stalking them and finally reach out for coffee chats.

I did a lot of research on the school, spent hours on forums reading about students' experiences, from those who'd been admitted to other programs to those who had not. Because the MMKG program was new, there wasn't a lot of information on it yet. Most of what I read was about the MBA program and how competitive it was. I didn't think I *wasn't* going to get into my program, but I didn't exclude that possibility either. Once more, I was only going to tell people about the program only if I were admitted.

My application was as good as I could make it. I'd been attending webinars about the program since 2018, so in my essays, I incorporated some of the information I'd gathered from those webinars and from my conversations with current students. I submitted my application on October 20th and paid the fees with the money I'd saved from working at The Peninsula.

CHAPTER 18

MENDED HEART

O n October 24th, I was sitting at my desk finishing up the equity investments topic of the CFA Level I exam when my phone lit up with another email notification. It came from a talent acquisition manager at Duff & Phelps, a company that had previously rejected one of my applications.

From: Rose

To: Me

Subject: Duff & Phelps—Unclaimed Property Tax Position

Date and Time: 10/24/2019 at 3:48 p.m.

Hello Danielle,

I am reaching out to you regarding another position that we have just posted online. I have included the link below.

If you are interested in the position, please apply using the link and email me once you have completed the application.

Please reach out to me at 123-456-7890 or send me at least three available time slots and I will reach out to you then.

Regards,

Rose

We'd never spoken before. I guess some companies really do keep candidates' information on file for future opportunities. I smiled a fake smile. *Is this one of Your jokes again? Okay, let's have some fun. You're not going to get me this time.*

I wasn't going to let myself be fooled again. I looked at the description and didn't even like the job. I didn't understand anything, and the title itself didn't appeal to me—I didn't like tax.

I didn't respond to her email, but I did apply for the job and called her the next day to let her know. The call ended up being more of an interview than me simply informing her that I had applied. Toward the end of the call, she asked the million-dollar-question:

"Thanks for your time today, Danielle," she said. "But before I let you go, I just have one last question. Do you require sponsorship now–?"

"No," I responded, before hearing the end of her sentence.

"–Or will you in the future? Oh okay, U.S. citizen. Perfect!" She sounded like she was taking notes.

She said goodbye before I could say anything else and hung up. The end of our conversation happened so quickly I didn't have the time to let her know I wasn't a U.S. citizen, as she'd started to think. I actually wanted to call her back and let her know I wasn't. But I didn't. *I'm not going to get the job anyway, so it doesn't matter.* I let it slide and carried on with my studying.

———— ⌖ ————

Two days later, it was Sunday. I hadn't been to church since the beginning of the month, and I was bored. I didn't miss God. I was bored, and that's exactly what I told Him before heading to church.

"Don't think this is me coming back to You. I'm just bored, and I want to get out of this apartment. This means nothing."

I could've done anything. I could've kept studying, or if I wanted to take a break that bad, I could've watched a movie. I could've gone to the grocery store, or for a walk. I hadn't seen Christie in a while and could've asked what she was up to. Or I could've taken a nap. Or I could've done nothing for one and a half hour. But instead, I went to church; I don't know why.

I walked fifteen minutes to St. Mary of the Lake. When I got there, I sat on one of the last pews instead of somewhere in the middle, like I usually did. I didn't sing, say any prayer, stand when everyone did, or pay attention to the readings. I just sat there doing nothing. I didn't know why I was there.

Then the priest did his homily, and I listened because I felt spoken to again. The homily didn't even have anything to do with the readings, so I don't know why he talked about what he talked about. But he talked about being hurt. He talked about coming back to God. He talked about love. And I almost lost it again. My attitude didn't change for the rest of the mass, but when I got home, I let it all out.

"Why is it so hard to love You, God. Why?" I was sitting on my loveseat in the living area of my studio apartment, facing the wooden cross I still hadn't removed from my nightstand. As I started speaking, my eyes turned into clouds on a rainy day.

"Why do You do this to me? What am I supposed to do now? Why do You always have to break me? Haven't You done that enough? Haven't I endured enough pain? How am I supposed to come back to You? What do I do with this pain? Do You even know how much it hurts? My heart has never been this broken, and I'm just trying to make it whole again. I've asked You thousands of times not to let life break me again, not to make me go back to dark places, but You don't listen. How do I know You won't rip off the bandage on my heart, then break it again if I come back? This is so hard, God, this is so hard. I want to come back, but I don't know how to do that."

I spent the rest of the day doing regular Sunday stuff, like laundry and cooking. While I was cooking, I remembered some of the things God had done for me in the past. Like how He helped me find apartments, go to school when I didn't know how that would be possible, and graduate in the semester I initially wanted to. I remembered how He provided food when I had no money to eat, how He helped me sleep through nightmares and anxiety attacks. I wanted to return to Him, but I didn't know how. I wanted to return to Him, but I was broken. My heart was a battlefield where two forces were competing for nonexistent resources.

When it came time to sleep, I sat on the edge of my bed. I stayed there, head down, silently watching my fingers fiddle with my pajama shirt, unsure what else to do. Several minutes later, and like the days and nights that followed, I prayed for my family, friends, and the rest of the world. I didn't know what to ask for myself. Well … actually, I did. I just didn't know *how* to ask for it or *if* I even should. I wanted to be fine. To *feel* fine. I wanted to be whole. To *feel* whole. I wanted the pain to go away. But I was scared of being hurt again. So, I just prayed for other people.

———— ⌧ ————

On the morning of Tuesday, October 29th, I got an email from a recruiter at The Kraft Heinz Company. I'd applied for a financial analyst role in their marketing division, and she wanted to know my availability for a phone interview. I didn't think anyone would even look at my resume. It was such a large company and from what I'd seen on LinkedIn, it, too, mainly recruited from renowned universities and top business schools.

Later that day, someone else from Duff & Phelps reached out to me to request my availability for another phone interview, this time with current senior associates. I still didn't like the job. I still didn't care. I liked Kraft Heinz better, but I also constantly reminded myself that it was too big and too good for me. That the job was finance and marketing-related was too good to be true.

I had both phone interviews the following Thursday. During my interview with Kraft Heinz, the recruiter asked about my salary expectations. I'd previously answered that question when I submitted my application online and had put $55,000. When the recruiter asked about it again, I got scared and thought I'd priced myself too high, so I gave a range of $50 to $55,000. I also said I was open to negotiation. And by *open to negotiation,* I meant they could pay me less if they hired me. I obviously didn't say it, but that's what I had in mind.

We had a good conversation overall, but I couldn't let myself think or even imagine walking into the Aon Center for an in-person interview, let alone for the actual job. Every time I drifted into daydreaming about working there, I quickly snapped back to reality, once more agreeing with the voice telling me I would be too happy if I worked there, and that God couldn't let that happen.

I moved on to next rounds of interviews with both companies. I was scheduled to meet the director and managing director at Duff & Phelps on November 7th, while I had to do another phone interview with the associate manager of finance and marketing at Kraft Heinz. I could not believe it–literally. I always had to remind myself that none of these opportunities would work. I had to make sure I didn't get attached to any of them, regardless of how they made me feel.

My second phone interview with Kraft Heinz was on Wednesday, November 6th. During our call, the associate manager asked if I was pursuing other opportunities, to which I answered yes. I let her know I had another interview the next day but did not disclose the company. To my (pleasant) surprise, that created urgency, and she now wanted to expedite the interview process and make me go on site for an in-person interview as soon as possible. But first, she had to check with her director.

In addition to Kraft Heinz and Duff & Phelps, I was interviewing with another company, a capital markets firm, for a portfolio analyst role. I had done the phone screening and two rounds of three-hour in-person interviews and was waiting to hear back. I wasn't sure what to make of everything that was happening.

Is all this real? Does Kraft Heinz really want to interview me that bad? Did I really move to an in-person interview with Duff & Phelps?

I still didn't like the job at Duff & Phelps but interviewing at a large multinational firm was no longer something I thought possible.

This is all too good for you. You can't have it. You're not good enough. You can't let yourself get caught in the trap of hope again. You'll be broken again. These jobs are not for you.

And I agreed.

———— ⌘ ————

On the morning of Thursday, November 7th, my in-person interview with Kraft Heinz was confirmed for the following Monday at the company's headquarters. Later that Thursday, I took the train to 311 South Wacker Drive for my final round with Duff & Phelps.

I walked into the sixty-five-story building right across the street from the Willis Tower and checked in at the lobby. A young lady gave me a visitor pass with my name and the company I was visiting printed on it. She was Black and had beautiful nails that I complimented her on. I took the escalator to the second-level lobby where I was greeted by two gentlemen. Two Black gentlemen. I then made my way to the elevator bank on my left, as indicated by the receptionist, and placed my pass on a speed gate card reader to get through.

I was going to the forty-second floor but had to take an elevator to the sky lobby on the forty-sixth floor first, then another one down to the forty-second floor. After a lot of walking and confusion trying to navigate the building, I finally arrived at the main office. I was almost late; not that I cared. I checked in again, then sat in the waiting area, facing floor-to-ceiling windows and indulging in the afternoon sunlight.

———— ⬥ ————

I spent around two and a half hours speaking with a total of four people. I had three consecutive interviews: one with two senior associates and two separate interviews with the director and managing director. They were all White, except for the director, who was the only Black woman I'd seen in an interview since arriving in Chicago in 2017. In fact, she was the only Black *person* to ever interview me for a corporate job.

Looking down at my resume and pointing out my credentials, the director asked what I was doing in a customer service position at a hotel. She didn't make it sound degrading, but I could tell she was genuinely curious. I wasn't going share the story of my life, so I simply said I was there to develop my communication skills, which was not entirely false.

I didn't prepare for interviews anymore, and having no expectations helped me be more relaxed. I now treated interviews like conversations, during which I was learning about my interviewers and the firm as much as they were learning about me. Being enrolled in the CFA program also gave me something more to talk about with one of the senior associates, who was studying for Level II.

By the end of my interviews, I had a different outlook on the job and possibly even liked it a little bit. Even though it was tax-focused, the fact that it was a consulting job made it more attractive.

"You should be proud of yourself for arriving at this stage of the interview process," Sam, the managing director at Duff & Phelps, said to me as he walked me out of the office. "We had multiple candidates to interview; there are currently two finalists, and you are one of them."

"Well, I look forward to hearing back!" The smile on my face was too big to look real. I called the elevator to the forty-sixth floor.

With all the confusion trying to find the office a few hours earlier, I didn't get to appreciate the beauty of the building. The sky lobby had high ceiling windows that overlooked Lake Michigan. The marble floors and walls, the dark wood tables, the neutral-colored chairs, and the white suspension lights gave the area a sophisticated feel. It was around 4:30 p.m., and some people were already leaving their office. As I walked by, looking around and listening to them, I wondered what it was like to work in the building. To have lunch at the sky lobby's café or a drink at the bar after a long day of work. I smiled and shook my head a little, then pushed the elevator button down to the lobby.

Standing on the escalator down to the first-level lobby, I marveled at what was in front of me. Grey and white marble floors and walls, a dark green fountain statue staring back at me from its oasis of greenery on the lower-level atrium. A high glass ceiling covered the atrium, which the lustrous late-afternoon sunrays pierced to permeate the entire lobby area. As I descended, the sunrays moved at the same pace. I squinted at their glistening reflection from one side of a wall to the other.

This is so beautiful. Blindingly beautiful. Too bad I won't get to see this again. I had accepted it and was OK not seeing it again.

———— ⌀⚏⚏⚏⊃ ————

It wasn't too cold out, and I didn't have much left to study for that day, so I decided to walk a little bit before taking the bus back home. I walked twenty minutes to Target on State Street to get a snack, then waited for the bus 146 right outside the store. As I entered the bus, I felt my phone vibrate in my bag. I struggled to take it out while trying to tap my Ventra card on the reader to pay for the ride and, at the same time, be mindful of everyone standing in front of and behind me.

The phone number area code was Atlanta. The only person in Atlanta that could call me at that moment was Duff & Phelps' talent acquisition manager overseeing my application. A frown creased my forehead.

"Hi, this is Danielle." I picked up the call, scrambling to find a seat inside the bus.

"Hi Danielle, this is Rose from Duff & Phelps. Is now a good time to talk?"

You know you didn't have to call me to tell me I didn't get the job, right? An email would have been fine. "I'm actually quite busy at the moment. Any chance we can discuss later?" I responded, trying to avoid an awkward conversation.

"Oh okay, I'm not gonna be too long. I just wanted to let you know that the team really liked you, and they want to offer you the job!" I could tell she was smiling. My heart sank into my stomach, then jumped to my throat. *Wait, what?* I swallowed my heart back into place.

"Oh ... oh ... okay, uhm ... that's ... that's really exciting. Thanks for letting me know!" I didn't know what to say.

"Of course! I'll give you another call tomorrow morning with the details; I just wanted to give you the good news before the end of the day!" she said, still smiling.

"Yeah, thank you so much. I look forward to our call tomorrow!"

I could not believe it. Literally. My lips tried to form a smile, but I quickly shook it off, remembering that I could not let myself fall into this kind of trap again. This was certainly another sham. Another heartbreak was waiting somewhere ahead, if I chose to believe I'd really gotten the job. The pain in my heart reminded me not to use it.

When I got home, I didn't thank God for the offer. I didn't believe it was real. But I couldn't focus either. I couldn't study, as I couldn't believe what had just happened. I was in a haze of contradictory emotions. *Did it really take them thirty minutes to make a decision? Didn't the managing director say they were considering another candidate? Did they really choose me? This is too good to be true.*

The next day, Rose called me as promised. I didn't wait for her call, but I would be lying if I said I wasn't pleased that she kept her promise. She went over the usual HR stuff and onboarding procedures. She never asked about my salary expectations; during this call, she mentioned how much I was going to get paid, but I wasn't listening. I couldn't believe I was having this conversation. Well ... it wasn't really a conversation since I didn't say anything the entire time. I just thanked her at the end and said I looked forward to getting the offer in writing to review the terms.

She sent the offer right after our call.

> **From:** *Duff & Phelps*
>
> **To:** *Me*
>
> **Subject:** *Offer of Employment for Analyst, Unclaimed Property: Please respond online*
>
> **Date and Time:** *11/08/2019 at 11:55 a.m.*
>
> *Danielle Ndende,*
>
> *On behalf of Duff & Phelps (D&P), I am pleased to extend the attached offer of employment to you for the position Analyst, Unclaimed Property.*
>
> *Please review the details of this job offer and provide your response online. You may be required to respond before the offer's expiration date, so please click to visit the site soon.*
>
> *Log in with the username and the password that you created when applying.*
>
> *Please feel free to contact your Talent Acquisition Manager with any questions or concerns.*
>
> *We all look forward to you joining the D&P team!*

So, this is what a full-time job offer email looks like? This is how it feels to receive one? I clicked on the link and logged in to review the offer, which expired on November 22nd. I scrolled down to look at the salary: $58,750. I did a double take. *Wow!* I couldn't believe my eyes, and my ears were definitely not working during the call. Just like the day before, I couldn't focus anymore. I couldn't study. I was confused, but I wanted to believe that this was real. I wanted to *hope* that this was real.

I got up from my desk to sit on the loveseat. And I finally asked God for help.

"Thank You. Thank You for showing me that I too am worthy of nice things. But why? Why did I have to go through that much pain? Why do I always have to get to a point where I am bone-weary and can't take it anymore? Why do I always have to almost fall off a cliff before You remember me? Why couldn't You give me this job three months ago when I had more strength and hope? I would've still been thankful, You know. I am so confused, God, and I am so sorry. I am sorry for being confused and I am sorry for all the mean things I said to You. I was just so hurt. I still am, but I just … I don't know. I guess I'm asking for help. Help to deal with this pain. I want to be whole again. And please don't break me, not now. My heart is bruised; it can't take any more pain right now. Please, please, please, I'm begging You. Do not break me again. Maybe wait until next year before my next heartbreak? I am not as strong as You think I am, God."

I stayed there, elbows pressed on my knees and palms pressed on my forehead, listening to the only sound of tears dropping on my jeans.

And I went back to church the following Sunday, and every Sunday after that. And I sat on the pews in the middle, and I sang, said prayers, stood up with everyone, and paid attention during the readings and the homilies.

Until March 2020.

CHAPTER 19:

RENEWED HOPE

I t was around 1:10 p.m. when I arrived at 200 East Randolph Street on November 11th. I was twenty minutes early for my interview. If finding the Duff & Phelps office inside its building was confusing, I don't know how to describe my experience trying to get to the seventy-second floor of the Aon Center. After a lot of walking around in confusion, the elevator doors finally opened to big letters boldly painted in dark blue and bright red on a white wall: Kraft Heinz. I checked in at the reception, then sat on a chair in the waiting area, yet again facing floor-to-ceiling windows. I was in the clouds. Literally and figuratively. I waited there in awe. *How did I get here?* Of course, I'd just taken an elevator to the seventy-second floor of a building I used to walk by, wondering how it felt walking into, but like, *how?* How did Kraft Heinz become interested in me? How did I get there?

"Danielle?" A deep voice from behind pulled me out of my thoughts.

"Yes!" I got up and turned around.

"Hi, I'm the finance and marketing director. Sorry I'm late, just came out of a meeting." He stretched his hand, and I shook it firmly. "How are you?"

"Doing well. It's very nice to meet you!" I didn't even notice he was late.

"You as well! Did you get a chance to take a picture with Mr. Peanut?" He gestured to the giant statue of a dressed-up peanut in the waiting area, the mascot of the Planters snacks brand, which Kraft Heinz owned at the time.

"I took pictures *of* it, but I'm sure I'll have time after the interview for plenty more." We shared a few laughs before heading to a room for my interview.

The road was covered in thick snow that crunched under my boots, and my breath turned into a cloud of vapor every time I exhaled. I'd just finished my interview and wasn't going to walk anywhere other than the nearest bus station. When I got home, I took out my journal.

Date: 11/11/2019

So, for a change, today I don't come with pain in my heart and tears in my eyes. I wouldn't go as far as to say that I'm happy, but I do feel better, at least about myself. After deciding to unsubscribe from job boards, I actually went back to apply ONLY for finance-related jobs (and I mean the "nicer" ones) and not just any job anymore. I didn't want to "waste" my time somewhere when I could be studying for my CFA instead.

Anyway ... so these past few weeks I've been going to interviews not really hoping for anything, but I thought if I did get something, at least it'd be somewhat related to my CFA. And guess what?! I got an offer from

Duff & Phelps! I know, right?! Like ... who am I? I so wasn't expecting this to happen, especially since they don't even recruit from my school. Plus, I didn't really "like" the job (it's tax-related), so I thought, Whatever. But not even an hour after my interview, they extended me an offer! It really made me regain some sort of confidence in myself, which, as you know, I'd totally lost. I was so shocked! I still can't believe they want ME in their team, knowing they interviewed other people as well. I must say ... it feels good to be on this side for once, and I feel like God showed me I am valuable, and I can get a corporate job and can make my dream come true.

Now, on to something less joyful ... I lied. I told them I wouldn't require sponsorship, and they are really looking for someone to grow with them, which I won't. I honestly just want to save up some money and leave by July 2020! I'm afraid once they see my EAD card, they'll rescind the offer.

I also just got back from an in-person interview with Kraft Heinz at the Aon Center!!! (I know, right?! WHO AM I?!!) Still can't believe such big companies looked at me and actually wanted to speak with me.

Anyway, I don't have an offer from them and honestly, I'm already thankful that they at least wanted to see me. I do want to work there, but then again, there's the sponsorship issue. But I also don't even feel like I did that well during the interview. I do, however, want to do a side-by-side comparison between Duff & Phelps and Kraft Heinz, should I have to decide between the two (can't believe I'm doing this).

Duff & Phelps		Kraft Heinz	
What I like	What I don't like	What I like	What I don't like
Corporate, nice building and views.	I felt Black.	Corporate, nice building and views.	Dress code is too casual.
Dress code is business casual.	Small team, I feel like I won't have anyone to hang out with.	Nicer people, younger workforce.	
Consulting-style job.	Kind of stuffy/ uptight culture?	Work/life balance.	Salary would be lower (I need as much money as I can get).
Not many people like me (could be used as motivation).	Didn't feel like I belonged or could blend in well.	Brand-name company.	
National travel, work on different industries.	Not many people like me.	Felt like I could belong (though the demographics are the same).	Single industry (Consumer Packaged Goods).
Salary.	Work/life balance.	Marketing-and-finance-related job.	

The excitement around the Aon Center comes from, well, walking by that building, wondering how it felt walking in. It very much gave corporate vibes and housed companies such as Microsoft and KPMG. I'd walked into the building only once during the summer, when I had a coffee chat with an employee at Slalom, a consulting company also located in the building. Back then, I'd only experienced the ground level, which was already big and confusing enough that I exited the building on the wrong side. When I got out, I didn't think I would walk in again. Definitely not to interview at Slalom, because in addition to recruiting from specific schools, the company's interview process for entry-level consulting roles comprised anywhere from three to five consecutive interviews. At the time of my coffee chat, I didn't think I could interview for that long. But now that I had done it a few times, and now that I had entered the Aon Center again, you can understand my excitement when I wrote in my journal after interviewing with Kraft Heinz.

The next day, I was sitting at my desk studying alternative investments when I got a call from an unknown number. The area code was Chicago, so I assumed it was Kraft Heinz.

"Hi, this is Danielle."

"Hi Danielle, this is Sam calling from Duff & Phelps. How are you?"

I knew it, they don't want me anymore. They want to rescind the offer. I knew it! I knew it!

"I'm doing well, thanks for asking. How are you?" My throat tightened and my heart started racing.

"Doing great! Look, I wanted to check if you received our offer and see if everything was alright."

Wait, what? "Yes, I did, thank you for that!" I swallowed to make the knot in my throat disappear. "I spoke with Rose last Friday, and I let her know I would decide by the end of this week. I had an interview yesterday and am waiting to hear back from another firm as well, so once I have more clarity, I'll definitely update you."

"Oh alright, I understand. Let us know if you have any questions in the meantime, okay?" He sounded busy. He mentioned he was at the airport on his way to a client, like managing directors in consulting often are.

"Will do! Thanks for the call, and safe travels!"

Okay, what just happened? Oh, God, who am I?

⋯⋯⋯⋯⋯

On Wednesday, November 13th, the recruiter at Kraft Heinz called to let me know the position I'd applied and interviewed for had closed. They'd decided to no longer hire (anyone) for it. She apologized for the inconvenience and thanked me for my time. I thanked her back. I wasn't sad at all; I was truly thankful for the experience. Maybe I just needed to see that no job or company that was too good for me, that I too could interview at a brand-name company, despite not having gone to a brand-name school. Maybe that was the sole purpose of interviewing at Kraft Heinz.

I'd been weighing the pros and cons, trying to decide which firm to join if I got an offer from Kraft Heinz as well. Though I'd started to like Duff & Phelps more, I felt like the Kraft Heinz brand would have more weight on my resume. The call with the recruiter was my confirmation to go with Duff & Phelps.

The next day, I got an offer from the capital markets firm. *Oh, God, who am I?* I kept repeating this to myself. I was overwhelmed with everything that'd been happening. I liked Duff & Phelps better, so that's the offer I was going to accept.

The talent acquisition manager at Duff & Phelps called me the next day to see if I'd made up my mind. I asked if there was room for negotiation. Though my other offer was lower (at $55,000, which I didn't tell her), I wanted to leverage it to get something even better with Duff & Phelps. Worst-case scenario, I'd still have something to fall back on.

In true HR fashion, Rose told me she wasn't sure there was a budget for more money and had to check with the managing director first. A few minutes later, Sam called me.

"Hi Danielle, I heard you got another offer, congratulations!" I could tell he was smiling.

"Yes, Sam, thanks very much!" I was smiling as well. "And as I told Rose earlier, I wanted to see if there was room to negotiate your offer. I really like the job and want to join your team, but compensation is also something I need to consider. Would it be possible to at least match my other offer?"

"That's understandable. Look, if there's not a huge difference, I can see what I can do. How much are they offering you?"

I thought about his question for a split second now because I hadn't thought about it before. "Sixty-two thousand dollars." I tried to say it slower than the pace of my heartbeat.

"Okay, that's fair. We'll revise the offer and send it over to you by tomorrow."

"Sounds great! Thank you, bye!"

Oh, God, who am I?

I received the updated offer on Friday, November 15th. The annual salary was $62,000, and the start date remained December 2nd. Rose had called me beforehand to let me know she'd updated my compensation and to ask if I would now accept the offer, to which I answered yes. And that's exactly what I did when I logged into my account. I couldn't believe it when I sent the email turning down the other offer. I even felt bad for that company, though I knew there were other candidates.

As I started my journey to a hopeful heart again, fear and anxiety plagued my thoughts. Fear that this was all a lie. Fear that my heart would break again, and my pain be even more profound. Fear that once I showed my EAD card, my offer would be rescinded.

I knew this was illegal—as long as an employment authorization document was valid, employers couldn't withdraw an offer because the document had an upcoming expiration date. I knew that, but still, if Duff & Phelps withdrew my offer, I wouldn't have had the resources or even the strength and courage to sue the company.

In trying to avoid disappointment, I decided not to tell people about my job until I started working, until after I'd passed the background check and the firm had verified my employment authorization. I didn't want to give false hopes to anyone–including myself–in case Duff & Phelps didn't work out.

Dreams come true. I picked up the triangular wooden sign on my desk and looked at it for a few seconds, brushing my right thumb across the letters. I smiled from ear to ear, then put it back down. *Maybe they do.* I stuffed my head back into my books. *Dreams come true, and mine will too.* I stopped reading and sat upright. My eyebrows rose all the way up, and my eyes and mouth opened wide on their own. I put my left hand on my chest and looked straight ahead, struck by what had just crossed my mind. It not only rhymed, but it also sounded good. I giggled and did a *happy* dance. "Dreams come true, and mine will too." I said it once, then louder before letting it play in my head while I studied. This was sometime before the end of November on a day I do not recall.

———⟨⟩———

As I finished getting ready on the morning of December 2nd, I stared at my reflection in the mirror, in awe. I was stunning in the black-and-white pencil dress I'd bought specifically for my first day, that I paired with light makeup. And of course, my nails were done. But that's not why I was amazed: I didn't recognize myself. Not because I looked amazing; I just couldn't believe I was getting ready for my first day of working as a full-time analyst at a reputable firm downtown Chicago. *How did I get here?*

I thought about the past months, the past year, and the past two and a half years.

The journey. The sweat. The pain. The blood. The tears. The exhaustion. *The pain.*

And there I was that morning, about to start a day I thought would no longer come. *Oh God, who am I?* I snapped a few pictures, then sped out the door.

I walked into 311 South Wacker Drive (again) at 9:12 a.m., and the building was even brighter and more beautiful. Or maybe it wasn't. I was twelve minutes late to the first onboarding session, even though I had left my apartment at 7:45 a.m. for a trip that normally took forty-five minutes by train. The Brown Line train to Quincy somehow decided to stop unexpectantly in the middle of nowhere, for twenty minutes, that morning. But that didn't ruin my mood—I just had to run. Luckily, one of my senior associates recognized me as I was running around the sky lobby, still confused how to get to the forty-second floor. He was on the same Brown Line train, so I didn't have to explain myself too much.

The two other employees who started that day were already there when I walked into the room where orientation was taking place. They looked like they'd been waiting for me. A young lady smiled at me, and I smiled back. I said hi to the young man and sat on the empty chair next to him.

"Sorry I'm late," I said, rolling my chair forward and trying not to look nervous. "That's okay; you didn't miss much," the gentleman in charge of our IT orientation said, handing me my laptop and login information.

Oh, so we get phones as well? Had no idea. This was my thought when he asked if we wanted to register to get a company phone. If we chose to get a work phone instead of just having our current phone bill paid for by the company, we would get an iPhone XR with the option to upgrade every two years, as long as we stayed at the firm. Not applicable to me. I didn't want to carry two phones around all the time, and I don't like iPhones anyway, but I was even less thrilled by the idea of my personal phone being controlled by my firm. So, I chose to get a work phone and continue to pay my personal phone bill myself. After all, I had a job.

———⬡———

After the tech onboarding, someone else gave us a tour of the floors that Duff & Phelps occupied in the building before taking us to our respective cubicles. The other new joiners were on different teams, but we were all going to work on the thirty-fifth floor. I was happy, grateful, excited, but also a bit anxious. I didn't know if I would *fit in*.

We walked to the other young lady's cubicle first and as we came close, she ran to her friends who were already waiting for her, and they all cheered and started chatting. They were friends from college, it seemed. We walked to the young man's cubicle next, and it didn't seem like he would have issues finding friends either. He was an experienced hire from EY, and there were quite a few ex-Big 4s at the firm. In fact, my director and managing director were both KPMG alumni. We walked to my cubicle last, and that's when my anxiety subsided.

"And there you are. Have a great first day!" the lady giving us the office tour said to me.

"Thank you so much, have a great day!" I replied, totally distracted.

My cubicle was the same size as everyone else's but more spacious than I had envisioned. My name and position were written on a golden plaque affixed to the outer side. I smiled from one ear to the other. My plaque was the same as everyone else's, but different.

Office 3548-B

Danielle Ndende

Analyst

Wow! My name looks so good written like this. I took a picture of my beautiful name before hanging my coat on the edge of the cubicle divider like I saw everyone else do. I dropped my bag on the chair and placed my laptop on the docking station beneath my two monitors. I then headed back up to the main office on the forty-second floor to verify my employment authorization. At that point, I'd already passed the background check.

I showed my EAD card and other documents to the office manager. He then asked me to enter all my information into an online platform. I was surprised my hands weren't shaking, considering the chaos that was going on inside of me. My heart was beating too loud in my ears when it wasn't trying to explode out of my chest, as the office manager looked at my documents and watched me type. *Please help me. Please don't let this go away, please.* He made copies of everything, then handed me my documents back without a word. I mean … he did smile and say, "Thank you," but that was it. I took the elevator back down. As soon as I sat at my cubicle, I got an email.

> **From:** *Schulich School of Business*
>
> **To:** *Me*
>
> **Subject:** *Great news from the Schulich School of Business!*
>
> **Date and Time:** *12/2/2019 at 2:48 p.m.*
>
> *Dear Danielle,*
>
> *Congratulations, you are being offered admission to the Schulich School of Business! Please read the attachment for all the details.*
>
> *To understand your next steps, get information on course enrollment, and other important details for new students leading up to the start of your program, please visit the New to Schulich website.*
>
> *Congratulations once again on your admission to the MMKG program for fall 2020. I look forward to welcoming you to Schulich.*
>
> *Recruitment & Communication Coordinator*

Is this the best day of my life? I smiled from ear to ear for the second time in a single morning. *Dreams come true, and mine will too.* My hardest task of the day was to contain my excitement. God also probably got tired of hearing me thank Him.

———— ⊂═⫯═⊃ ————

My first week at Duff & Phelps was spent completing online training modules and other onboarding tasks. I enrolled in benefits, requested my business cards, employee ID, and building access cards. I also applied for my corporate credit card, to be used for work-related expenses such as travel or for meals when I worked more than ten hours in the office. Because it wasn't a personal credit card, it couldn't help me build my credit. But that wasn't a big deal.

I was excited but scared at the same time. The fear that everything would fall apart crept around. And as much as I knew that wasn't the case, I felt like a fraud and every day felt like the day I would get caught. It took me my entire first week to understand it was all real and nothing bad was going to happen. Only at the end of that first week did I finally let people know I had started a new job. I also updated my LinkedIn profile as well as my SEVP portal with the December 2nd start date.

That first week is also when the firm had its Christmas party, on Thursday, December 5th. It was hosted at The Metropolitan Club on the sixty-seventh floor of the Willis Tower. The building was right across the street, so some of my co-workers and I walked there after work.

The view was breathtaking through the floor-to-ceiling windows. Servers roamed the venue with platters of sparkling wine and snacks while people were chatting and laughing and drinking and eating. I was surprised at how much the school people went to was part of their identity. They all added the school they attended to their introductions, and I heard "Where did you go?" or "What school did you attend?" too many times in one night. With me being one of the few people from Roosevelt University at the firm, it was awkward at times not to be able to fully participate in conversations because I didn't share the same college memories as my colleagues. Weirdly enough, I also had to tell some people where my school was located, even though it was right downtown on Michigan Avenue, and I'm sure they'd all passed by it at some point.

I stepped away from the busyness and chatter after a moment to recharge. I stood by a corner to look through the windows and confirm I would never get used to the beauty of the city. The skyline was a constellation of dazzling lights; the sky itself was a concert of stars dancing to the rhythm of the music. All were singing: *Congratulations, Danielle!*

How did I get here? Of course, I had just taken an elevator to the sixty-seventh floor of Chicago's tallest building, but like, *how?* After all I'd been through, I couldn't imagine myself going to such places or attending such events. Once more, God may have been tired of hearing me thank Him.

When I gazed back inside the room, I sadly realized there weren't many people like me. Sure, there were women, but we weren't the same race. Those who shared my race were roaming the venue with platters of food and drinks, or were at the reception checking guests' coats, or were part of Duff & Phelps' administrative assistant teams. Nothing wrong with any of these jobs, of course. But you get the picture. For a second, I wondered where all the Black women graduates went to work. I made my way back to the party and looked for my director—another Black woman—to no avail. When I asked where she was, people said she worked a lot and didn't join these types of events very often. I didn't fully understand it then, but I do know.

I left the party early because I had to study for the Level I CFA exam, which was now two days later. My team knew that, so they allowed me to take the Friday off to finish studying. I didn't actually *finish* studying because I had too many exercises left to do. But I did what I could.

Sophie came back later that month for the holidays, and we had a lot of fun as usual. The difference, this time, was that I could finally also treat her to restaurants or other things, which felt good. When she left, I did my usual end-of-year exercise.

For 2020, I got myself an Erin Condren LifePlanner that I customized. There was a dry-erase section on the reverse side of the front cover. I reached for my colored felt-tip pens and started writing.

In the title space at the top of the page, I wrote:

My Lifetime Mantra

And below, I wrote:

Dreams Come True
And Mine Will Too.
BELIEVE!!

That mantra effectively kept playing in my head throughout the month of December. I then proceeded to do my year in review in my journal and write my goals for the upcoming year. Here were some of them.

2020 Goals and Wishes and Fears and Hopes

Things I am labelling as wishes because I'm too scared to label them as goals for fear that I won't achieve them:

- Take and pass the CFA Level II (provided I pass Level I).
- Get my study permit and study at Schulich.
- Attend Deloitte events and take more intentional steps toward making my dream come true.
- Not sure this applies to 2020, but I (maybe) want to write a book one day or have some type of platform where I'll share my, hopefully, success story and hopefully inspire people.

Fears:

- Suffering, being depressed again.
- Not doing a good enough job at my job.
- Pain.
- Applying to my dream job, getting interviews, and not getting an offer. Failing to get that job again and again. The thing is, I don't even know what I'll do if I don't get my dream job. Sure, I'll find something else to pay the bills, but I feel like I will never be (professionally and even personally) happy and fulfilled until I have that dream job.

Goals:

- Trust God with ALL my heart, avoid holding back; surrender to Him, get closer to Him.
- Be more flexible with my plans.

- Build back my self-confidence and find the right balance between humbleness and confidence.
- Not let fear get the best of me.
- Be outside of my comfort zone as much as possible.
- Stop being such a hoarder. Use or wear what I buy.

Hope: Find myself, know myself better, who and what I am, be okay with being different. Find my identity, my unique self.

I wrote my monthly goals in a separate journal (are you keeping track?). Then I prayed, unaware that a pandemic was looming ahead.

CHAPTER 20:

DCTMWT

Date: 01/09/2020

Dear Heavenly Father... It's been quite some time since I last wrote here because I'd lost hope and didn't feel like writing to You anymore. But here I am today, with a grateful and hopeful heart.

Thank You for... 2019, its downs, but mainly its latest ups (job and admission to my dream school), family and friends. Opening my eyes to see You are here; You listen to me; You know me; You love me; and You want my dream to come true as well. All Your blessings.

I am worried about... Not being good enough at my job. Not getting my study permit for Canada. Feeling THAT pain again this year. Schulich not being in Your plan for me this year.

People I am praying for today... People going through hard times. Family and friends. The homeless in this cold weather. Anyone in need of a prayer.

Here's what's happening in my life... I don't know how I'm going to attend Schulich. But I know and now really believe nothing is impossible to You.

I need... Guidance as usual. Strength to face this year's challenges. Your help to fight my fears.

Other things on my heart that I need to share with You, God... I just want to say thank You for this season that I'm in. It's not perfect, but I feel more at peace. I love You. Happy New Year!

Being admitted to the Schulich School of Business meant that I needed to start planning for my study permit application and my accommodation in Canada. I'd already started doing my research on how to get a study permit; as soon as I got my admission, I started attending the study permit webinars hosted by Schulich's international student services. I also already knew where I wanted to live if admitted, and when applications for those student residences opened in January, I immediately applied. Basically, I took care of everything I could control and pay for.

The biggest and scariest part was the tuition fees. I had no idea how I was going to pay them, and I wanted to finally leave my mom alone. She'd already helped me with the $3,000 tuition deposit required to accept the admission offer–since I didn't have enough savings yet–and the deadline to accept the offer (and thus pay the deposit) was one month after receiving it. My goal was to find a way to finance my stay in Canada all on my own.

———— ⌾ ————

Three days later, I pulled out another journal (I told you I have many). This time, it was the one where I write my dreams and goals and wishes, the things I hope for and want to accomplish in the future.

Date: 1/12/2020

Not sure this is a goal or even a wish, but I guess it is a wish, lol. Anyway, I have the desire (there you go) to inspire people. I kind of want to write a book one day (I know, that's crazy), or have some kind of platform where I'll share my, hopefully, success story, especially with people who will relate the most to me. I want to talk about dreams, my absolutely not-perfect spiritual journey. I want to talk about passions, school, work, having or wanting to get multiple degrees and/or certifications, being a woman and having firm principles. In short, the things I've been through and my experiences. Hopefully my story in a couple of years will show that my work paid off and that my challenges were surmountable; and hopefully they will have made me a better person. I hope to have the legitimacy and authenticity to inspire and uplift other people.

Yeah … so this is how it all started. I'd been thinking about writing a book since December 2019, but I didn't write anything about it in my journals until January 2020. (I wrote about it in a *planner* first, not a journal.)

March 3, 2019, was a Sunday. And like every Sunday morning, I'd gone to church. At the time, I lived on South Morgan Street in the West Loop and still attended Old St. Patrick's Church. During his homily, the priest talked about being a credible and authentic companion to others thanks to our own experiences. (I kept church notes in my planners; that's how I know exactly what day it was.) He explained how these experiences give us the legitimacy to help others who may be going through the same things.

Back then, and even though I hadn't gone through nearly as many things as I had by the end of 2019, I already wanted to help others through my experiences. I remember trying to help Christie, who at the time was looking for a job, by sharing what I'd done to get my internship at CIVC Partners, but I wasn't satisfied. It didn't feel like that was *the thing*. I wanted to do more, to give back to God and to people around me. I remember asking God for help many times. I remember feeling frustrated for months when I still had no idea how I was going to be a legitimate and authentic companion to people in my life, especially since I, myself, was struggling. I remember feeling like He hadn't heard my prayers. And when I lost hope, I lost hope for everything, including becoming a legitimate and authentic companion to people in my life.

And here we are.

A month later, I wrote in my other regular journal after getting my CFA exam results.

Date: 2/17/2020

I am starting to feel a little overwhelmed with the things I want and now have to do. The CFA Level I exam results came out a couple of weeks ago, and I failed. I was sad, and I questioned a lot of things. Before they came out, I told myself if I didn't pass, I would not register again. Fast forward today, I've registered to take the exam again because I really like finance now and want to work in the industry and some point in my career. It's absolutely NOT about the money; it's a newfound passion for portfolio management, valuation, and even corporate finance (mergers and acquisitions). Who knew?! Anyway, the thing is I haven't been motivated at all to study. I've been procrastinating a lot and feeling tired. Even today, I have the whole day off and instead of studying, here I am journaling and it's 2 p.m. already. I really don't know why that is, especially since no one is forcing me, and I paid the fees out of pocket! I just don't have the same motivation as the first time, but I still want to be a CFA charterholder.

The overwhelming part is that I was also admitted to my dream school (yeah, school again) for the MMKG program that starts in September. Sometimes I feel like I'm doing too much, and it doesn't make sense to pursue this many degrees/certifications. But at the same time, I'm really passionate about marketing and finance. Plus, that school is one of the best in Canada and has lots of connections with top firms, especially my dream firm. So, to me, this is a pathway to my dream. But with the CFA that will now extend to 2022 if I do pass all exams consecutively, I feel like it's a lot, and I don't know how I'm going to do that. I wanted to be completely done with school by 2021, which is not going to happen. I also feel pressure regarding the things I want to achieve but don't know where to start, and I feel like I'm running "behind schedule."

I am about to turn twenty-four in less than a month, which means next year I'll be twenty-five and still in school, and it seems to me that I should have already done more by now. This is not healthy, I know, but I can't help it.

Anyway ... going to try and study. Good luck, Danielle. 🩶

The CFA exam results came out on January 30, 2020. After crying in the office bathroom for ten minutes that day, doing a lot of thinking throughout the week that followed, and speaking with my senior associate at Duff & Phelps, who was taking Level II for the second time, I decided to enroll in the program again.

It's never fun to fail an exam, but the crying wasn't so much about not passing the exam as much as it was the time and effort I put into studying. While I was looking for a job and couldn't find one, and after Marquette Associates broke my heart in October 2019, I tried justifying the situation by telling myself it was probably best for me to focus on studying.

I also have to admit that seeing how well things were starting to go gave me the impression that it was the beginning of a life without too much trouble. So, when I got the results, nothing made sense anymore. But I wanted to give it another try.

Duff & Phelps sponsored the CFA exam, but not retroactively and only if the employee passed. So, I didn't get reimbursed for the fees I'd paid in September 2019 because that was before I started at the firm, and I wouldn't get reimbursed for the fees I paid in February 2020 because the exam was supposed to take place in June, and I was going to leave the U.S. right after, whether I passed or not.

———————— ⌘ ————————

My 2020 birthday fell on a Friday, which I took off from work to treat myself. That is also the day I opened the birthday gift I'd gotten for myself a couple of days earlier. I glanced at the box next to my nightstand multiple times a day every day, impatiently waiting for my birthday to come so I could finally open it, even though I knew what was inside.

That Friday morning, I opened the box, pulled out the overflowing mountain of pink filler paper to reveal a perfectly folded pink dust bag with a logo printed in the middle. It read *Kate Spade*. I smiled. Below it was a medium-sized leather satchel. It was all black, but the soft pink accent sides added a nice contrast. The logo was printed on the front, at the top, in small golden letters. The last thing in the box was a bright pink envelope. I opened it and smiled at the card I forgot I'd written to myself.

From me to me. Happy birthday, Beautiful! 😊

I took pictures of and with my beautiful bag before heading out to my day of pampering, fully aware of what that gift meant to me.

The next day, on March 14th, I celebrated with my friends. I'd made a reservation at BLVD, a sumptuous steakhouse in the West Loop. No one knew a stay-at-home order would soon be issued, so everything was still operating as usual. I had on a mauve off-the-shoulders dress and black strappy heels. You could tell I'd started working out again. The scars on my chest had faded, while my makeup covered the acne and scars on my face. A sparkly necklace decorated my neck and was my only piece of jewelry. And you already know my nails were done. I had a great time. And I had cake.

When Chicago entered lockdown the next day, I was thankful to have been able to celebrate my birthday before everything closed and before leaving the country. I didn't know it then, but I would not go out again. So, I guess my birthday party doubled as a farewell party.

With the COVID-19 pandemic in full swing and news of layoffs across the country, I was thankful I hadn't lost my job. I worked from home and was able to continue paying rent and other bills on my own, while saving money for my goals. However, going back to staying in my room all day every day was not something I enjoyed. What initially started as a two-week lockdown turned into one that lasted a month, then several months, which made me want to go home to Cameroon even more. That USCIS did not show any flexibility toward international students did not help either.

The flight ticket I'd bought in April with a June 5th departure date got cancelled because of border closures. The CFA Level I exam, initially scheduled for June 6th, had been cancelled. This was a relief, because it meant no longer forcing myself to study. It also meant I no longer had any reason to remain in the U.S. after my EAD card expired on May 26th. If the exam hadn't been postponed, I would've taken it during my sixty-day grace period that expired on July 25th. But now I wanted to leave as soon as possible at the end of my OPT.

On April 29th, I emailed the international student advisor at Roosevelt University to tell her about my situation and ask what would happen if I couldn't to leave the U.S. on time. She responded saying *unfortunately* USCIS had not issued any new guidance, and I would still fall out of status if I couldn't leave before the end of my grace period (even though it wouldn't have been my or anyone else's fault). She said a student had asked a similar question directly to USCIS two weeks earlier and was told to either change their status to a B1/B2 visitor visa (which costs money) or re-enroll into another academic program (which costs even more money). *Great!*

When you add to that all the shooting and murdering of Black people, all the protesting and looting and street violence during a pandemic, I just couldn't spend one more day in the U.S. I wanted to leave. I *needed* to leave.

———————— ⌨ ————————

I quit my job at Duff & Phelps on Friday, May 15th, 2020. I'd first called Sam, my managing director, to let him know of my intention to leave. I explained that the main reason for my departure was the pandemic and everything happening in the country, which wasn't a lie. It just wasn't the complete truth. He understood my decision, and to my surprise, he said he would consider rehiring me if I came back to Chicago later in the summer, "once the pandemic was over." Obviously back then, no one knew how long this thing was going to last. I thanked him, knowing very well that even without a pandemic, I would not go back to the firm.

All the positive feedback I received when I sent my goodbye email on my last day was also a pleasant surprise. People thanked me for my hard work. Those with whom I'd started working toward the end of April said they'd heard good things about me, and they wished me well. The HR professional who did my exit interview tried to make me stay, and though I knew she was doing her job, it still felt good to feel valued.

She asked why I was leaving, if I'd found a new job and how much that job was going to pay me. When I told her Chicago was a bit lonely, she suggested transferring me to the Dallas or New York City office where there were many more analysts, with the firm paying for my moving expenses. The offer was tempting, but I couldn't stay. Even if I could, I wouldn't have stayed because I didn't want to. And there's no amount of money, no additional benefits, nothing and no one that could have made me stay.

I wanted to leave. I *needed* to leave. So, I left.

While packing my laptop, phone, and other work accessories to ship them back to the office, I reflected on how much of a journey it'd been to get to Duff & Phelps. I was thankful for the experience and for the sense of financial freedom it'd brought back into my life, albeit temporarily.

On Friday, May 29th, 2020, at 2 p.m., I was officially unemployed. Again. But this time, I wasn't looking for another job. I was looking forward to being home.

———— ⋐⋙⋑ ————

I was eventually able to book a flight back home that didn't get cancelled; it departed on June 7th. I'd sold or donated whatever I no longer needed or could not fit in my bags and kept the cash to pay the overweight baggage fees I knew I'd have to pay at the airport. There was now only one issue left, perhaps the biggest.

I'd packed winter clothes and other personal items (such as my journals) in boxes that I wanted to ship to Toronto. But I spent sleepless nights wondering if that was the right thing to do considering I wasn't a hundred percent sure I would get my study permit for Canada. I didn't know what to do if I didn't ship them to Toronto. Shipping them home wasn't an option because shipping services had stopped sending packages beyond a certain distance, and Yaoundé was just too far from Chicago.

Selling or donating would mean losing a lot of personal things and having to buy winter clothes all over again if I got my study permit. And if I did send the boxes to Toronto but didn't get my study permit, I didn't know what was going to happen. I didn't know anyone in Toronto—or Canada—who could ship my boxes back home or keep them for a while. And what about money? Shipping those four boxes north of the border was going to cost more than $1,000, in addition to the monthly storage rental fees. Plus, all the storage services I'd contacted required someone to sign the contract and take possession of the keys in person. Again, I knew no one in Toronto or Canada for that matter. At the same time, I'd already paid the first and last month's rent deposit at the student residence where I wanted to live if I went to Schulich.

On June 2nd, my application for a private student loan submitted in March was approved. International students in Canada didn't qualify for government and most bank loans either, so I had to go the private (and unfortunately more expensive) route. I'd been saving aggressively while working, accumulating about $10,000 by the end of May. However, that wouldn't be enough to show as proof of funds for tuition and living expenses. I planned to use the student loan for tuition, while allocating my savings to living expenses.

Getting approved for the student loan was my sign to ship my boxes to Toronto, which I did the day before I left. I'd eventually found a storage service that had agreed to receive my boxes and keep them without me having to get the keys. I signed a digital contract for a small self-storage unit and paid for three months upfront. This was how long I thought my items would stay there, considering the MMKG program and my apartment lease started in September.

My older sister Naomi spent my last week in Chicago with me and took me to the airport on the morning of June 7th. I walked through security with tears still running down my cheeks and before I disappeared into the hallway to my gate, I turned around to wave goodbye to Naomi for the last time.

Bittersweet. As much as I'd been hurt in that city, I was going to miss Chicago and its beautiful skyline. But I was finally going home. No more worrying about finding my next apartment or job, no more stressing over finding ways to remain in the U.S., no more F-1 visa, no more I-20s, no more CPT, no more OPT, and no more restrictions. Just peace and freedom.

I couldn't wait to eat all the good food my mom had prepared for me.

Hmmm … fried plantains.

CHAPTER 21:

NO PLACE LIKE HOME

"Danielle!!!" Emma yelled from across the airport parking lot. She jumped at my neck, taking me by surprise and ignoring the cart full of bags I was pushing into the parking lot, trying to find my family. I wrapped my arms around her, leaving the cart in the middle of the road, blocking people behind and cars beside me. They were annoyed, but I didn't care. My little sister and I were a mess of tears and happiness. I moved over to take Nora in my arms; I felt like the old aunty noticing how tall she'd gotten. Maybe we were the same height, maybe she was taller. But that's beside the point. And my mom … oh, my mom. "Ming Mang Moung!" I cheered, squeezing her in my arms like I hadn't seen her in another decade. "My Person!" I jumped at my brother, ignoring his comments on how ugly Emma and I looked because we were crying. I gave a hug to his partner and immediately took Luna out of her hands. She was such a big girl; for a moment, I wondered if the clothes I'd gotten for her would fit. I greeted my dad, too.

We were missing a few people, but I'd have the time to see everyone, anyway. Luna was quiet on my hip, probably wondering what all the bustling was about. She was quiet, sweet, innocent, and completely unaware she was the reason I did not delete my social media apps again in February 2019.

I helped put my bags in the trunks, and off to eating okok and fried plantains with braised chicken I went.

My first month in Yaoundé was filled with laughter, rest, freedom, peace, and lots of food. I don't know how or when exactly it happened, but one day, it was gone. I was in my room, sitting quietly on my bed, recharging both my phone and my personal battery from having just spent hours chatting and laughing and eating and dancing with my family. Something felt weird. I frowned in confusion and ran my right hand from the front to the back of my neck, stretching it from side to side. Something was missing. I then ran my hand down my chest. *There.* I smiled from ear to ear, realizing that the pain, that once pea-sized hole on my heart that then grew into the size of a coin, the pain that shrank a little at some point then came back deeper, the pain that tore my heart wide open and exploded through my body, that pain was gone. I'd become so used to having it in my heart all the time that I didn't even notice when it went away. I just didn't feel it anymore.

Unfortunately, it wasn't all rainbows, butterflies, and fried plantains. I shed some tears as well, tears that were not of joy. I hadn't realized how much of a culture shock I was going to experience going back home. And I'm not even talking about the words whose French equivalent I sometimes couldn't remember or didn't even know. Having been gone for just a little over three years, I didn't think anything would be too different from before I left. After all, Yaoundé was home; its people were my people. I knew these people talked a lot and always had something to say about everything. I'd just forgotten how unfiltered (and quite honestly, inconsiderate) they could be. I realize those traits are not country specific and can be observed across the world, but I experienced them differently when I went back home.

Americans talk a lot; that's the first thing I noticed in Chicago. For almost my entire first year, I was taken aback by people's responses when I asked how they were doing, especially those I didn't know. The strangers in elevators *actually* told me how they were doing instead of just returning the "I'm good" answer I had just given to them. When I asked if they had a good weekend, some people went on about what they had *actually* done every single day of that weekend instead of just answering "Yes" like I did. Still, other people openly talked about what was wrong with their day and how frustrated they were, to which I never really knew how to respond besides, "That's too bad" or "Sorry about that." So yes, I thought Americans talked a lot, sometimes too much for my liking.

What no one did, however, was comment on my skin. Granted, I didn't meet a ton of people and pretty much spent ninety percent of my time in a room, but in my three years and three months in the U.S., no stranger in the bus or on the street told me how bad my skin looked. And I knew people saw my skin. I could tell when they looked at my face because of how damaged my skin was. Yet, I got no comments.

When I got my job at Duff & Phelps and could finally afford it, I decided to get personalized facials every month to help heal my skin. I only got to do that once, a couple of weeks before my birthday. Then the pandemic hit, and everything closed, so I couldn't continue the treatment I'd just started. That was unfortunate, but my plan was to start another treatment once I got home, as things weren't as bad there.

On the afternoon of Saturday, July 4th, I went to my first facial appointment at a pretty reputable spa, and that was by far my worst experience. As soon as I took off my mask, the esthetician who was "helping" me started criticizing my skin. At that point, I'd already received too many comments on my skin from different people. Every person I met for the first time (besides close family members and some friends) started with a comment on my skin. I managed to brush off all those comments until the day of my facial.

When I got home from my appointment, my throat was full of repressed tears. I didn't have any of my journals, so I poured my heart and tears onto my laptop.

Date: 7/4/2020

Title: My Skin

How am I supposed to be confident with such bad skin? Every day I am reminded, one way or another, that my skin's condition has drastically deteriorated and neither yesterday nor today was different.

Can you imagine going into a beauty salon to get a facial, and the esthetician starts criticizing your skin so much it hurts in and out? People assume I don't do anything or enough about my skin and that must be why it looks the way it does. People assume I do not take my skin condition seriously, and that must be why it hasn't improved yet. Everyone is trying to give advice on what to do, what products to use, like I don't already do my research, like I don't already spend hundreds of dollars on skincare products.

Those who give advice are not coming from a bad place, and I know that. It just hurts to be reminded that my skin looks bad. What they don't know is that my skin actually looks so much better now than it did last year or two years ago, and I actually gained a little bit of confidence back when I saw some improvement. I felt like I could own my skin and be confident in it despite the remaining imperfections. Ever since I came back, I feel like I just can't work on my confidence because my skin looks bad. I ... I feel ugly. As bad as it sounds and even though I know I shouldn't say this, I just don't feel pretty.

I've had comments like I don't look like myself anymore, that I am not as pretty as I used to be, which, in all honesty, is actually true. I tried looking past my pimples; I tried looking at my skin and think it's not that bad, but clearly it is, and I just don't know what to do anymore. It's been three years, three years of struggle. What am I supposed to do? The worst part is that all of this is also a reminder of what I went through and what initially started damaging my skin.

I know my skin is not what it used to be three years ago before I left. I know my skin is not perfect. I know I have skin issues. But why are people so inconsiderate? Why can't they just see and not say anything if they have nothing nice to say? Isn't that how it's supposed to be? With so many people commenting on my skin, I know there are some who have something to say but refrain, and I truly appreciate them for that.

Here I go again, not wanting to go out or to see people because of how my skin looks. Coming back here has made me so much more self-conscious than I already was and I am now always nervous about seeing people, especially my old friends who only know what I used to look like and think I at least look the same or better. It is not the case. Not only do I not look the same, I am also not a reflection of what they think someone coming from abroad, especially the US, looks like. That in itself wouldn't bother me as much if I had at least gotten my skin back.

"Why aren't you as pretty as before?" "You look old." "You don't look like yourself." "You look so dark." "Why couldn't you get lighter?" "Your skin needs so much work." "We were used to pretty you." "You should use Clinique." "You can't just get a classic facial; your skin is too damaged for that." "Did you really think you were going to get a classic facial with such bad skin?"

But I have to build thick skin (haha) and not pay attention to this, right? Right! OK, done! You just had to ask. :-)

Maybe I should just give up on my skin already and learn how to live with it as it is. I probably won't get my twenty-year-old skin back.

Every time I met someone who hadn't seen me since coming home, I felt the need to "warn" them beforehand that I didn't look like what I used to. That eventually stopped as I got used to comments, but I also found a much, much better spa with much, much better customer service, and I started seeing some improvement within a few months of starting my treatment.

July is also when I applied for my study permit. To study in Canada as an international student, you need a study permit, and in some cases, a temporary residence visa (TRV), depending on your country of origin.

I like to think of the study permit as being similar to an I-20 in the U.S. It's a document that contains a student's personal and school information, is proof of status in Canada, and determines how long the student can stay in the country. There is also a ninety-day grace period after the document's expiration, similar to the I-20's sixty-day grace period. On the other hand, a visa is simply a stamp on your passport that allows you to enter a country.

I was going to need both the study permit and the TRV, but I only needed to submit one application—the study permit application. If approved by Immigration, Refugees and Citizenship Canada (IRCC), I was going to get my visa together with an approval letter to show at the Canadian border so my study permit could be issued. Essentially, getting a visa and/or being approved for a study permit does not guarantee entry into Canada as an international student; the study permit is issued at the border, and it is the border officials who make the final decision. And yes, they could send me back, even if I'd made it all the way to the Canadian border, if they judged that my supporting documentation was unsatisfactory.

I couldn't apply for my study permit while I was in the U.S. because my passport expired in June. Plus, I only had a few months left on my EAD card, which was not sufficient evidence of ties to the country of residence. And I didn't hit my savings goal until the end of May. I'd already prepared all the other documents so that by the end of June, the only missing piece was my new passport. As soon as it was issued in July, I applied for my study permit.

Later that month, the private lending company where I'd applied for a student loan cancelled my contract because they faced pandemic-related challenges. They could no longer accept new applications or service loans approved after February 2020. I continued to enjoy my summer, optimistic about finding a solution. I was calm and cool about it, until I wasn't.

I resumed studying for my CFA Level I exam sometime in August. The exam was now going to take place on December 5th. I'd previously changed my exam location from Chicago to Toronto, hoping I would be there by then.

By the end of August, my study permit application was still pending. Luckily, the Canadian government acknowledged the challenges facing international students because of slower processing times. They allowed students to start their programs online from abroad as long as they showed proof they'd applied for their study permits before the start of their programs.

I applied for my study permit in July and my program started on September 14th, so I was good. My plan was to stay home for a maximum of three months, hoping to start the program in-person. But most schools–including Schulich–were not offering in-person classes during that fall anyway, and Canadian borders were still closed to non-essential travel. So, even if I'd gotten my study permit and visa, I wouldn't have been able to travel.

What bothered me most was that I'd already paid $2,600 in rent for two months at my Toronto apartment, as required when my application was approved. That amount was non-refundable and could not be applied to other months, because my lease contract effectively started in September. I would also have to continue paying $160 every month for the storage space I was renting for my boxes.

———— ⌬ ————

Starting September 14th, I attended class every weekday afternoon, which corresponded to morning time in Toronto. I loved my classes, though I wished I had them on campus. Coordinating times to meet for group projects was a challenge because of the time difference between my classmates and me, who were all scattered around the world. Some days I had meetings at 11 p.m.; others I had to wake up at 2 a.m. The same was true for networking events with companies, which were usually scheduled at the end of the Toronto workday, so around midnight in Yaoundé. Not fun.

Even less fun was the fact that by the end of September, I had no news from the embassy. I began to wonder if it was worth it to continue attending classes. Plus, I hadn't made any additional tuition payment and hadn't figured out another solution. There were so many times when I wanted to give up and stop attending classes. I kept going, some days feeling like a complete fraud, and others just appreciating being in the program.

By the end of October, nothing had changed. Living in two countries simultaneously took a toll on my body. I studied for the CFA from 8 a.m. to 12 p.m. before attending class at 1 p.m., then I met for group projects or extracurricular activities or networking events at night. I also tried to see my friends here and there and be with family as much as possible, and I *tried* writing this book on Sundays. Whether positive or negative, I needed a response to know where to focus my limited energy.

Date: 10/26/2020

Title: I Miss Writing to God

Hey God, I hope You're doing well. I am writing here because I do not have my physical journal with me, and I miss writing to You and putting my thoughts down in a journal. It may sound corny, but it really felt like I was talking to You when I wrote in my journal. It was also a good way for me to just express how I felt.

I've been missing You, and I tried, maybe not hard enough, to do a fast to get closer to You. It didn't quite go well. I was only able to fast 4 days out of the 21 days I was supposed to, but I still gained some value reading the Bible every day for 21 days. I will try this fast again next year when I am hopefully in Canada and can be a vegetarian for 21 days (hihi).

I don't feel well today, and I haven't been feeling very well lately. I have no idea what Your plan for me is, and if it includes me going to Canada this year or ever. I am taking classes that I don't know how I am going to pay for. I am paying rent for my storage space in Toronto every month without even knowing for sure if I'll go. I am thankful that I even have enough money to pay for that, it hasn't always been the case. I saved some money from the job I had, and I am grateful that I was able to do so. But the thing is, I definitely did not save enough money to pay for school. Even if I were given my entire annual salary at once, it still wouldn't have been enough to cover my tuition and living expenses. I couldn't get a student loan, and yet here I am still attending classes, doing assignments, and getting involved in activities. Sometimes I am so into it that I even forget I don't have the money to go to that school. And based on my past experiences, I am so scared that I will end up not going. And to be honest, that would not be a surprise. This is not me lamenting. This is not me not trusting You. This is not me letting fear get the best of me. I am just lost, and I am not sure what You want for my life.

It's October 26th, and I still don't have my visa. Studying here has been so challenging with the time difference. I know I am not the only one taking classes from abroad, and I am not trying to make it sound like I suffer, not at all! I'm just saying it's not always easy, and I try to be thankful for what I have and where I am, but sometimes I also get frustrated because I am not comfortable. I know I am not the only one who is not comfortable, especially this year with all the challenges it has brought, but ... I don't know, I'm just saying.

I don't feel well ... I've used up all my skincare products and some of them I can't find here. I also sometimes feel lonely. I want to leave, but then again, I don't have the money to support myself there ... I've been looking for jobs, but no luck so far. I have to admit that with me being here and with the content of my program, I can't really have a job because of how demanding the program is.

Speaking of jobs ... If I do get to go to Canada, I don't know if I should pursue my dream job right away ... I don't feel ready enough to do so, and I am also unsure if I'll be eligible to join next fall, considering Deloitte has already closed its recruiting season for jobs starting next fall. If I do not join Deloitte, I do have a plan B: RSM. I am just trying to have options; I am not saying this is exactly how it'll happen because I know life is unpredictable and I am not really in control...

Anyway, the thing is, by targeting RSM after graduation, I don't feel like I am aiming high enough compared to where other people want to go. I know I am comparing myself here, but other students, especially MBAs, have ambitions to get into top banks for example. That is great and legitimate. I myself want to work at Deloitte and hope to work at an MBB firm later in my life, but I just don't feel like I can access those types of jobs now, and I think I should start "small." But then when I hear everyone, it's like I'm not ambitious enough … I am not really sure what to do. I really like RSM, but not for longer than a year. My dream is Deloitte, but I am not sure I can join next year.

Also, I don't feel good enough; I don't feel smart enough; I don't feel well. Also, my book scares me sometimes. I don't know the outcome of my "life" yet, and since the end of my book hasn't happened yet, and I don't know if/when/how it'll happen, it's a bit scary. I also think I am pushing to get into RSM because it'll fit well within the story in my book, but is that a valid reason? Should I really pursue RSM? If not, then what do I do, where do I go?

I am sorry this is all so sad, but I needed to get this out. Sometimes I wish You could give me a hug. I love You, God, and I trust You. Whatever You decide, I'll follow, even if it hurts. I know You have my best interests at heart. Thanks for listening/reading.

RSM's consulting practice focuses on the middle market and is not as big as the Big 4 or MBB. But when I discovered the company back in Chicago, I immediately wanted to join it to kick off my consulting career.

I'd wanted to attend one of its networking events at DePaul in January 2019. I obviously wasn't a student there, but RSM didn't come to my campus, and I wanted to get as much exposure to the firm as possible. So, I'd gone, hoping my previous status as an ELA student would get access. The recruiter and event coordinator dismissed me as soon as she saw on my resume that I was attending another school, citing that the event was exclusive. So, I didn't get to speak with anyone from the company or ask any of the questions I'd carefully prepared.

Later in the summer of 2019, I tried joining the firm again. I reached out to employees on LinkedIn and had a coffee chat with a current associate, but that still didn't work out. I applied for a few roles independently, but all my applications were rejected.

I saw my admission to Schulich—a better ranked school—as another opportunity to try RSM before joining Deloitte.

In terms of financing my education, I'd hoped the academic results from my MBA would help me get a merit-based scholarship, but I learned from my conversations with Schulich's financial aid office that international students in one-year master's programs were not eligible for scholarships. I looked for external grants and scholarships but couldn't find something that wasn't STEM-related and still accepting applications.

On November 7th, I finally received my passport request letter, which meant my visa was going to be issued. At that point, the Canadian government already allowed international students with a valid study permit and visa to enter Canada without an essential reason.

Knowing that visas are printed at the Canadian embassy in Senegal rather than at the high commission in Cameroon, I needed to submit my passport as soon as possible. I did so the following Monday. Usually, it would take one to two weeks to get the passport back, but because of the pandemic, there were going to be delays. I didn't want to wait until my passport came back to book my flight, so I booked it a few days later for a November 30th departure date.

On November 20th, IRCC notified me that my study permit approval letter—the letter I would show border officials with other supporting documents so they could issue my permit—was ready. However, my passport was still not back from Senegal, and I'd already missed the deadline to cancel my flight for a refund. Also, because I had to do a mandatory fourteen-day quarantine upon arrival in Canada, I'd already applied for accommodation through my school and provided my flight information so they could prepare a room for me at the partner hotel. I tried not to worry too much, but my anxiety eventually returned, keeping me up at night until my passport was finally ready for pickup *two days* before my departure date. Again, I was thankful, but this constant last-minute thing in my life was exhausting.

The same people who welcomed me on the night of June 8th took me to the airport on the night of November 30th. As is the case every time I'm at an airport, tears were still streaming down my face even after saying goodbye. I was going to miss singing random songs at the top of my lungs and dancing with Emma while we were cooking with our mom and Nora. I was going to miss our chats and bursts of laughter over dinner. I was going to miss my brothers' silly and not-very-funny jokes, and the happy moments we shared when we were all reunited on the weekends with their partners and children. I was going to miss eating fried plantains any time I wanted.

"Your dreams will come true, okay?" I murmured into Emma's ear as we were once again a mess of tears in each other's arms. "Never forget this. Your dreams will come true." She nodded on my shoulder.

She didn't know I was writing a book—no one did. We'd spent quite a bit of time talking about her dreams and the things she wanted to accomplish, and I wanted her to one day see *my* story, not just Instagram influencers' stories, as proof that dreams really do come true.

Before disappearing into the check-in line, I turned around to wave goodbye to everyone for the last time. I boarded my plane with the hope of making my dream come true.

Deloitte, I am coming for you.

CHAPTER 22:

NEW BEGINNINGS?

Date: 12/25/2020

Dear Heavenly Father... Hey God, happy birthday! 😊 I hope You're doing well. I am writing from Toronto, but You already know that because You made that happen. I am still very thankful, though it was another stressful process.

Thank You for... Allowing me to come to Toronto. I really hope this is the start of something better. My little Christmas celebration with a friend and her family. The fact that I've found a job here already and didn't get to a point where I lost hope before I found one.

I am worried about... How I'll pay for my education. I only made one payment, and it was the deposit. I have no idea how I'll pay the rest. I don't know what kind of miracle will happen and what I should be doing to help. Not being able to make my dream come true this year.

People I am praying for today... My friends and family. Anyone going through a hard time. People who feel lonely during this festive season. Those who are grieving or mourning a loved one. Those who have lost hope.

Here's what's happening in my life... My skin has started acting up again, and I honestly don't know what to do anymore. I spent so much time and money trying to fix it. It finally cleared up, but that only lasted a month! Please help? I hope this is a valid request.

I need... Help making my dream come true. Help writing my book. 😊 Help with my skin. 😟 Guidance as to what to do to pay my tuition.

Other things on my heart that I need to share with You, God... My book is not (yet) coming together very well, mostly because I've been managing my time poorly lately. But at least now I know for sure I want to (and should) write this book, and that's because of You, so thank You. The thing is, I don't know if it'll be good enough, and I'm worried about what people will think. I also don't know what my life will look like by the time I launch the book. I'm scared, but I'll still write it. I love You, God. 🖤

By the time I got to Toronto, it was my last week of classes, and I only had a few more assignments to submit. I spent most of my quarantine continuing to look for jobs; three days before Christmas, I was offered a part-time sales internship for the winter term. My savings wouldn't last much longer, so I needed something to keep paying the bills.

As an international student in Canada, I wasn't required to have studied for any amount of time at an academic institution before being eligible for work, and the job, whether on or off-campus, didn't have to be related to my field of study. However, I couldn't work more than twenty hours when school was in session. I would also need to have a Social Insurance Number (SIN) for tax purposes, which I applied for after my fourteen-day quarantine.

The Canadian SIN is similar to the U.S. SSN but unlike the social security number that is valid for a person's lifetime, the social insurance number is issued to temporary residents of Canada for the duration of their stay in the country, based on current immigration documents. It is only when a temporary resident becomes a permanent resident that they get a new SIN that will no longer expire.

The day after Christmas 2020 was the beginning of an Ontario lockdown that was initially set to end a few weeks later, so I spent the rest of the year organizing my studio apartment, watching TV shows, and *trying* to write this book.

I was living in yet another student residence, where the amenities were similar to those of the building on South Peoria Street in Chicago, but better. Unfortunately, because of the pandemic, all the building amenities were closed, except for the unique laundry room on the first floor. I went for a studio apartment this time so I could continue living on my own and have the kitchen to myself. Just like that first Chicago apartment, this studio was furnished. Heating worked in the apartment, thought it was controlled centrally and never set to a high and comfortable enough temperature for me. So, sometimes I'd still wrap myself in a blanket throughout the day.

Unlike the building on Peoria Street though, the student residence at The Pond Road wasn't located in downtown Toronto; it was right across the street from York University in North York, where the Schulich School of Business was also located. I paid the $1,300 monthly rent myself, as well as the utilities. When I got out of my self-quarantine on December 14th, I picked up my boxes from the storage space where they'd been for the previous six months. I only needed to buy a few more things to make my place nice, cozy, warm, and more like me.

I did my usual year review on December 31st, 2020, and laid out my plans and monthly goals for the upcoming year. Here are some of my thoughts from that day.

Dreams and Wishes and Hopes and Goals and Fears for 2021

THE BIG DREAM: Get into Deloitte as a consultant in the Strategy, Analytics and M&A service line.

Overarching objective: Be more confident in myself and my abilities. Do not let fear get the best of me or my life. Own my goals and stop labeling them as wishes because I fear that I won't reach them. Hope again and know that I too can be happy.

Challenge: Take a leap (or leaps) of faith and dare to hope with ALL my heart. Whatever happens, I don't want to be mad at God. I want to trust that He knows what He is doing. Please Danielle, try. Dare to have goals that you want to achieve.

Fears: I am scared that my journey in Canada will be a continuation of what started in the U.S. I am scared of being stressed out. I am scared of not being able to launch my book because my dream did not come true.

Goals: Graduate with my MMKG with a GPA of at least 3.5. Finish writing my book by August. Make my dream come true. Pass CFA Level I (February) and Level II (August).

Wishes: Launch my book in October. Get a nice apartment in downtown Toronto.

Hope: Look back at this in December and be proud of myself.

My first few months in Canada didn't go as well as I'd hoped they would. By March, I was back to a state of mental and physical exhaustion I knew all too well.

Date: 3/18/2021

I meant to write here last week when, for the millionth time, I felt like I wasn't good enough. I didn't because, for starters, I hate feeling this way and writing about it all the time. I feel like there's already enough of that here. Then, there's my book. I didn't want to write stuff that will potentially end up there. I know I can choose to leave out some things and have been doing so already, but just knowing that I might even remotely consider including last week's thoughts in the book made me shy away from writing altogether. Also, I don't want to write in my journals just because I can talk about it later in the book. I really want to preserve the initial intent of journaling.

So anyway … why am I writing today? I don't know, maybe because something wild happened to me a couple of hours ago? I don't know. I've been feeling so inadequate at my job, and last week was just terrible. I felt so unfit and wondered how I would even work as a consultant if I wasn't already performing well at this internship. And it was by birthday week, my twenty-fifth birthday week. This may not be a huge deal, but I really wanted to celebrate my twenty-fifth birthday, especially since I didn't get to celebrate my twenty-first. And so there I was, last Friday, the very day before my birthday, being sad because of my performance at work.

So today they … fired me (WOW!). Yeah … is that even a thing? Do people get fired from part-time internships after two months on the job? Like, I know I wasn't a good fit and, to be honest, the job wasn't a good fit for me either, but I thought I'd be able to stick it out until the end of April as initially planned. I was shocked and sad for a while, but now I don't know how I feel.

My grades have been suffering this semester partly because of that job. I'm not performing as well as I would like, and I wasn't doing a great job at work either. That job made me really anxious every Sunday thinking about work on Monday, and that has never happened to me before. I've also been overwhelmed with everything I'm doing, and being locked up in my room every single day doesn't help. But I also needed, and still need, money, especially now that I ran out of savings and spent what I had left on this case prep program that I really hope will pay off. Glad to have more time and be able to focus on other things, but I was still fired. Do people get fired from internships?

Also, it's now mid-March, which means the CFA Level I results are coming out soon, and I'm scared I won't pass that either. I've been doing so many things and feeling burnt out, and I don't want my results to reflect that. Oh, and did I mention I didn't get the job at Deloitte? Haha. To be honest, I wasn't really surprised, and I was absolutely not prepared for the case interview, anyway.

With my firing, I just kinda feel crazy for still wanting to apply to BCG or even Deloitte again. Preparing a resume and cover letter for such big companies when I couldn't keep an internship at a small company just sounds ridiculous. But oh well, I'll still do it. Plus, I've already paid for the case prep program, so might as well take advantage of it. I really hope I can still be a strategy consultant and publish my book.

Case interviews are an important part of consulting interviews, and they are *not* easy. At least they weren't to me when I practiced. The idea of networking to increase my chances of landing an interview, in consulting or elsewhere, was reinforced in Canada. It is through networking that candidates often get referred for jobs. Though these referrals are not mandatory, they are common practice. And especially if a candidate has an unconventional background, the recommendation is often that they get a referral from someone inside their company of interest. You can't get a referral if you don't know anyone at the firm, and you can't know anyone at the firm if you don't network.

I'd been reaching out to consultants at Deloitte since I was back home and continued to do so when I came to Toronto. I had a few virtual coffee chats, mainly to learn more about the firm's various consulting service lines. I still felt very uncomfortable asking for referrals, so I never did. I didn't plan on applying for a job before June because I wasn't prepared for case interviews and didn't want to rush anything. But I was still hoping to get a job—my dream job—before the end of the summer so I could focus on other things. Cute. Let's revisit this later.

Toward the middle of January, Deloitte posted several new graduate jobs set to start in September. I applied for a strategy consulting role and immediately started preparing for case interviews. I was part of a consulting club at my school, but we didn't meet very often to practice. Our career center had also organized students interested in consulting into small case practice groups, but the group I was in wasn't very active. So, I booked case prep services with freelance case coaches on Fiverr and started preparing.

A few weeks later, I got a rejection email. It didn't affect me as much as I thought it would. I knew from a conversation I had with a career counselor that Deloitte was going to post more jobs in the latter half of the year, so I just told myself I would try again at that point. Also, I somehow developed an interest in BCG, one of the top 3 strategy consulting firms. That was very scary for me because BCG was even more selective than Deloitte, and the interview process included *six* cases, compared to Deloitte's two. I didn't know if I could pass that many case interviews.

The case prep program I'm referring to in the journal entry is different from the freelancers I hired to help me prepare for a potential interview with Deloitte. After my application was rejected and because I was still confused about case interviews, I decided to enroll in a case interview prep bootcamp. I enrolled in the program before losing my job and had already committed to paying about $1,500 every month for the following three months. Pretty steep, but the program was comprehensive, and I thought if I received a consulting offer, my sign-on bonus was going to more than offset that cost. However, had I known I was going to lose my job, I certainly wouldn't have enrolled in the bootcamp.

During the first few months of 2021, I was probably the busiest I'd ever been. I had a lot on my plate with even more classes that term, assignments, studying for the CFA exam, trying to prepare for cases interviews, networking, extracurricular activities, my internship that started every day at 7 a.m., and trying to write this book. Everything happened on my laptop in my studio apartment because the lockdown kept getting extended, and it didn't take long before I burnt out. I went out for walks whenever I could, that is not very often. My days went by too fast, and when I had a second to myself, I used it to catch up on sleep. Plus, walking in minus twenty degrees Celsius weather was not very invigorating. Refreshing, maybe, but not invigorating.

North York wasn't very lively either, and it didn't seem to have anything to do with the pandemic. But because of it, many restaurants, for example, remained closed. Stores were operating on reduced hours, and a curfew was in effect everywhere. A handful of fast-food restaurants were open; some only taking drive-through orders, while others accepted customers inside but with no option to sit. What I'm getting at is it wasn't fun to stay inside my apartment, but outside of it wasn't any more fun either.

I kept pushing, convincing myself I should be able to manage all of it. In addition to needing money, I felt like I owed it to myself to work while I was going to school, because I had finally come to a country where I could do so without too many restrictions. I kept reminding myself there was a time I wanted to be busy but couldn't, and I remembered how sad that made me feel. So, I didn't want to take the opportunity to be busy for granted and not grab it while it was there.

Unfortunately, the job wasn't a good fit for me, and I wasn't a good fit for it either, which I now know is OK. I am not very good at pushing people to buy stuff, and that's essentially what the job entailed. I didn't have the best experience with my manager either, which my feeling of inadequacy stemmed from. Sometimes, he would imply or blatantly say that my work wasn't worthy of a student attending a school like Schulich. I'd never mentioned to him that my goal was to work in consulting, but he once told me that if I were a consultant at Kearney–a large strategy consulting firm–I would've already gotten fired.

These words did not immediately affect me. In fact, I didn't even care. If anything, I thought my manager didn't know what he was talking about. But after a while, they started playing in my head, and, coupled with my poor performance and subsequent firing, they made my career goals seem delusional.

Now, I did make my fair share of mistakes while on the job. With everything that was going on, I wasn't performing at my best. There were tasks that I didn't do, thinking I'd catch up later, so I lied and said I'd already done them. I was reporting to a project manager, and we both reported to the Chief Operating Officer (COO), who I referred to as "my manager" earlier. When they both found out I hadn't completed the tasks, it was too late.

I remember breaking down in front of my laptop during the meeting with the project manager the night he confronted me.

"This is not me," I said, shaking my head inside my hands. "I don't usually do this."

But how could he believe me? The damage had already been done. He then asked if I would be willing to work additional hours to complete the work, but again, international students in Canada were not allowed to work more than twenty hours during the school year.

I never told anyone at the company that I was an international student; I feared that *admitting* it would prevent me from getting a job, like it did in the U.S. I didn't lie about it; I just did not mention it. They wanted someone to join full time, but when I interviewed, I simply said I couldn't work more than twenty hours because of school, which, in itself, was true.

So, when the project manager asked about the extra hours and I said I couldn't do them because of my status, he got angry. And I broke down in tears. That night is when I thought they would fire me. I apologized for lying about my tasks and for not saying I was an international student sooner, then said I would work the extra hours without the extra pay. And that's exactly what happened. This was my way of not only "redeeming" myself, but also remaining compliant with immigration laws. I worked on weekends as well, hoping my work would finally be "acceptable."

All this took a toll on me, my body, and my mental health. To be honest, at some point, I wanted to quit. By the end of February, I was counting down the days until the end of that internship, wondering how I was going to make it to the end of April. The micromanaging I was now under was unbearable. Meetings every couple of hours to see how things were going, but mostly to check that I was working. And if I ever missed a call or was just a few minutes late, that was an issue.

I was attending classes on my personal laptop while simultaneously trying to work on my work laptop. No time to eat during the day because I didn't want to waste one second that could be spent working, with the constant fear that it was still not going to be enough. I had stomach cramps almost daily thinking about work. I had less than five hours of sleep because of work, school, extracurricular activities, and the CFA exam. It all became a lot to bear.

I wanted to quit, but then again, I needed money to pay the bills. I wanted to quit, but I felt guilty and weak for wanting to quit a four-month part-time internship. I wanted to quit, but I thought I was giving up too fast—I had to stick it out.

But then, the decision was made for me. I felt bad the day of my firing, especially since I didn't see it coming. I'd spoken with the project manager that morning, and there didn't seem to be a plan to let me go. Things had actually been going better, at least from what he was telling me. When he sent me a meeting invite that morning with no context, I couldn't imagine what was going to happen. The COO did not join the meeting, but when I saw the HR manager—who I was meeting for the very first time—I knew.

The project manager stayed on the call five seconds, maybe six.

"We can't do this anymore and have decided to let you go," he said before dropping the call immediately.

I didn't hear anything after that. The sound was muffled, less because of the speakers' quality and more the daze surrounding me. The larynx in my throat shut down. My brain froze. Luckily, my eyes still worked, but they only captured the blurry screen in front of me. The call didn't last much longer. When I found my voice again, I asked the HR manager if something specific had happened that morning that prompted the decision. She gave a very long version of the answer "no." I didn't insist.

I remained seated at my desk after the meeting window closed in complete silence. I was paralyzed. Getting fired wasn't something I thought would happen this soon (or ever) in my career, and I definitely wasn't prepared for it. Do you prepare for a firing? How? I don't know. What I do know is I wasn't feeling well. Once more, I felt lonely and overwhelmed.

After about ten minutes of not moving, I remembered how to use my hands. I reached for my journal, but I needed to talk to someone, ideally someone who didn't know me. I also wanted to know if other people had been fired from internships before. So, I opened the YouTube app on my phone and searched for "I got fired from my internship" storytimes. I found nothing. Especially with the pandemic still underway, most stories I found were of people who'd been laid off because of it, not because of poor performance. And these were full-time employees, not students or interns. I felt lonely and overwhelmed.

Schulich's mental health resources website had a list of mental health providers. I picked one, Good2Talk, a free helpline for students in Ontario. I initially wanted to call them two weeks earlier when I felt lonely, overwhelmed, and inadequate at my job and the government had just extended the lockdown again, but I never found the courage. This time, I needed to. The counselor didn't have a solution to my loneliness or the fact that I'd just lost a job, but it felt good to be heard. It felt good to talk.

When I came out of the office the next day after returning my laptop and access card, the weight on my shoulders and the ball in my stomach disappeared. On my way back, I was actually glad I wasn't doing that internship anymore. The night before, I'd had my first good night's sleep since January.

———— ⬤ ————

The CFA Level I exam had been postponed again, this time to February 2021. This worked out well for me, considering I was still in quarantine on December 5th, 2020. The results came out on April 13th. Once again, I had failed. This time, I wasn't shocked, and I didn't cry. Of course, it would've been nice to pass, and that was the goal, but I also knew I wasn't at my best. My results were actually a relief. I'd been praying and hoping to pass, but somewhere deep inside, I didn't want to. I knew the pressure I was going to put on myself to study for and pass Level II in August if I had passed the Level I. And there was *no way* I was going to do that while in school full-time, looking for a job, preparing for case interviews, networking, and writing a book. So, I was glad that was off my plate.

Oh, and in case you're wondering, I didn't re-register for Level I. I'm not giving up, just taking a break from constantly studying. It's exhausting, physically and mentally. I may or may not try again in the future, but for now, it's not a priority. Also, I now know and understand I don't need a degree or professional certification in *every single thing* I am interested in. Believe me, I had to convince myself I didn't need a writing or English degree to write this book.

———— ⬤ ————

Before my second school term ended on April 23rd, I applied for a student loan again with the same company I'd used a year earlier, as they had just started accepting applications again. I couldn't register for my summer classes set to start on May 10th because I still hadn't made any payments besides the deposit.

The Master of Marketing at Schulich was a one-year program with three consecutive and mandatory terms, each building on the previous: fall (September to December), winter (January to April), and summer (May to August). As such, all students moved together from one term to the other. Unlike my MBA program at Roosevelt University in Chicago, there was no flexibility to choose when to take certain classes, with no option to skip a school term or expedite the time to graduation. There were elective classes, though, but they could only be taken within specific terms. This configuration reminded me of what I was used to back home, when I attended the Catholic University of Central Africa.

This worked for me because I didn't want to be in school longer than a year. But if I wanted to graduate from the MMKG program, I would have to complete the third and final school term in the summer of 2021. My only hope was to get that student loan.

During the break between the winter and summer terms, I worked more closely with my coaches in the consulting bootcamp. I had two: one who helped me craft a new resume and cover letter, and the other who helped me with case interview prep. Both were former BCG and Bain consultants in the U.S. As part of the program, I had a total of six sessions with my case coach. After three sessions during which my performance wasn't great, I decided to wait until I had an interview before using the remaining three. In the meantime, I went over my weakness areas by doing targeted exercises also provided in the program and practiced cases once a week or every two weeks with other participants in the bootcamp. Sometimes I did well, sometimes not so much. I also continued to reach out to consultants on LinkedIn, focusing on Deloitte, MBB, and Accenture.

This routine gradually wore on me. I tried to remain positive until I couldn't anymore. I was once more lost and confused, overwhelmed and exhausted with pursuing a job that seemed too big, with preparing for case interviews when I had none scheduled and didn't know when or if that was going to happen, with wondering what the point was of everything I was doing, with wanting to give up one day and finding the strength to keep going the next, with spending my days in a small studio apartment doing the same things over and over again, with not knowing how I was going to pay for tuition at a school I'd been attending for months, with pushing myself to continue writing a book about dreams that come true when mine hadn't yet, and with wondering if this was really going to be worth it or if it was all another sham. Going back to my mom for help with rent wasn't thrilling either. And my skin, oh, my skin…

One night, I was on the phone with a friend. After a few minutes of trying to ignore my feelings so we could have a normal conversation, I broke down. I was overcome by a wave of frustration I couldn't push off. I was exhausted. The government had just announced they would extend the lockdown until the end of May, and I just couldn't take any more of these types of news. I was tired of trying to find the strength every day to keep going. I was tired of counting down the days until I would finally be out of a lockdown that had been going on for years for me. I was tired of telling myself it was all going to be OK and that this was just another trial. I was tired of holding back my tears. So, I didn't, unaware how much they would flow.

"Danielle? What's wrong?! Are you OK?! Is it something I said?" My friend sounded worried on the other end of line.

"Yeah … no, I'm fine," I started, but I wouldn't be able to lie for too long. "I just… I'm just tired of being on lockdown. It's been five months, and they've now extended it for another month. You don't know how much energy it's taking me to live like this, to try and have normal conversations with people. And it's not that I'm faking it or anything; I just try to be positive, and I keep telling myself it's not that big a deal, but I can't keep doing this anymore." *And it's been four years, but you don't know that. And I'm broke again and don't know how to pay for school, but you don't know that. And I'm scared my dream won't come true, but you don't know that.*

I continued to cry, for the reasons I mentioned and the ones I did not.

Two days after the summer term started, I still had no update on my loan application. I spent the day trying to get a hold of someone at the company for the third time that week to ask about my loan status, but no one picked up the phone. Later that night, and like every night since April, I opened my DCTMWT Word document to continue writing this book. I stared at my screen, unable to write.

Why am I even doing this?

I felt the pain grow back in my heart. A few minutes later, I wrote in my digital journal instead.

Date: 05/12/2021

Title: I Don't Know

After everything I've been through, after all He's done for me, I should be able to not get stressed out anymore. I should know that this is just a phase and that there is a solution. And it's not that I don't trust Him or that I don't think there is a solution, it's just ... I'm just wondering if I did something wrong or if there is something I should have done. I feel like I shouldn't be in this position. I feel like had I done that thing, I wouldn't be. I feel like I could have prevented this. But I don't know how. I feel like maybe this wasn't His will. Maybe He never approved of me coming here, and I was just being stubborn traveling across the world to study at a school I can't afford. But then why did He let me have my visa and study permit? I asked Him not to let me come if it wasn't part of His plan...

Classes for what is supposed to be my last semester have already started, but because I made no payments and have an outstanding balance, I am not able to enroll. Don't get me wrong; I know He is there, working, helping, but I just don't know how to play my part. I don't know what I should be doing to make something happen.

Days keep going by, and nothing happens. I just keep reading about assignments, group projects, and stuff like that in the class group chat, and I don't know what to do. People have asked where I am, and I keep lying, saying I don't feel well. Well ... it's not like I do, but you know what I mean.

Whatever He decides, I will follow and trust that it's the best thing for me; I'm just scared it'll mean not finishing the program this summer. And I am so tired of staying alone in my bedroom. Yes, I have a roof over my head. Yes, I have food and I am physically healthy, but He knows how uncomfortable it is to be alone 24/7 for months on end! And this is not the first time. This just feels like Chicago all over again. And if I don't finish the program this summer, what am I going to do? And I also have to move out by August because I won't be a student anymore. Do I just have to spend all my summers like this when I am abroad? This is so tiring.

I have started crying almost every day again. I thought these days were behind me. This thing in my heart, this pain that I thought was gone for good, there it is. I keep pushing through the days, I keep calling upon Him, and He is just SO silent. I know He is there; I just don't feel Him.

It was back. The pain, that once pea-sized hole on my heart that then grew to the size of a coin, the pain that shrank a little at some point then came back deeper, the pain that tore my heart wide open and exploded through my body before disappearing a few months later, that pain was officially back.

The pain that you've been feeling cannot compare to the joy that is coming.

"I know it's true, but it hurts."

I closed my laptop and cried myself to sleep.

CHAPTER 23:

DO DREAMS REALLY COME TRUE?

Date: 7/10/2021

I feel like I have to brace myself for another heartbreak, another very painful and shattering experience in the coming weeks. I have so many things to take care of, and I honestly don't even know if I'll still launch my book this year. I'll keep writing it, but sometimes I just don't know where I'm going with it.

So, I didn't even know that, but I have to move out by August 20th. Writing my book also makes me realize how long I've had to wait, all the things I had to go through, all the brokenness I had to experience before a breakthrough. And now that I am looking for a job again, looking to move again, looking to get work authorization again, looking to finish paying for school again, the cycle repeats itself.

I feel like I'll have to go deep into darkness again. Deep into pain, heart-shattering pain, before something finally happens. And I've started looking for just any job again, not just my dream job anymore. I just need something to pay the bills, you know?

My deadline is August 20th, but based on past experiences, I just know that I won't find anything before like August 18th, if it even happens before the deadline. I don't even know how to prepare for the pain that's coming. I want to pray and hope it doesn't happen, but this wouldn't be the first time. And all the times before, it still happened. I don't know that this time is different. I don't know what the truth is.

I've run out of savings again, but thankfully I can still buy food. I don't know how I'll pay for rent. I don't know how I'll pay for moving expenses. I don't know how I'll pay the remaining tuition fees. I haven't even started paying interest on my loan, which I'm afraid is going to affect my credit and thus my chances of getting an apartment. So many mountains, and as usual, they're intertwined. Everything is beyond me. And it's not that I don't know or trust that He will help me. I know He will. But I also feel like life (He?) will have to break me first, and that's what I have to brace for.

I wish it didn't have to be that way. I wish this ONE TIME would be different. I wish I could find a job before my deadline with no heartbreak. I wish I could move to a nice place without too much trouble. I wish I didn't have to be stressed out because deadlines are approaching, and nothing looks different. I don't know ... maybe it's a lot to ask, and I should just ask for strength? But I feel like strength sometimes (always?) comes with additional challenges. I wish this time was different.

Well … It wasn't exactly different. I effectively found a new place on August 17th but to be honest, I didn't start looking for an apartment until early August precisely because I knew this would happen. I didn't want to "waste" my time and energy looking for a place, only to find it a couple of days before my deadline.

The American and Canadian financial systems are similar; knowing how important credit is for just about anything, I knew when I came to Canada that I would need to start building my credit as soon as possible. Luckily, international students in Canada have more credit card options compared to those in the U.S., albeit with some restrictions. I'd already researched Canadian credit cards available to international students while I was still in Chicago, and I spent my first two weeks in Toronto researching some more. By the time I got out of my quarantine in December 2020, I'd selected the credit card I would apply for once I got my SIN.

In Canada, credit scores range between 300 and 900 (compared to 850 in the U.S.), and the principle is the same: the higher the score, the higher the creditworthiness. The five factors I mentioned previously (payment history, credit utilization, length of credit history, credit mix, and recent activity) also affect credit in Canada.

By June 2021, I'd built enough credit for my score to be in the high 700s, which is considered good credit. However, I couldn't afford and wasn't eligible to live on my own because I had no job and thus no proof of income. Unlike the I-20 in the U.S., the study permit in Canada does not include proof of funds for tuition or living expenses, so its only purpose during my apartment search was to prove my status. For these reasons, I ended up renting a room in the townhouse that I shared with other people. I shared the house, not the room.

The house had three floors and included no other amenities than a washer and a dryer on the second. Each floor had two to three rooms, and mine was on the third. My housemates were a mix of young women and men, some university students, others who'd recently started working, and still others who were on a short stay in the city. Thankfully, the rooms were furnished and had their own in-suite bathroom, which is also rare in Toronto. All tenants shared the single kitchen on the second floor. It didn't include a dishwasher, but the oven worked.

I was finally in the city. The townhouse was located in the Annex neighborhood of downtown Toronto, on Dalton Road. Rent was about the same as what I was paying for my studio apartment in North York but included all utilities. Overall, I liked the place. The only inconvenience, I would later find out, was the unique thermostat that controlled the temperature for the entire house. Here too my housemates and I never agreed on the settings. Later in the fall and into the winter, I would sneak out at night to raise the temperature, only to wake up a few hours later to a cold room.

But while it was still summer, all was good.

I went out for walks and watched the red-and-white streetcars and buses drive by, looked at the reflection of the sun on tall glass buildings during the day and marveled at how they blended into the sky and its stars at night. I walked past shops and bars and restaurants and food trucks, listened to people chat and laugh, watched them stroll or jog, and I smiled at those walking past me. I rolled my eyes every time someone zoomed by in their unnecessarily loud luxury car or motorcycle, and every three to four minutes when an ambulance or fire truck drove by blasting its sirens. I looked at, listened to, and appreciated everything that reminded me I was in the city. The tree-lined streets and the brightly painted houses that contrasted with modern architecture. The liveliness of the people and places. The busyness that makes me feel *alive*.

———— ⊂▨▨▨⊃ ————

By the end of the summer, I still hadn't found a job, despite looking for full-time roles and even internships outside of consulting. I networked across industries and firms, interviewed for three out of more than a hundred jobs, but did not get an offer. These rejections did not tear me down. I wouldn't say I was used to it, but by then, I'd experienced rejection multiple times already. What affected me, however, was the exhaustion from looking for a job and networking, realizing that the only time I looked for a job and didn't wear myself out, that specific job resulted in a termination.

My finances were now at their worst, but I tried my best not to see myself as a burden or an unprofitable investment. I was reliving another version of my summers in the U.S. One day I wanted to give up on everything and go back home, then the next I found the strength to push forward. There seemed to be no end to the cycle. *New beginnings don't exist*, I would tell myself at times. When I moved out of North York, I was thankful for my new place in Toronto, but I longed for more stability. I desperately tried but failed to make my dream come true. I desperately tried but failed not to spend days crying.

———— ⊂▨▨▨⊃ ————

Two weeks after the summer term started, and about a month after the registration deadline, a student services coordinator at Schulich reached out to me; she'd noticed I hadn't enrolled in any of my classes for that term. After explaining the issues I was having with my loan, she gave me until May 30th to get instructor permission for those classes. I reached out to professors individually to request permission to join their classes already in session. Classes were still held online, but because I wasn't registered, they didn't appear on my learning platform, and I didn't have access to Zoom links. Even if someone shared the links with me, they would not work with my student account.

My requests were approved, and I emailed them back to the student services coordinator. Before the block on my account could be lifted, the school needed a more detailed explanation of my situation, which I provided in an email. They then lifted the block, allowing me to join my classes on the fourth week of the term, on May 31st, on the condition that they received the funds by June 20th. If not, they would de-enroll me from my classes. The funds arrived in my student account a few days before the deadline, but in the meantime, my mom made an additional payment.

To be honest, I wasn't too worried while waiting for those funds to come. Not until the week of June 20th when I frantically called and emailed the loan provider every day to check on my loan disbursement status. I was grateful to the coordinator for reaching out to me and helping me attend classes for my last term. When I thanked her in my last email to her, I wished she realized what she'd done and to what extent she'd helped me. I completed the MMKG program in August 2021.

———— ⊂⥤ ————

When September rolled around, and despite not having found a job, I started to feel more optimistic. Fall is usually recruiting season at many companies. On-campus recruitment happens at that time, together with a variety of information sessions and networking events.

Seeing that some companies were more flexible with their start dates—offering additional ones in January 2022 instead of September 2022 only—gave me hope I wouldn't stay unemployed for too much longer. The interview turnaround at most firms was also pretty quick, lasting from two to three weeks. Their timelines indicated that interviews would be conducted starting mid-August, with final decisions made starting in September. I was hoping to get a consulting job and negotiate my start date for November or December 2021.

My calendar was full of networking and recruiting events, in addition to the case practice sessions I booked more frequently to prepare for a potential interview. I attended as many events as I could, as long as they were relevant to my career goals, even if not directly related to consulting. I did the same with my applications, applying to financial services, telecommunications, and other types of firms.

From: Deloitte Canada Campus Recruitment

To: Me

Subject: Congratulations! Deloitte HireView Interview

Date and Time: 9/10/2021 at 4:04 p.m.

We want to learn more about you! We are excited to invite you to participate in our digital interview, for the Consulting - Strategy, Analytics and Mergers & Acquisitions - New Grad 2022 role you applied to with the Strategy and Business Design Team.

You should have received a 'HireVue Interview with Deloitte' invitation that includes important next steps on completing your digital interview. We encourage you to check your junk mail if you have not yet seen the email.

Please note that the deadline to complete the video interview is **Sunday September 12th at 11:59 p.m. ET.** I am happy to further assist if you have any questions around this process.

Best of luck,

Campus Team

The Strategy and Business Design team is housed within Monitor Deloitte, the firm's strategy consulting practice. Over the years, as I learned more about the consulting industry, my interest narrowed from general management consulting to strategy consulting specifically, which is relatively more difficult to break into. So, rather than simply wanting to get a job at Deloitte, I now specifically wanted to work at Monitor Deloitte. From what I'd found out, their projects were similar to those of McKinsey, Bain, or BCG.

To say that I was happy to get the interview invitation email would be an understatement. I'd applied on August 16th, my seventh time applying to Deloitte Canada in the past year alone. The other six times were for a mix of roles across different consulting practices, but I never made it past the resume screen. Those rejections didn't affect me at all. But after my last unsuccessful application, I told myself I'd just wait for on-campus recruitment instead of applying as an experienced professional as I'd been doing.

This time I was hopeful but didn't want to have high expectations. I told myself it would be my last time applying to Deloitte, at least for a while. If it didn't work out, I would still go after consulting jobs, but focus on the other firms I'd been increasingly interested in. That said, I was happy to move on to the next step.

The interview had to be completed within two days of receiving the invitation and included a mini case, so I quickly scheduled a practice session for the next day with one of my case partners from the consulting bootcamp. I would schedule another session with my case coach when I moved on to the next step again. I also spent that Saturday evening practicing my answers to behavioral interview questions.

I spent half an hour the next morning setting up my desk and making sure that everything looked good, from the lighting to my background and surroundings to my sound and image quality. I practiced my answers one last time before sitting in front of my laptop to start my interview. *Smile, remember to smile. You got this, Danielle. We're almost there.* My heart was racing with nervousness and excitement. I answered the questions the best I could.

When I closed my laptop, I was feeling pretty good. I didn't want to get ahead of myself, but I was hopeful. Only one more round of interviews and that would be it. My dream would come true. If I received an offer, I would negotiate the closest start date, though it wouldn't bother me to start a year later. My dream would finally come true, and that would be my early Christmas gift. I would finally write the last chapter of this book. I would move out and get my own apartment where I'd stay longer than a year. I would have enough money to start saving, investing, paying off my debt, and living my life. I would finally have good news for my mom. I would finally be stable and *happy*. I reminded myself not to put too much weight on this to avoid being crushed if it didn't work out, but I was hopeful.

The update came in four days later at 12:31 p.m. I was sitting at my desk doing I can't remember what, so I opened the email on my laptop. The subject read *Digital Interview Follow-up*. Seeing that it didn't include the word "Congratulations," I knew I hadn't made it to the second round. But something inside of me wanted to believe that maybe this was how they sent updates to everyone, and that once I opened the email, good news awaited me. That wasn't the case. They regretted to inform me that I was not selected to move forward in the interview process.

The familiar taste of pain took over my throat. My tears knew the way, so I let them run their course. It hurt much less than

October 2019, but much more than I thought it would. I thought I was "stronger" than that. I thought I was past crying over a rejection email, considering how many of them I'd received over the years. But that week had been especially difficult—I received a rejection email at least once a day, and when I saw the one from Deloitte, I caved.

Date: 09/16/2021

I didn't know job rejection emails could still make me cry. So far, this week has been one of the worst this year. Every day came with at least one rejection from a job I've applied for and today ... Deloitte rejected me. Again. This time, for good. I mean ... not like I can never join the firm again, but this was my last chance for trying to join as a new grad. I didn't expect it to hurt as much as it does because over the past few months, I found myself other dream firms. But the thing is, pretty much all of them have rejected me already, and I'm honestly just tired and want to move on. I don't even want to have a dream firm anymore. I'll take whatever pays me. Yes, I still want to be a consultant and if I had more time and energy, I'd go for a big firm. But at this point, I'm just tired. You know what the worst part is? It's that despite being heartbroken, I also feel like this is not even the point where it starts to get better. I feel like there's worse pain ahead because I am not as tired or as broken as I can be. I am so tired of living like this. Like, is this how it is for everyone? Constant heartbreaks before things get better? Waiting beyond your deadlines for something to happen? Feeling and being lonely ninety-nine percent of the time? Watching seasons change every year, yet having the same issues? Feeling lost all the time? Struggling with confidence and knowing your worth?

As usual, I don't know where to put myself. And I am always trying to balance being humble and content with wanting more for my life. I always feel like there's a type of "more" I shouldn't want because I should be content and grateful for what I already have, but even when

I try "smaller" things, they don't succeed. I am tired, but I don't think it matters how much I say it or how much I feel it. What has to happen will, regardless of how I feel. I just need to be strong or ask for more strength.

I was so close. So close to the finish line. I could see it. Feel it. Smell it. My dream. It was about to come true after all these years. After all these tears.

I was fifteen years old when I decided I wanted to be a consultant. Nineteen when my mom invited me to attend one of the Institute of Internal Auditors' conferences with her in New York City. All Big 4 and other major firms were there, but I fell in love with Deloitte. I didn't want to work in internal audit; I wanted to work in consulting. At Deloitte. I was twenty-one years old when my mom came to visit me in Chicago, and we walked along Wacker Drive, a street I knew all too well. I showed her the skyscraper at 111 South Wacker, saying I would work there one day. It was the Deloitte Chicago office, one I walked by frequently, dreaming of entering. I was twenty-two years old when I started dreaming about moving to Toronto and glued pictures of the Deloitte Toronto office in one of my journals. Twenty-four when, on my first trip to downtown Toronto after quarantine, I made it a point to locate the Deloitte office. I walked by and took a live picture of the skyscraper at 8 Adelaide Street West, my heart full of hope that my dream would soon come true.

It was all going to make sense. The pain. The struggle. The sweat. The blood. The tears. The wait. This was the moment I'd been preparing for. I was ready to live my dream. But then it was ripped out of my heart.

I was twenty-five years old when I applied to Deloitte Toronto, again and again. Twenty-five when my applications were rejected by Deloitte Toronto, again and again. And the pain, that once pea-sized hole on my heart that then grew to the size of a coin, the pain that shrank a little at some point then came back deeper, the pain that tore my heart wide open and exploded through my body before disappearing a few months later and making its way back, that pain further expanded.

As you've read, one of my goals since 2020 has been not to let my circumstances drive me away from God, no matter what they are and no matter how hurt or upset I may be. It's not easy, at least not for me, especially in situations like these. I was once more in a lot of pain, crying on my desk. I turned around in my swivel chair to get up and head toward my bed. This time, when I walked past the nightstand with my cross on it, I told God I wasn't mad at Him. I opened my *Renewed Hope* playlist on Spotify, put the song *Hills and Valleys* by Tauren Wells on repeat, then laid down. I curled under the blanket, my back to the cross, and cried myself to sleep.

I woke up from my little nap around 4 p.m. and decided I wasn't going to give up. Deloitte may have been off the table, but the other companies were not. I thanked the recruiter and asked for feedback on my application, then moved on.

On the days I had no case practice session scheduled, I would do some exercises on my own, which is what I did that evening as well as the following days. This preparation eroded my energy overtime, especially as I wasn't hearing back on my applications and had been maintaining this rhythm for months.

By October, no other consulting company had gotten back to me. I applied to all the Big 4 but did not hear back from KPMG, PwC, or EY. I applied to IBM, Kearney, Accenture, Richter, but nothing.

Nada. Rien du tout. I tried RSM again, but no luck. I tried CGI and Cognizant Consulting, but no luck either. I even tried Duff & Phelps again, but still no luck. And these are the results from consulting companies only. I'd already applied to Bain and BCG over the spring and summer, but that hadn't worked out. I had a pending application with McKinsey, and despite the silence and not feeling ready for the job, I continued to practice. *Maybe this will work. Maybe this is why it's all happening this way. There is better. There is bigger. This is the end of my book.*

I still hoped and believed I would hear back soon from at least one firm, despite starting to see posts on LinkedIn from students and recent grads who were excited or humbled or thrilled to share or announce that they were going to join this or the other firm in the winter or fall of 2022.

Attending a top school and having connected with several people at top companies over the past year meant that the content on my LinkedIn feed came from them, as well as from students attending similar schools who applied to top companies. I am not saying everyone got in; of course not. But I had never read that many job update posts with such a high concentration of top companies across all industries. I wanted to believe that I too would hear back and that my application dates were just different from everyone else's, until the LinkedIn posts started to dwindle, and it became clear that all the offers had been made to successful candidates.

I didn't want to lose hope. I truly didn't want to feel bad about myself, especially as I'd written part of this book by then and was aware of certain patterns. I tried, until I caved.

After spending days speculating on the status of my applications, I decided to email recruiters or send a message on LinkedIn to get a clear answer. I didn't contact them all. The day that I emailed KPMG, the recruiter confirmed that my application was not selected. I asked for feedback like I always do, and for the first time, I actually got a response, albeit generic.

"No direct feedback at this time, we had an extremely competitive applicant pool this cycle. Feel free to reach back out in the coming months and we can sync back up to see if there are any openings at that time."

I know this is not what he said, and it may have not been what he meant, but I was already so beaten down that I couldn't help but think that my application wasn't competitive enough. That *I* wasn't competitive enough. That I wasn't good enough.

I wish I never had a dream. I wish all I wanted was to live a comfortable life. I wish I could be happy and fulfilled with any decent job that gave me that comfort. Aren't some people happy this way? Why can't I be too? I feel so inadequate for the things I desire.

A cloud of shame settled over my head and followed me wherever I went. It stayed above at first, then wrapped me around so that I couldn't ignore its overwhelming presence. I was ashamed of myself for not getting into one single consulting firm. I was ashamed of myself for not getting one single job.

Where did I go wrong?

I worked with a coach and previous consulting recruiter to craft a good resume and cover letter. I met several times with career counselors at my school's career center. One also reviewed my resume and was looking forward to when I would tell him I'd gotten an interview. I updated my LinkedIn profile. I networked more in my ten months in Canada than I did in my three years in the U.S. I attended info sessions and recruiting events. I followed up and asked for feedback on my unsuccessful applications. I practiced for interviews. I kept my options open and applied to non-consulting jobs. What more could I have done to get a job? Just anything?

I didn't cry, but I wasn't feeling well and couldn't sleep that night.

One thing that I'd heard from some of the people I networked with, to whom I had sent my resume, was that I lacked experience. I knew that, which is why I was willing to start over, to start at the very bottom of the ladder and work my way up. I didn't care that I had an MBA. I didn't care that I had just gotten another master's degree. I was willing to get an entry-level job, as long as it was aligned with my career goals. Other people pointed out my three-year employment gap, having had six months only of full-time work experience between 2016 and 2020. But I tried to gain that experience. I wanted to work. I didn't *not* work intentionally. All these rejections and remarks made me feel like I was being punished for something I had not caused.

———⚬⫘⚬———

The next day, these thoughts were still swirling in my mind as I was once more at my desk, getting ready for yet another personal case practice session. The cloud of shame was still there, above and around me, reminding me of the situation I was in.

We had an extremely competitive applicant pool this cycle. I am not competitive enough. If you worked at Kearney, you would have already gotten fired. Why am I even still practicing? Maybe this isn't for me. I wish I didn't have a dream.

As I dove deeper into those thoughts, I didn't realize I wasn't writing anything on the blank sheet of paper in front of me. That's until the Outlook notification ping pulled me back into the real world. I unfroze my right hand from above the sheet of paper I was staring at, and the pencil it was holding dropped onto the table. I moved my hand over to the mouse to navigate to the email tab on my laptop screen.

It was Siemens congratulating me for getting an offer on the internship position I had interviewed for.

Something else I didn't realize was that I'd been holding my tears. As soon as I read that email, they rushed down my cheeks without my permission. When I caught my breath, I turned around in my swivel chair to face the cross on my nightstand.

"Thank You," I said, still sobbing.

I turned back around, rested my head on my right hand on the table, and continued to cry. I don't know why I was crying. These were not tears of joy, but they were not tears of pain either, because I did not feel *the pain*. When they stopped flowing, I put everything away and closed the practice exercise tabs on my laptop. I was no longer going to practice for case interviews. I was exhausted and needed a break to figure out if I even still wanted to do consulting. And maybe, just maybe, there was a lesson to be learned.

The rejection email from my pending McKinsey application came in later in October, beautifully closing out my fall recruiting season and letting me focus on Siemens. I did not cry. What made me cry, however, was getting paid one Friday in November and having to spend my entire paychecks on my bills, student loan, and credit card debt.

My savings completely ran out in June, so I relied on my credit card for daily expenses while my mom helped with rent. With my moving and living expenses, I quickly reached and even exceeded my $1,000 credit limit, which generated interest and fees on my balance. This is in addition to my unpaid student loan interest payments, which were also accumulating late fees. By November, my credit score had gone from good to poor.

Siemens paid me $25 an hour, which I had negotiated up from the initial $22 the company offered. But after tax, that was barely enough to cover my rent, debt, and other expenses. I knew when I got the offer that this would be the case, so I continued to look for another job, something I would do part-time to supplement my income and help me breathe a little. Luckily, I found a part-time marketing contract that I did on the side. It paid me $1,000 a month, essentially replacing the taxes deducted from my Siemens income.

I was thankful for those two jobs, but that Friday evening, I was crying because I had just gotten paid from both; however, it still wasn't enough. After paying my bills and only a part of my debt, I had less than $50 left in my checking account, and no savings at all. I knew this situation was temporary, but the feeling of working entire days just to pay the bills and always struggling financially didn't seem all that temporary.

My internship with Siemens lasted four months, from October 2021 to February 2022. I knew that my last internship experience (combined with my many rejections) had affected my confidence, but I hadn't realized how much.

I was working in the Smart Infrastructure business unit, reporting directly to the vice president, who worked directly with the CEO for all of Canada. While I wasn't particularly intimidated by them, I always worried that my work was not going to be good enough. And because I was the only intern and only lower-level employee on that team, I had little reference for what constituted good work. I was also the only Black *person*. That said, my manager—the vice president—supported me when he wasn't too busy. There was also Zarin, another Schulich alumna who had interned in my business unit a year earlier but was now working full time in a different area of the company.

The fear of getting fired followed me throughout my internship at Siemens. I didn't know what value, if any, I could bring to the company. I didn't know what I was capable of. I braced myself whenever I got a call or email from my manager, thinking it was negative feedback or a comment about something I had done wrong and how unacceptable it was.

One Friday, my manager emailed me after hours. A cold wave immediately travelled through my body, freezing everything on its way except the blood pounding in my ears. And maybe my heart too. Two weeks before I lost my previous internship, I'd gotten an email from the project manager around 7 p.m. on a Friday, saying how dissatisfied he and the COO were with my work. I thought this time was similar. It was not. This time, the VP at Siemens was thanking me for my hard work throughout the week and encouraging me to enjoy the weekend *to the fullest.* The wave made its way back, warm and delicate, unfreezing one cell at a time. I let out a soft sigh. *Wait what? What kind of manager says that?*

I didn't believe my manager whenever he said he was happy with my work. One time, I even thought he was being sarcastic because I didn't feel like I had done much, and yet he had thanked me again for my work. It's only when Zarin joined me on a project, and he showed that same appreciation to both of us at the end that I believed his comments had been sincere all along.

He thanked me for my work. He recognized me publicly (including in front of the CEO). I tried hard not to miss any of his calls, but whenever I did, he didn't get angry. When I apologized, he said he understood I was working from home and that he did not expect me to be glued to my desk. He took note when we worked extra hours and encouraged me to finish early the following day if there was nothing urgent. When I told him I was interested in consulting, he forwarded my resume to a director in Siemens Advanta, the consulting arm of the company. He said I had a promising career and that the future held countless opportunities for me.

Of course, it wasn't all rainbows and butterflies. He wasn't perfect, and I wasn't either. But not once did I count down the days until the end of February.

———— ⌘ ————

Halfway through the internship, around mid-December, I did something I'd never done before but always knew was necessary—I scheduled a midpoint check-in meeting with my manager to discuss my progress and get feedback. To my utmost surprise, he responded by asking *me* to prepare feedback for him as well. *Wait what? What kind of manager does that?*

That meeting helped ease my anxiety, but only for a short while. The feedback was positive, and he reiterated his appreciation for the work I was doing. There were areas for improvement, but the way he communicated them didn't make me feel unworthy of working there.

But even after that meeting, the fear of getting fired continued to follow me until my very last week, when I realized it would be too late to fire me. My manager even asked to extend my contract, but I turned down his offer, because, as you'll discover, other things were happening at that time.

When I thanked him during our last meeting and in my farewell email, I wished he realized how much of a positive impact he'd had on me, both professionally and personally.

"The world awaits you to grow and prosper. Siemens doors are always open. :)"

I took a picture of his email before packing my bag. When I went to the office to return my laptop and access card on February 25, 2022, there was no weight on my shoulders and no ball in my stomach.

Only gratefulness in my heart.

CHAPTER 24:

THE LESSON

L et's take a step back to December 2021. When the last day of the year rolled around, I did what I always do: I took out my journals and planners to reflect on the ending year and plan the year ahead. However, this time looked a little different because I didn't have specific plans or goals. This excerpt explains why.

Date: 12/31/2021

It's that time of the year again. So ... 2021. Another year during which almost none of the things I planned for actually happened. To be fair, my biggest goals were out of my control, and the most disappointing thing was not making my dream come true and not publishing my book. I held on to that dream and to that book so tight, I didn't realize they had become obsessions. Hard pill to swallow, but I eventually saw them as what they were.

Definitely painful and unfun to see that dream fall apart after trying so hard for so long to make it a reality, but I think that made me learn the biggest lesson of my whole life: my happiness does not depend on my dream coming true. I now truly believe there is more to life than accomplishing goals, and for this reason, I will not have any for 2022.

This time, not because I am broken or disappointed. There are still a few things I want to achieve and honestly, I lowkey hope to finally start my consulting career sometime in 2022, but I am not putting a deadline on that and will not obsess over it.

What I am proud of:

- Holding on to God (or at least trying) and not letting my circumstances completely drive me away from Him.
- Starting another journey to get closer to Him (Bible study)
- Realizing that life doesn't revolve around my dream.
- My graphic design skills!!! 😊
- Writing almost an entire book.
- Making my website on my own + everything around DCTMWT.

My "Goals" for 2022

I just want to enjoy life with whatever I have and whenever I can, whether I have friends or not. I want to see what there is to see, do what there is to do as much as I can and to the extent that my finances allow it. I hope to still have a job throughout the year, whether in consulting or not. I want to set aside $50 every month to do something new, no matter what it is. I also want to be consistent in the gym, not so I can be skinny anymore, but just to be and feel better in my body.

I finally got it. The Lesson, the one I didn't know I needed to learn. Even before the fall recruiting season, I was already suspecting that there might have been something I was missing, some sort of lesson I needed to learn. But I truly didn't know what it was. I tried to figure it out in vain throughout the summer of 2021.

Did I need to have a more targeted approach to networking? Did I need to cast a wider net when looking at consulting firms? Did I need to be more patient and trust that good things do take time, or actually go harder and not let my fears hold me back? Did I need to be brave and strong and push through rejections, disappointments, self-doubt, and other challenges in my personal life, or did I need to take a break and start afresh? I looked for the answer. I prayed for the answer. I couldn't figure out the answer.

While all these questions were relevant, and I did apply a little bit of everything, they all still revolved around one single thing: making my dream come true. This dream had been a blindfold over my eyes since I was fifteen. How could I possibly have seen that my conception of happiness, purpose, and fulfillment had become distorted by the very pursuit of that dream? How could it be any wrong to base my worth on something that I so very much desired? After all, if I didn't make my dream come true, if I didn't achieve my goals, if I didn't go after what I wanted, what was I doing with my life?

I had heard, read articles and LinkedIn posts, watched YouTube videos of people warning against becoming so attached to a job, a project, a dream that it becomes part of (or entirely) our identity. They encouraged to instead find fulfillment and happiness outside of whatever that *thing* was. While I absolutely agreed with them and liked, supported, celebrated, loved, and sometimes saved these posts, I still couldn't see that I was doing the exact opposite. Probably because I had managed to convince myself that my situation was different.

So, how did it happen? How did I learn?

Let's wind back to October 2021, when I decided to take a break. Now that I was no longer trying to get into consulting, I had more time on my hands. And now that October 10th–World Mental Health Day and my initial desired book launch date—had passed, I was no longer in a rush to do anything regarding this book. I started designing the book cover in the summer, but I wasn't very skilled at Photoshop, so I thought I'd do a simple draft as a reference to show to an actual graphic designer. The same was true for all the other things I wanted to design. But since there was nothing at stake anymore and no more deadline, and despite the occasional fear that it would all be pointless, I wanted to try and design these things on my own. First, that would translate into a lot of money savings, but second and more importantly, I actually like graphic design.

I enjoyed working on my website throughout that summer—finding the perfect shade of every color, trying different fonts and styles and page layouts, incorporating a little bit of my personality, etc. It was overwhelming at times, and with it being the first real website I was building, there were lots of trials, errors, Google searches, iterations, crashes, unsaved changes, and frustration, but that was one of the few processes I can honestly say I enjoyed. So, before my internship at Siemens started and even after it started, I spent a few hours every day designing the book cover, watching YouTube tutorials, and designing again. I also continued working on The Website.

Every step closer to a completed design brought a smile to my face and excitement to my heart. What brought the biggest smile, however, was creating the logo and finally figuring out the right shapes, color combinations, fonts, spacing, and dimensions. It was not a very complicated design, but once it was done, I felt so proud.

I can't believe I have a brand. I got up from my desk to look at the DCTMWT logo on my laptop screen from a distance, to make sure it looked as good from afar as it did up close. It did. I came back to my desk, sat, and stared at the screen some more while tears welled up in my eyes.

I am so happy.

There it was, a thought I hadn't had in a very long time. It crossed my mind without me noticing and when I did, my eyes opened wide in dismay, allowing the tears to travel down. I never planned for #DCTMWT to evolve from a hashtag to a brand. I never even thought I would have a brand, not because I didn't feel capable of having one but because it wasn't one of my goals. It was not something I planned.

Granted, the logo was about dreams and my dream hadn't come true, but it looked so good!

Could this be why my dream didn't come true this year?

I'd been wondering and asking God why my dream hadn't come true, what would have happened if it had in the spring or in the summer or even in the fall. When I couldn't figure out the answer, I thought maybe there were none, that maybe this time everything happened for no reason at all. As I continued my graphic design journey, I became increasingly interested in other forms or art, such as photography and videography. All this made me realize so many other things that could bring me joy and happiness.

Going to the gym also brought me joy and happiness. As I mentioned earlier in this book, I started developing a much better relationship with my body throughout the latter part of my teenage years. By the time I was an adult, I was actually very confident in my body. But I would be lying if I said the occasional comments on my chubby cheeks or whenever I gained weight didn't sometimes bring me back to my childhood and make me feel like I could lose a few pounds. When I went back to the gym in November 2021, it was the first time I was going for no other reason than to be healthier. And stronger. And more toned. But mostly healthier. It was the first time that I didn't weigh myself with the goal of shedding a few pounds.

In fact, I didn't weigh myself at all and wasn't going to start a diet or a cleanse, nor was I going to stop eating the food I love. I no longer wanted to let people's definition of beauty influence, even just a little bit, how I looked at my body.

So, by the end of the year, I was doing better physically and mentally. I wouldn't go as far as to say that I was a hundred percent happy, but I was trying, and I wanted to keep trying throughout the upcoming year. I was doing better, and I wish it'd stayed that way.

———— ⊂▦⊃ ————

On the morning of January 3, 2022, I was casually scrolling on my phone when I stumbled on the news that the Ontario government was going to make an announcement regarding possible new restrictions because of the nth variant of the Covid-19 virus.

Please don't close the gyms. I'm begging you, please don't close the gyms. Oh God, let them close everything else—restaurants, theatres, nail salons, everything else—but not the gyms, please. Please don't let them close the gyms.

The announcement came at 11 a.m., and they closed everything. Including the gyms. And my heart broke. I cried the rest of the morning. I cried the entire afternoon. I cried the entire night. The pain, oh, the pain...

I texted my older sister Sophie around 2 p.m. to tell her the news, mentioning how tired I was of living this way. It was 1 a.m. in China, where she still lived, so she called me when she woke up a few hours later. And I let it all out.

"I can't do this anymore. I am so tired of living like this. They've closed everything again, even the gyms. Going there is one of the few things that was getting me outside of my room, and it actually made me happy. Why is it that every time I find something that brings me just a little bit of joy, it gets taken away? Couldn't they have just further limited capacity at the gyms? To 5%, to 1%, I don't care. I am vaccinated. I wear a mask the few times that I get to go out. Why do I have to go through this again? It's minus fifteen degrees outside, and it's only going to drop lower. Is taking a walk in the freezing cold all I'm supposed to do to take care of my mental health? How am I supposed to keep living this? I have to work tomorrow and the rest of the week. How am I supposed to keep working, to keep talking to people like everything is fine? How strong can I be to always have to go through such things? Do I not get tired? Why can't I be stable? Do I not deserve it? Am I asking for too much? I feel so stuck. I feel like I'm in a prison. Even when I try to be positive when things aren't going well, there's always something that's going to come and tear me down. Now we're on lockdown again, and they say it's for three weeks; that's what they said last time, but then it lasted eight months! How do I know this time is different? I've been through this before. I've been through this a million times already, and I am so tired. I am tired of living like this. I can't do this anymore. I am tired of this life. I try to keep a smile on my face. I try to stay positive despite the challenges. But there's always going to be something that'll keep me in this infinite cycle. I can't do this anymore. I am tired."

My head was on fire, but I did not stop. Not until I sensed Sophie was starting to worry that I was going to hurt myself.

"I understand," she said shortly after, "but please stop crying like that. Please. I … I don't even know what else to tell you. I don't know what to do. If only I could visit to keep you company, even for a few days, I would. But even here things are complicated. Danielle, calm down, please. I know you've been through a lot. I can't imagine how you feel, but please don't do anything … don't think of the worst."

The words never came out of her mouth, but I knew what she meant. She didn't know I had *thought of the worst* earlier in my life. No one did. She'd never heard me cry *like that* either, not even in the summer of 2019.

I was sobbing. Nothing new for me—I'd been crying the entire day. But I think the sobs combined with nonstop talking was new to her. What I had never heard before was the powerlessness in her voice. She was stuttering at times, trying to find the words to calm me down. I felt bad for putting her through this and didn't want to scare her, so I tried to calm myself down. I wasn't going to do the worst, but I *was* tired of my life. I can understand that hearing me say it so many times in a single conversation may have been scary.

Sophie texted me the following days, more frequently than I was used to. Maybe she was simply checking in to see how things were going, or maybe she wanted to ensure I hadn't done *the worst*. She said I could call her at any time if I needed to talk or wasn't feeling well. She told me not to feel like a burden. And I cried. I cried because I'd never heard those words from anyone before. I cried because despite not saying, thinking, or writing it, deep down, I'd been feeling heavy. Heavy on her. Heavy on my mom. I could tell she was still worried, so I told her I was fine and doing better and better every day. Some days that was true; other days, I lied so she wouldn't worry.

Days went by, and I eventually got used to spending entire days inside my room again. I continued to work my two jobs and to design when I wasn't too tired or unmotivated. I started a new series to help me fall asleep at night, and sometimes I was on the phone with a friend. Some nights, I felt nauseous and dizzy, but it wasn't as bad as 2017 or 2018. Plus, I'd since learned to always keep mints or cough drops on my nightstand to help with the nausea just in case. I also dedicated some time to prepare for an upcoming interview.

On December 9, 2021, a recruiter from Accenture reached out to me about an analyst position that opened in a development program within the Interactive practice, with an early 2022 start date. I guess some companies really do keep candidates' information on file for future opportunities. I was very surprised, especially since the company hadn't given me the courtesy of a rejection email when I applied to the strategy development program back in September.

"Are you still interested in a role with Interactive?" the recruiter asked me after a brief introduction.

I'd never applied to Accenture Interactive. In fact, my cover letter was all about strategy consulting, though I did mention liking the opportunity to work on Interactive projects as well.

"I initially applied for a position in strategy," I responded, "but I'm open. However, I just started an internship that may turn into a full-time job."

"Oh, that's strange; it shows here that you applied to Interactive." She proceeded to ask questions about my current role. "Let me know if you're interested in learning more about this opportunity, and I can always give you a callback to discuss."

"Yeah sure! Thank you for reaching out!"

My guess is my application was rerouted because of my marketing degree. Accenture Song–at the time Accenture Interactive–is the firm's digital agency. Or God may have had something to do with it.

The recruiter called again on December 20th for an official screening, during which we talked more about the role, my experience, and the interview process. Moving forward, I would only need to do the final three interviews: a case presentation and two behavioral interviews. That is because I had already passed the initial digital assessment from my first application, which I didn't know because no one got back to me.

I was interested, but not really. First, my negative recruiting experience significantly lowered my interest in the firm, and second, I was tired of interviewing for jobs. I wanted to stay with Siemens, even if I didn't love my job, if that meant being stable for a while. Plus, I had a great manager. But at the same time, this was Accenture we were talking about. This was a *consulting* job we were talking about.

The mid-point check-in meeting with my manager at Siemens was two days later, on December 22, 2021. I told my manager I wanted to keep working at the company once the internship was over. He had hinted at this possibility during my interview, asking if I had a "hard stop" in February, or if I could see myself working there full time if the opportunity presented itself. I obviously said I would take that opportunity, but that was because I didn't have any other options. At the time, I wasn't thrilled by the job description, but I was tired of looking for jobs and tired of having only bits of work experience on my resume.

So far, I had a two-month internship at CIVC Partners, a six-month full-time work experience at Duff & Phelps, and an internship I got fired from after a month. I didn't include my time at The Peninsula Hotel because it was both too short (three weeks) and not relevant to corporate jobs. If I didn't stay at Siemens, that would mean yet another item on my resume that only lasted a few months, which recruiters would see as a red flag again. I wanted to stay somewhere for at least a year and finally show that I, too, could keep a stable job.

Unfortunately for me, there were no open roles within the Smart Infrastructure business unit or elsewhere at Siemens Canada that fit my profile. The open roles required an engineering or other technical degree, which I didn't have and had no interest in. My manager was happy to help me find something and started recommending my profile here and there within the company. As mentioned before, he shared my information with Siemens Advanta, but there were no available roles there, either. Plus, the North American Advanta practice operated in the U.S., and I didn't see myself starting yet another immigration process to go back to that country if I even got a job there.

It was frustrating because, again, I was tired. That is when I started considering interviewing with Accenture more seriously. The recruiter contacted me again in early January 2022 to let me know my virtual interviews would be on Friday, January 14th. So, as I put together my case presentation, I tried to reignite the flame I once had in my heart for Accenture and for Interactive. I was grateful to interview with the firm, but I can't say I was happy. At least not yet.

I had my interviews as scheduled that Friday afternoon. While I waited to hear back, my stomach was in knots. I wanted to believe that this opportunity hadn't showed up for no reason, but at the same time, I didn't want to hope and be disappointed again. Most importantly, I didn't want to have to look for another job and go through countless rounds of interviews. I had no Plan B. Staying at Siemens was no longer an option, but I hadn't been looking for another job either. So, I hoped but not too hard. I hoped, not excluding the possibility that I wouldn't get the job. I hoped but reminded my heart not to stray. I hoped and told God I would accept whatever outcome was on the other side.

The recruiter called me the following Monday, January 17th, with good news—I'd gotten the job! Another quick turnaround. I *could* believe it, but not really. I didn't think Accenture was too good for me; I just couldn't believe all that it took to finally get to this point. I was ... *happy*. But even more than that, I was proud.

When the recruiter hung up, I was overcome by an immense sense of pride, one that I was feeling for the very first time in my life. It didn't simply stem from getting a consulting job at Accenture. Not at all. It was the culmination of my efforts over the previous five years. The holding on when I wanted to give up. The fighting of mental battles. The pushing through the pain. The perseverance. The learning of the most important lessons of my life. I was proud of myself.

Starting that Monday, the only song I listened to was *I believe in You (Je Crois en Toi)* by Il Divo, Celine Dion.

The job was scheduled to start on March 21st, and it felt good not to have to worry about what was next. The only thing I was a little worried about was my pending application for a post-graduation work permit (PGWP).

The PGWP is similar to OPT in the U.S., but with notable differences.

For starters, the PGWP can only be issued once in a lifetime, compared to OPT, which can be done at every degree level earned in the U.S. For example, if I had gotten a bachelor's degree in the U.S. prior to my MBA, I would have applied for my first OPT after completing that degree and still be eligible for another OPT after my MBA. However, if I had done my master of marketing in the U.S., I wouldn't have been eligible for an additional OPT because both my MBA and master of marketing would be the same degree level. The next time I would qualify for OPT would be if I pursued a PhD.

Additionally, the EAD card for OPT was only issued for one year (but recall that STEM students could usually apply for a two-year extension). The post-graduation work permit, on the other hand, has a validity between one and three years depending on the duration of the program. A one-year program usually grants a one-year PGWP, and programs three years or longer grant a three-year PGWP. Sometimes, a one-year program can lead to a three-year PGWP, for reasons that are arbitrary. However, no degree of any length can lead to a work permit longer than three years.

And while neither the OPT nor the PGWP require a job offer at the time of application, the PGWP doesn't limit how long an international student can be unemployed, or the type of work they can do, and there's no trying to figure out a preferred start date. Perhaps more importantly, an international student may start working while their PGWP application is processing, as long as they applied when their study permit was still valid and respected a host of other requirements. As soon as a decision is made, they either continue working if the application was approved, or immediately stop if it wasn't.

The expiration date on my study permit was February 20, 2022, but as with the I-20, that date is not what determined the validity of my status. Because I completed my program in August 2021, my study permit became invalid three months later, in November 2021. I applied for my PGWP in October 2021, since proof of application was required before I could start my internship at Siemens (or any job at all). That document indicated I was eligible to work for any employer until February 20, 2022, or until a decision had been made, whichever came first.

I negotiated my Accenture compensation package and was able to increase my sign-on bonus to $12,500 from the initial $5,000 they offered. I negotiated the base salary as well, but the recruiter said it wouldn't be possible to get anything higher because the firm kept analysts at the same salary level. I was actually pleased to hear that, so I accepted the $75,000 annual salary.

By the time I received my final written offer on January 19th, I only had one month left on my work authorization document, with the job starting another month later on March 21st. Seeing that my PGWP had still not been issued and knowing that I would soon engage in background checks and employment authorization verification, it felt like Chicago all over again. This time though, I was less stressed out.

The Ontario government effectively lifted some restrictions at the end of January. As soon as I saw the good news, I texted Sophie to let her know. When I thanked her, I made sure she realized how much she had helped, how grateful I was that she was there for me. And when China entered a lockdown of its own a few weeks later, I made sure I was there for her as well. In the meantime, I went back to the gym. I also met some people who I sometimes went out with. I did my nails. I took care of myself physically and mentally as best as I could.

As mentioned previously, my last day at Siemens was Friday, February 25, 2022. My manager was happy about my Accenture offer, but knowing I wouldn't start until a month later, he offered to extend my contract. While I appreciated the offer and surely needed the money, I needed a break even more. I knew my new job would be more demanding, having signed a document agreeing to work in excess of regular work hours (9 a.m. to 5 p.m.) as part of my contract. In addition, I was going through other personal challenges, so I turned down the offer.

On March 1st, IRCC notified me that my PGWP application had been approved. It had a three-year validity. Again, I am not sure how or why that happened considering I had done a one-year master's program, but that was certainly the highlight of my day. I saw it as an early birthday gift.

Later that month, I went to a Service Canada location to extend my initial social insurance number, which was only valid until February 20th, based on my study permit. Now that I had a work permit, my SIN needed to be extended until the work permit's expiration in 2025. A few days later, I also applied for a new visa, because the one issued to me back in 2020 also expired in February 2022. Fortunately, unlike in the U.S., it is possible to apply for a visa from within Canada.

My visa was issued for the duration of my work permit.

CHAPTER 25

NEVER QUITE THERE YET

Date: 04/01/2022

~~Dear Heavenly Father...~~ Hey God, I hope it's okay if I just spend time with You here instead of reading the Bible. There are many things on my mind, but You already know that. Still ... I want to write here. But I don't know where to start.

~~Thank You for...~~ I guess first of all, I'd like to thank You for my job at Accenture again, even though my start date got pushed. I am also thankful for the fact that while I'm waiting to start, I at least have a part-time job to hold me up. But ... there is a "but." If I am being completely honest, I am a bit tired of how complicated things always seem to be in my life.

~~I am worried about...~~ It feels like nothing ever goes smoothly. It feels like nothing will ever go smoothly again, especially my moves. I know I may sound a little dramatic, but am I really? Have You looked at my past five years?

~~People I am praying for today...~~ Why can't I ever move without too much trouble? Why does everything in my life always have to be some sort of miracle? Is it such a bad thing that I also sometimes want a regular life? Please don't take this the wrong way.

~~Here's what's happening in my life...~~ If You have chosen me to do great things, I am very grateful for that and by no means am I trying to stop Your plans, but sometimes I get tired and I just want ... I guess an easier life? Just for some time? I know I don't understand it now, but I truly hope there is a good reason why things are happening this way. Also, constantly job-hunting for the past five years has been so tiring that I think I won't even last that long in the workforce.

~~I need...~~ Once more, I feel like what's going on right now with Accenture or my overall job and living situation didn't really need to be this way. I get it, maybe this is testing my patience and all ... but haven't I demonstrated enough that I can be patient? Why are there always setbacks and delays whenever I get closer to something good? Something that gives me a little bit of stability? What would have happened if I had started last week as initially planned? Is this even coming from You? If it is, okay, great, I don't want to derail Your plan. But why, God? Why always so much trouble? I just want sustainable stability.

~~Other things on my heart that I need to share with You, God...~~ If this is all a test, I'm sorry that I failed, especially on those first few days of getting the news. But God, can You really blame me? I always feel like I'm running a race with no finish line. I'm never quite there yet. Never. Will I get there, God? Will I even get there? If so, when? When is this over?

I had to move again, and this time, it took me by surprise. When I moved into the townhouse on Dalton Road, I signed a month-to-month contract instead of an annual or other longer term rental contract. The main reason was I didn't want to stay there very long, and I thought I wouldn't have to.

Back in August 2021, I thought I was going to get a job, hopefully in consulting, that would allow me to move again three or four months later into a studio, but preferably a one-bedroom apartment. I obviously did not share this with the landlord. Most landlords try to push for annual contracts, but this one didn't, which made me appreciate that place even more. What I didn't know, and what he didn't tell me, was why a month-to-month contract also worked for him.

"Have you found a new place yet?" Samir, one of my housemates asked, joining me in the kitchen as I was cooking dinner. This was sometime in late January 2022.

"Uhm… no…" Confusion was evident on my face. "Not planning on moving out anytime soon. Why are you asking?"

At that point, I truly was no longer planning on moving out anytime soon. Although I had found a new job, I wanted to save as much money as possible during the first few months and move out again sometime at the end of the summer as I had become accustomed to.

"Oh, so you don't know? The landlord is about to turn this thing into an Airbnb or something, and he needs everybody out by April," Samir replied.

"Wait, what?!" The knife made one last chop to the onions before my hand froze, and I looked up at him. "Are you serious? Well, he didn't tell me anything when I moved in, in August." I continued to chop the onions, confident that this news didn't apply to me. "Maybe that's just the first floor?" Samir's room was on the first floor.

"Yeah, I don't know, but rent prices are just crazy right now!" He laughed a little, scratching the back of his neck before heading back down.

I didn't think much of that conversation at that point, because the information had not come from the landlord himself. Even if that were true, it was probably only going to affect the people on the first or second floor. The landlord would've told me if it affected the third floor where my room was located. I was wrong.

A month later, at the end of February, two more roommates asked me the same question, and I kept hearing people talk about moving out soon. That is when I started taking the situation more seriously. I texted the landlord to ask, and he responded two weeks later in March, confirming that we all had until April to vacate the house. No formal notice. Not even an email. A phone call. Nothing. When I complained and reminded him that this was never communicated to me in any way, he said all he could do was give me until the first week of May, as renovations were scheduled for the second week. *Great!*

By then, I was more upset because the landlord hadn't given me proper notice. I didn't like the idea of moving again after finally accepting I would need to stay there longer than four months, but at the same time, I always considered that place temporary. This explains why I never took all my stuff out of the moving boxes. Well, seventy-four percent for that reason, and twenty-six percent because the room didn't have enough storage space.

I was upset, but grateful that at least this time I had a full-time job to help with my rental applications. By the end of April, I would've already worked a month at Accenture and would be able to show my two most recent paystubs required as proof of funds. I was also planning on saving most of those two paychecks (since in Canada, too, you're usually paid twice a month) so I could pay the first and last month's rent required almost everywhere. My sign-on bonus would also help with moving expenses, basic furniture and Wi-Fi setup, as I would no longer look for student housing or shared arrangements. Additionally, because I'd been focusing on paying off my credit card bill and making more consistent payments on my student loan, my credit score had improved. All of this even made me look forward to moving into a nice condo, now that I would be making enough money to afford that. Well, (wrongfully) ignoring my debt.

The background check procedures at Accenture started on January 24th, the Monday after I got my final offer letter. They were going to be performed by the same company who did my background check for employment at Siemens, so I was already familiar with their process. With Siemens, it took eight days to complete, but after two weeks of providing additional information for Accenture, my background check was still pending. I began to worry when by the end of February, nothing had changed. I made multiple calls to the company to inquire about any issues or additional requirements, until they told me they couldn't continue discussing my case and advised me to reach out to Accenture for any further inquiries. That is exactly what I did, but that too was a deadend. I didn't insist and tried to be patient instead.

On March 10th, I emailed the recruiting specialist with whom I was in contact regarding employment verification and other pre-onboarding tasks. My start date was just eleven days later, and my background check had still not cleared, so I wanted to know if that would affect my start date in any way.

From: *Me*
To: *Fernanda*
Subject: RE: *Update*
Date and Time: *3/10/2022 at 11:09 a.m.*
Hi Fernanda,

Thanks for the update. My initial start date is on the 21ˢᵗ. Will that change or will I still receive onboarding information in the next few days?

Thanks,

Danielle

From: *Fernanda*
To: *Me*
Subject: RE: *Update*
Date and Time: *3/10/2022 at 11:12 a.m.*
Hello Danielle,

Your start date is confirmed, and you should be receiving the onboarding information closer to your start date. 😊

Kindly,

Fernanda

The recruiting specialist's email reassured me, especially with that smiley face at the end. I was excited. The following week, I effectively started receiving onboarding information through the Accenture new hire portal. I alternated between completing the tasks there and touring apartments. For someone who wanted to take a break and recharge before starting a new job, I can't say I did much of that. But I wasn't going to complain. The tasks I was completing and the welcome package I received from the firm made me even more excited to start a few short days later. Plus, by then, I was an expert at moving, so no big deal.

———— ⟨☰⟩ ————

I spent the morning and afternoon of Friday, March 18th–the business day before my initial start date–touring several apartments and condos. Around 3 p.m., I was speaking with my last leasing specialist of the day. We were discussing the available units in the building when I received a call. Seeing that it was the Accenture recruiting specialist, I excused myself to take the call.

"Hi Fernanda! How are you?" I answered cheerfully. I thought she wanted to confirm that I'd received my laptop and login information, which were still on the way.

"Hi Danielle," her voice was low. "I wanted to let you know that, unfortunately, we're going to have to postpone your start date."

Wait, what? My shoulders dropped, and the smile on my face disappeared. I felt *something* on my heart. The pain, it was the pain. I paused before answering.

"Is it because of the background check?"

"Yes. It still hasn't cleared; they're still verifying your U.S. information."

"What's wrong with my U.S. information? What are they missing? I gave them everything I had. It's the same company that did my background check at my previous company where I applied with the same resume, and it didn't take this long. Is there something I can do?" I tried to contain my frustration, but I doubt I succeeded.

"Unfortunately, there is not. You will be starting on April 25th and your login information will be sent to you a few days before."

"April 25th?!" I exclaimed, surprising myself at how loud the words came out of my mouth. Until this point, I thought my start date would be postponed by a week or two, not *five*. "Can't I start earlier?"

"I am really sorry. I know you were excited to start, but that is the next available start date we have for analysts in North America." She did sound sorry.

I remained silent for a few seconds before sighing an "Okay," then we ended the call.

———— ⬦⬦⬦ ————

How am I going to find a place now? Everything is so expensive. Why are things like these always happening? I could have continued to work at Siemens. How could I have avoided this?

My new start date now almost matched my move-out date, which means I wouldn't have two paystubs. The most recent ones were from February when I still worked at Siemens, but that was too far back in time, and my part-time job didn't pay me enough to use it as proof of funds. Because I'd spent the past months repaying my debt and trying to improve my credit score, I didn't have much savings. My sign-on bonus was to be included in my second paycheck, so I wasn't going to get that in time either.

My move-out date wasn't going to change. My scheduled debt payments weren't going to change. My bills weren't going to change. The rental application requirements weren't going to change. The one thing that changed was what would've helped me have a smooth move.

———— ⬦⬦⬦ ————

"So, this is the one that goes for $1,850; it's the cheapest one we have available," the leasing specialist said as we entered a one-bedroom condo.

I'd been swimming in my thoughts on our way there, simply nodding or smiling or saying different versions of "Oh okay, nice." The condo *was* nice, but I couldn't focus anymore.

"I'm gonna take a look at the den," I said, walking away from the living area.

"Sure! Go ahead, take your time."

I wanted to leave. I wanted to be home. I wanted to be alone.

I rested my head and back against the side of the den opposite to the living area, so that the leasing specialist couldn't see me. I pressed my eyes shut, trying not to let the tears fall. I pressed my eyes shut, trying not to dive into my thoughts. I pressed my eyes shut and silently exhaled.

"This looks really nice," I cheered, once I finished *taking a look* at the den. The smile on my face was the size of my disappointment.

We toured two more units before I left. I knew this was pointless, but I had scheduled these tours and the leasing specialist had made himself available, so I wanted to make use of that time.

Sitting in the 511-Bathurst streetcar on my way home, I was looking out the window. Warm tears sporadically made their way under my mask, which I hoped covered my face enough to hide them. I cancelled dinner plans I had that night and told my friend I'd gotten sick. When I got home, the package with my Accenture laptop was waiting for me on the porch. I picked it up, then headed straight to my room. As I started writing in my journal, the dam that was blocking the rivers of tears failed under their pressure.

As years went by and my perception of what a "strong" person is shifted, I decided to no longer bottle my emotions (especially when I'm on my own). Instead, I feel them, as intensely as needed for as long as needed, until I am ready to get back up. So, I let the rivers dripping from my eyes run their course and flood my room.

"Unfiltered" was the title of the journal entry. No sugar-coating. No trying not to sound ungrateful. Just raw thoughts. I promised myself not to include that entry here, so you won't see it. What I can say is my thoughts weren't suicidal, but the running theme was that I was *tired of living my life*. I wasn't thinking about death or anything related to it, but I was … exhausted. I felt like I was never quite there yet.

I scraped some energy the days that followed to go out and continue looking for apartments. More than wanting to have a nice place with my own kitchen, I'd started looking at nicer apartments and condos because I didn't want to move again a year later. I saw the surprise announcement about my having to move combined with a new job as a chance to settle somewhere, sign a lease of at least two years, and finally get a sense of stability.

———————— ⌼⫘⊃ ————————

Rental prices had gotten ridiculously high across the city, but I was determined to get a studio apartment, even if that meant moving away from the downtown area. Unfortunately, it didn't matter that I had an offer letter with a somewhat high salary. Especially because it was dated January 19th, leasing agents wanted proof (paystubs) that I was getting paid that salary. I asked Fernanda to provide an employment verification letter confirming my new start date and the full-time nature of the job. I used that letter in combination with my offer letter in my applications, but it still wasn't enough. My applications were rejected, either from the lack of proof of income or because I didn't have enough money to pay for first and last month's rent. Some places required three to six months' worth of rent as a deposit to compensate for not having a strong application, but I obviously didn't have that money. I knew I was going to find something. I mean … I had to. But I was … exhausted. Nothing made sense.

What made even less sense is that my background check cleared on Wednesday, March 23rd, two days after my initial start date. Because it had already been postponed, starting earlier was no longer an option. *Great!* I thought about looking for another job, but I didn't have the energy for it and didn't know if I could find a job that offered me at least the same compensation as Accenture in less than five weeks. Even if I did find something, I would've still undergone a background check with no certainty on how long the process would take. This would only further delay my finally starting a permanent job I wouldn't need to leave after six months and further delay receiving my first paycheck. For these reasons, I decided to just wait.

———— ⬥ ————

On Thursday, April 7th, a student financial services representative at York University called while I was cooking breakfast. I didn't have my phone with me, so she left a voicemail. She wanted to inform me that my account balance was going to be transferred to a collections service if I didn't make a payment by April 12th, the following Tuesday.

My account was past due with a balance of about $49,000, including late fees and interest charges. Tuition for the MMKG program was $75,000 when I started in 2020, but the loan I got in June 2021 was $29,000.

My mom paid my tuition deposit when I got my admission offer in 2020 and made partial payments while I was in school. But since there was an unpaid balance on the account, it started accruing fees in addition to interest charges. I was aware of that, but the truth is I never looked at my account because it scared me. When I thought I was going to get a consulting job in 2021, my plan was to use my sign-on bonus to pay for part of that balance and save enough to pay off the rest.

Fast-forward to April 2022, my student account had been inactive for over six months, which is why it was going to be transferred to a collections agency if I didn't do anything.

Transferring debt to collections negatively impacts credit. It means the organization you owe money to writes off that debt from its books and transfers the responsibility to a third party to *collect* it instead. Once the transfer is complete, the collections agency reports the information to credit bureaus, which considerably lowers your credit score. That information also appears on credit reports to be accessed by lenders, landlords, or other interested parties. It remains on the report for seven years, even if the debt is paid off *after* it was transferred to collections.

After listening to her voicemail, I anxiously contemplated whether to call the representative back. But then I researched the impact of collections on credit and concluded now was definitely not a good time for my credit score to take a hit. So, I called, unsure how the conversation would go. I wasn't able to reach her but didn't leave a voicemail. Instead, I emailed asking if she could wait. I said I was about to start a new job and that I would use my sign-on bonus to make a payment, though it would only be partial.

She responded a few minutes later, saying she sympathized with my situation and gave me the option to do a ten-month payment plan. Under this plan, I would pay $5,000 on the 10th of every month, starting with my first payment on April 12th and the last one on January

10th, 2023. For every month I made a payment, she would remove my account from that month's collections list. However, my balance would still accrue fees and interest charges.

I was relieved but overwhelmed. The payment plan was a start, but I didn't know where I was going to find $5,000 in three business days, and $5,000 every month afterward. Once I started at Accenture, my monthly income was going to be less than $5,000 after tax and other deductions, so that even if I wanted to use it entirely for these payments, it still wouldn't be enough. And what about rent? My private student loan payments? Daily expenses? Life in general?

I didn't know what to do, who to turn to. I was overwhelmed, but my eyes stayed dry. If this was another test, I didn't want to fail it, so I resisted having negative thoughts. Instead, I did some more research. This time, I was looking for other lending solutions available to me, a non-Canadian citizen or permanent resident. Not many.

As a work permit holder, I was considered a temporary resident, which means access to credit and other lending opportunities was very limited. I didn't qualify for bank loans or lines of credit or peer-to-peer loans or other types of traditional personal loans. Especially with my limited credit history, existing student debt, lack of savings, and as a newcomer who had lived in the country for just over a year, but was about to move into a third place with no paystubs to prove that I'd be able to pay back any loan, my profile wasn't particularly attractive to lending institutions.

The only option I was eligible for was a subprime loan, which is what I applied for. I found an institution that approved me (almost immediately) for an $8,400 loan to be repaid twice a month for two years at an interest rate of 47%. *Forty-seven percent.* When the agent was walking me through the contract over the phone, she paused at the interest rate, probably expecting a reaction from me. I knew the interest rate was outrageous, but I needed the money. I let her carry on, agreed to the terms and signed the contract once she emailed it.

The funds were transferred into my bank account on Monday, April 11th. The situation was not ideal, but I decided to take it one month at a time, ignoring how close to the deadline I was yet again. At least now, I had enough money to cover both the $5,000 payment due the next day and my moving expenses, as well as the first and last month's rent for wherever I was going to live next.

If you're wondering how I got my PGWP, considering I owed money to Schulich, well, that's a valid question. Final official transcripts are required to apply for a PGWP and those cannot be delivered unless a student has paid tuition in full. But because of the pandemic, many things were not running as usual, including my school which was still operating remotely. All staff members were working from home, and official transcripts could not be issued. This was the case at many if not all Canadian universities, which the government was aware of. So, IRCC accepted unofficial transcripts in lieu of official ones, as long as students also submitted the required letter of completion signed by the school, confirming they had completed their studies.

As much as I hated the pandemic, I want to acknowledge that certain measures that were taken because of it have supported my immigration journey.

After more weeks of applying for and visiting apartments, I received the long-awaited approval for my application for a studio apartment. With this many applications, I was even more thankful for one specific difference between renting in Canada compared to U.S.: the absence of application and administrative fees.

For every application I submitted, I didn't have to pay any fees at all. In fact, some agents were surprised when I asked how much it would cost to submit my application and have it processed. They'd never heard of such fees; one called them "absurd" and "ridiculous." I don't know if I've ever agreed to anything more in my entire life. They needed to keep finding these fees absurd and ridiculous, so I stopped bringing them up. My rejected applications may have been a waste of time, but at least they weren't a waste of money.

The apartment I found was also in the Annex neighborhood, not far from the townhouse on Dalton Road, where I lived. I walked twelve minutes to Spadina Road to tour the apartment, appreciating being able to book movers for only two hours, including travel time, if my application was approved. As was the case in each of my previous apartments, this studio was drenched in sunlight. I was literally blown away when I entered the unit, my eyes immediately attacked by the downpour of sunlight coming through windows that covered almost an entire wall.

The apartment had a similar layout to my studio apartment on West Sheridan Road in Chicago. The kitchen was tucked away at a corner while the main room had enough space for a queen-sized bed, a chair or loveseat, a coffee table, and a potentially small TV stand. There was also a nook that I visualized as my home office. The unit was spacious enough to comfortably fit everything I needed while being small enough that I wouldn't need to buy a lot of furniture to make it feel like home. It also had a balcony with a good enough view of the CN Tower. The building itself was old with no amenities but was undergoing light renovation.

It was the only place that accepted my offer and employment verification letters as proof of income. The building was also running a promotion at the time for one free month (the first one) on a thirteen-month lease contract. And unlike at other places, I could move in a few days before my lease start date at no additional cost. The leasing agent also mentioned they had deals with major telecommunications companies for reduced prices on home internet packages. If you've heard anything about Canada, other than how much it snows there, it's probably how expensive Wi-Fi is. To top it all off, new residents were eligible for a $500 Presto card, the Ontario public transit card.

The catch? Well … rent was about $1,700, excluding utilities, for a unit in an old building with no amenities. Also, they didn't provide any sort of window treatments (which I later found out was not uncommon for Canadian apartments, a striking difference from what I'd seen in Chicago), and there was no air conditioning. This last bit did not bother me, but at that price point, I didn't expect having to buy additional appliances to keep my apartment cool during the summer.

I liked the apartment and wanted to live there. Most importantly, I wanted to be done with my apartment search. With my start date postponed, I wanted to have completed my move before starting the job at Accenture.

My rental application was approved on April 20th. The standard deposit of first and last month's rent was required, but with the promotion still ongoing, I only needed to pay for my thirteenth month—in this case, June 2023.

I packed my boxes and moved two days later, on April 22, 2022.

CHAPTER 26:

ALMOST THERE, I PROMISE

On the morning of April 25, 2022, I woke up, got ready, and sat in front of my laptop not very far from my bed. Because of the pandemic, the two-week new joiner orientation at Accenture was virtual instead of in-person in Chicago. I would have loved to take a trip back to the Windy City, but still, I was excited. I'll admit it that I was also glad to have moved before starting the job; I was starting to see that maybe part of the delay was to help me move without the added stress of an ongoing job. I settled into my studio apartment pretty well, ignoring the promise I'd made to myself to take it slow in furnishing the place.

The second half of 2022 was a little quieter. That summer was the first one in years I wasn't attending school, looking for a school, or wondering how I was going to pay for the next term's tuition. It was the first summer I wasn't unemployed and looking for a job with pending or overdue bills, though I was deep in debt. The first summer my lease wasn't expiring, forcing me to spend weeks looking for my next place to live. I'd finished school with no plans of going back anytime soon. I had a full-time job with benefits. I was living in a studio apartment I could afford. I had a valid work permit and visa. I'd never had all these things at the same time. I got a taste of stability, and it tasted good. I was so grateful.

Despite the financial struggle of trying to repay the expensive loans I'd recently taken, my Schulich tuition balance, and my private student loan, that summer felt like a break.

Part of my financial struggle stemmed from no longer having supplemental income when my part-time marketing contract ended in June. But to be honest, I didn't manage my money very well. I had more income thanks to my Accenture job, but I had so much debt that even my entire after-tax monthly salary couldn't cover my monthly debt payments. By the time my $12,500 sign-on bonus reached my bank account, it was down to around $7,000 after income tax deductions.

I spent part of that bonus on my debt and on furnishing my apartment, and I saved the rest. I didn't travel or go out too often, but I spent money on items I didn't necessarily need. And I did all of this without ever checking my bank account and without a budget in place. I certainly knew better, but the truth is I dreaded looking at my finances. Seriously. I would get stomach cramps only thinking about opening my banking app. I let my bank account be charged for bills and other payments, vaguely estimating the amount available and crossing my fingers it would cover everything. If not, my next paycheck would certainly help. I paid off my credit card in full, but my credit utilization was very high.

As I struggled to make my $5,000 tuition repayments due every 10th of the month, I found myself applying for two additional subprime loans at similar outrageous interest rates. I cried the day I applied for the third one. By then, I'd used all my initial savings toward debt repayments, in an attempt not to borrow more money. But again, even without using a single dollar of my income, it wasn't enough to cover just debt. More debt meant more monthly payments going toward paying back money that I borrowed to pay back debt. I felt trapped. By the end of that summer, I could no longer make the monthly payments to Schulich and wasn't going to borrow even more money. Still, I didn't want to *look*.

Making a budget would force me to face my financial reality, which I was both scared and ashamed of. But after months of avoidance, guilt, and anxiety, I finally sat down to look. And it *was* scary. My credit score had plummeted. I thought about getting another part-time job, looked for freelance opportunities, but I didn't find anything. Now, I only looked for about two months, from late August to October, but the truth is I was exhausted. I wasn't thrilled at the idea of working extra hours on something I probably wasn't going to enjoy in exchange for money that would all go into debt repayment. Plus, although I had now looked at my finances, I still didn't have a plan. So, I decided to start by getting the money I had in order; I drafted a budget, identifying costs to cut down. I then made a loan repayment plan for all my loans and was going to start by paying off the most expensive ones (those with the highest interest rates).

Not everything I spent money on was futile, though. I already had plans to do so as soon as I got a full-time job, but certain events, combined with writing this book, prompted me to start therapy consistently for the first time in June 2022. I began working through past trauma during my weekly sessions. I learned more about myself through therapy and other mental health resources and books, all of which encouraged me to try new things, some of which I initially imagined myself only doing once my dream came true. Consistent with my goal at the beginning of the year, I decided to not wait until I had friends to enjoy life. I had met some people along the way, but I no longer wanted to wait until anyone was available to do the things I wanted to do.

———— ⚷ ————

By the end of 2022, I'd gone through lows, but many highs as well. I got to experience what, to me, was sustained stability, despite my massive debt. I was proud of the work I was doing on myself. I had a budget and a plan for paying off my non-Schulich debt. I was grateful for the people I'd met and the positive experiences I'd had. I'd gotten even closer to God. But as we were nearing the end, I realized this was it—the end of a year I told myself I would not have any goals. The end of a year when I had no goals and yet accomplished a lot. The end of a year I felt peace and freedom in not striving to achieve anything.

Now that it was almost over, what was the implication? I feared setting goals again. *What if I get hurt again?* But how much longer was I going to live a life without objectives? *What am I supposed to do? I am so scared*. This fear kept me up at night.

As usual, my end-of-year ritual happened on the last day, around 10 p.m. I wrote pages and pages on how grateful and how proud of myself I was for all the things I'd accomplished on many levels, despite not having specific goals at the beginning of the year. One highlight was being able to do my nails all year long. At 11:30 p.m., I was still writing; so was I fifteen minutes later.

It is now 11:45 p.m., and as the year closes, I first want to thank God for it, but also recognize that I've been worrying about goal-setting. After living an entire year with relatively no goals, I know this is not necessarily how I need to keep operating. Now that it's time to set goals again, I am scared. Scared of not accomplishing them and having my heart broken again. Scared that they won't be aligned with God's will and, therefore, not materialize. Scared to be broken and hurt again.

Also scared about my dream. Although I am no longer obsessed with it, I still have the desire for it to come true. And I need an end to The Book; I am open to anything else, but I would be lying if I said it wouldn't hurt if God's plan didn't include McKinsey or BCG.

As I enter 2023, I pray that He continues to be with me and guide me, that He watches over my family and us all on this earth, that He shows me His dreams and plans and goals for me.

Sometime in December, I evolved from writing to-do lists in my planners to using a project management tool, and it absolutely changed my life! I still don't understand how I was able to function without such a tool. In addition to not having goals for 2022, I tried to live outside of this book and barely worked on anything related to it. But for 2023, I wanted to start writing again or work on my website or the million other things I didn't realize I still needed to do. So, instead of writing goals in my journal, I upgraded to writing them in my project management tool. They looked *beautiful* in there. And this time, they were more reasonable and specific.

Now, that doesn't mean I wouldn't write in my journals anymore. In fact, I'd bought two more! I told you, stop counting. I was excited for the year ahead but took with me the newly found ability not to obsess over things I couldn't control.

———————⊂▥▥▥○—————

One of my goals for 2023 was to get rid of my subprime debt. Two of the three loans I'd gotten at the same financial institution had been consolidated into one. By January 2023, I had a balance of about $8,000 of subprime debt, spread unevenly across two accounts. My goal was to use the refund I'd receive once I filed my taxes in March to pay off part of that debt, then once I became a permanent resident, I'd apply for a line of credit and use it to pay off the rest.

Although a line of credit is a form of debt, this type of product has significantly lower interest rates. The only thing is, as a work permit holder whose immigration status was temporary, I did not qualify for bank loans or lines of credit. My priority as a new permanent resident would be to apply for a cheaper loan to get rid of the more expensive ones. At least this way, my monthly debt payments would be lower.

I applied for permanent residency in November 2021; in September 2022, IRCC approved my application, and the last step was the issuance of my permanent resident (PR) card. I still didn't have it by the end of 2022, but I knew—or at least I hoped—I'd get it within the first few months of 2023. And I did.

I realize I am casually mentioning this important milestone right now, but believe me, it was a big deal. Both in September 2022 when I got the approval email and on February 13, 2023, when I received my PR card. There were many tears of joy, celebrating the culmination of my arduous immigration journey.

Things didn't quite work out the way I had planned. They worked out even better in terms of repaying my subprime debt. While I did use my tax refund in March 2023 to pay off part of my debt, a line of credit isn't what covered the rest.

Remember how my previous landlord basically kicked me out of his townhouse with no formal notice because he wanted to renovate the place and turn it into an Airbnb? Well … I filed a complaint with the Landlord and Tenant Board (LTB) in May 2022, after multiple failed attempts at recovering my deposit. It took *a little bit* of time, but the LTB got back to me in March 2023, almost a year later, with a scheduled hearing. By then, I'd been rewatching *Suits* for weeks, so I was basically a lawyer. Getting help at a legal clinic probably also helped. My landlord's representative and I settled in mediation for $5,500. I asked for more money during the negotiations, but I internally set $5,000 as my threshold, knowing that was the balance on my subprime debt after using my tax refund.

So, at the end of April 2023, when I received the last installment of that settlement, I paid off the last portion of my subprime debt. And oh, how I felt free! I still had a long way to go with my other debt, but it almost felt surreal to no longer spend hundreds of dollars every two weeks toward debt payments that barely touched the principal and stifled my savings goals. It felt great!

Unfortunately, that feeling didn't last very long.

———— ⚬◊⚬ ————

My father passed away in May 2023, and I needed to get home to Cameroon as soon as possible. I didn't have enough savings to pay for my almost $3,000 flight ticket, so I resorted to debt again. Thankfully, by then, I was already a PR and had already gotten approved for a line of credit. Though I wasn't thrilled to borrow money again, at least it was cheaper this time.

What thwarted my efforts to get out of debt was having to put another $3,000 on my line of credit to come back to Canada at the end of the summer, because I couldn't board my plane back. I was unaware that with my passport, I needed a transit visa if my flight stopped in two or more countries of the European Union, so I didn't pay too much attention to layovers when I bought my first ticket. I was just looking for the cheapest option (yes, the cheapest), regardless of the number of stops. My flight home only had one layover, but my flight back had two: one in France and one in Amsterdam. That cheapest option turned out to be very expensive. By September, I had accumulated another $6,000 dollars in debt. *One step forward, three steps back.*

The gratefulness in my heart when I got back to Toronto in August 2023 contrasted with my feelings toward my new debt. Despite the bleak circumstances, it felt good to be home after two and a half challenging years in Canada. It felt good to eat good food and be around family and friends. This time was a much better experience, though I was still battling acne and scars. I was also practicing communicating boundaries and feelings, and my friendship with Olivia and Cedric had been restored.

And then I came back to my apartment. *My apartment.* When I left for Yaoundé on July 2, 2023, I didn't realize how it would feel coming back to Toronto on August 8th.

I remember being on the phone with a friend that day; I hung up when I entered my apartment building on Spadina Road, so I could comfortably bring up my two suitcases before calling him back right away. But when I entered my studio apartment, I was overcome by something I cannot describe. I was back in my apartment. *My apartment.* One that I paid for with my own money every month. One that was already mine before I left and would continue to be mine long after my return.

I stepped into the middle and stood there, awe-struck. I looked around. Everything was right where I'd left it a month earlier. No need to pick up any boxes from a storage unit somewhere far away. No need to pack anything to move somewhere else. I just needed to unpack my two suitcases, shower, and grab something to eat in the neighborhood I already knew. I took pictures of an apartment I'd been living in for more than a year. *Oh God, thank You so much.*

This was on top of breezing through airport security two hours earlier. For the first time, I entered a country that wasn't mine without border officials asking for my immigration documents. In fact, I hadn't interacted with any border official at all; I simply scanned my passport and PR card at one of the self-serve kiosks, and off I went. No questions asked. No proof of anything to show anyone. I was so grateful.

———— ⌐⧯⊃ ————

After a year and a half at Accenture, I was ready to leave. Actually, I'd been ready to leave for months. Yeah, I know, I know, but hear me out.

In addition to everything that happened between when I first applied for a role at the firm in September 2021 and when I joined in April 2022, I realized after a few months of working at Accenture Song that it didn't live up to *my* expectations from a diversity, equity, and inclusion perspective. Out of more than four hundred employees across Canada, I was one of a handful of lower-level Black employees, many of us hired in 2022 or later. And things didn't improve as you moved up the ladder.

Then there was the salary discrepancy I noticed among people working at the same level. You may remember when I negotiated my offer in January 2022 that the recruiter insisted she could not raise my base salary because the firm kept every analyst at the same salary *level* (not salary *band*). A few months after joining, I learned of someone who was offered the analyst position that year with a higher base salary and sign-on bonus. I checked with the other two Black analysts, and it wasn't any of them. In fact, one was offered an even lower base salary. Overtime, and with everything else I was seeing, hearing, and experiencing, I gradually detached from the company until I focused on strictly doing my job.

What really made me want to hand in my resignation was my experience with requesting a paid leave of absence (LOA). When my father passed in May 2023, I was already burnt out from work, in addition to the nights spent working on book-related activities. I was mentally exhausted. When I shared the news about my dad at work, my people lead—or PL as we called them—told me I could request a paid LOA under short-term disability insurance, which covers physical and mental health.

A PL at Accenture was a kind of career counselor, a higher-level employee the firm assigned to every employee for guidance throughout their career at the firm. Depending on the nature of the work, a PL may or may not have been an employee's direct manager.

The LOA request process involved some paperwork, including health forms to be completed by a family doctor. The firm also assigned me an LOA advocate to help throughout the request process. I filled out the paperwork, met with the LOA advocate, submitted my request, then took the five paid days of bereavement Accenture offered.

When I returned to work a week later, a case manager from the insurance company contacted me regarding my LOA request. She asked various questions regarding my health, my work, and the reason for requesting an LOA. Many of the health-related questions were hard to answer because I wasn't suffering from a physical illness. When she asked for proof that I could no longer perform my regular duties at work, I told her I was facing mental health challenges, and that although I could still type on a computer, I couldn't focus anymore. At the end of the call, she told me my request would be denied because she couldn't verify, based on our conversation and the forms I submitted with my request, that I was unable to continue working. The fact that I'd returned to work from my bereavement leave also seemed to indicate that I was doing just fine. I was never told it would help my case if I wasn't working. I wasn't back to work because I wanted to.

I discussed this with my Accenture LOA advocate, who told me I could appeal the decision by submitting more supporting documentation, which I did. While I waited for another decision to be made, Accenture was going to pay me my regular salary during my leave; if my request was denied again, I would need to pay that money back.

I came back from Cameroon on August 8th but returned to work on August 21st. For the remainder of the month and into September, I went back and forth with my LOA advocate and the insurance case manager, trying to get the appeal approved. The main issue was that they didn't find enough evidence that my mental health condition prevented me from performing regular work duties, despite the additional health form a doctor filled out or the very event of my dad's passing that triggered my LOA request. At last, I asked my LOA advocate to drop the case. I was tired of dealing with it.

Dropping the case meant paying back to Accenture any salary paid to me while I was on leave. But to do that, a family doctor needed to fill out yet another medical form. The issue with these forms is that they cost money–$100 on average–and were not covered by insurance. Additionally, they needed to be completed by a family doctor, not just any doctor. If you've heard anything about healthcare in Canada, other than the fact it's "free," it's probably how hard it is to find a family doctor who accepts new patients. When I first brought one of these forms to my family doctor, he told me he didn't typically fill them out but would do it as an exception, considering my circumstances. Lastly, most questions on these forms focused on physical health.

I asked my LOA advocate if I couldn't repay the money without a medical form, since my request had been denied again anyway; I shared how much financial and emotional stress this process had been causing me. He kept repeating it was standard Accenture process. I spoke with my PL at the firm several times, but she too was learning about this process and recommended I involve HR. That was a dead-end, too. Everyone advised me to get the medical form filled out and get it over with.

I spent the afternoon of Sunday, October 8th walking around Toronto, going from one clinic to another, trying to find a doctor who would agree to fill out my form. This was after weeks of calling doctor's offices and being denied, setting up virtual appointments that were ultimately cancelled when the doctors saw the type of form I needed them to complete. Finally, one doctor agreed to do it on that Sunday. I submitted the form to Accenture the following Monday.

The last step was to repay the $3,500 the firm paid me during my leave. By then, I had under $3,000 in total savings. I asked payroll if I could do a payment plan instead of them recouping all the money at once, but for tax reasons I didn't understand, they told me a payment plan would involve paying back the gross instead of the net amount, or about $4,800. The only way to repay the net amount was to make a single wire transfer. Well … I suppose I was lucky they at least gave me until December 15th—a month and a half later—to make the transfer.

While enduring all of this, with a desire to leave the company already ingrained in me, I tried to believe things were happening this way for a reason. Talent discussions for that year's promotion cycle had taken place in September. I had a very strong story and excellent feedback, both from my project team and from the client. Despite my desire to leave, I'd been performing very well. So, maybe at the end of all this was a promotion. I held on to that hope.

My people lead recommended me for promotion during talent discussions; she was confident, but cautious. I was confident, but cautious. If I got promoted, I would use my bonus to pay back the money I owed to the firm so my savings would remain untouched. If I got promoted, I would update my resume and leverage my Senior Analyst title when applying for new jobs.

The results came out on November 6th. My PL set up a meeting with me and as soon as I saw her face on the Teams call, I knew.

"I am so sorry, Danielle," she started, "You unfortunately didn't get it this time."

I didn't say anything.

"I was also shocked when I got the news." She broke the silence.

My people lead and I had a good relationship; we'd been working on a promotion since she became my people lead a year earlier, so I believed her when she said she was shocked.

So, what was the point of all this? I kept asking myself, phasing out of our conversation. When I refocused, I asked for feedback.

"Is there anything I could've done better? What did I miss?"

"Literally nothing," she responded. "This is not a reflection of your work; you checked all the boxes and were marked for promotion. It's just been a shitty year, and very few people are getting promoted."

I silently nodded.

Our meeting didn't last very long. I left the call wondering what I was still doing at that firm. I later found out several analysts who had joined after me got promoted. While their deserving of a promotion is not up for debate here, I have wondered what ultimately gave them the upper hand if I had, in fact, checked all the boxes. Well … I suppose I was lucky I still got a $2,000 bonus later that month, even though leadership had announced that people who stayed at the same level wouldn't receive a bonus or raise.

That bonus came out to $1,400 after taxes, which I used on November 30th with a portion of my savings to pay back the money I owed to the company. This is the day I wished I could also have handed in my resignation. But I had higher bills and expenses thanks to inflation, and, now, even less savings. I wanted to take some time off, but even that was not possible.

When I submitted my request for paid leave of absence back in May 2023, it was for two months. When it was denied for the second time in September, I retroactively applied most of my paid time off (PTO) and sick days to cover part of what was now going to be an unpaid leave, saving the rest to take off during the holidays. I did it so I wouldn't have to repay two months' worth of my salary to Accenture.

I couldn't quit with less than $2,000 in savings, and the only way to accumulate PTO and continue paying my bills was to keep working at Accenture. I felt like a literal slave.

———◦———

Since coming back to Canada in August, I'd been feeling my mental health degrade by the day. I could almost feel a unit of joy leave my happiness tank each passing day.

I am not depressed. I am fine. I am not depressed.

I repeated these words to myself on certain days, trying to push away what I felt was coming. But soon enough, I was back in an all-too-familiar mental state. By November, I was crying every single day of every single week. The financial struggles, the nonexistent social life, the unhappiness at my job and the frustration of not being able to leave yet, the impending winter with its cold days and longer nights, the holiday season that reminds me every year of how much I miss home ... I was exhausted.

It was one of those times when I wanted to disappear. Not die, just disappear for a while. I wasn't active on social media and hadn't posted anything in a few years, but I deleted my apps again. This time, I kept WhatsApp so I would still be reachable and TikTok so I could laugh.

"Wow, that's rough," a friend from Accenture commented, when I shared with him part of my LOA chronicles during one of our calls, together with the news about not getting promoted. "How are you managing?" he asked.

I didn't know how to respond. The truth is, I hadn't thought about it before he asked the question.

"I'm not managing. I don't know ... I'm just trying," I responded with a shrug.

"No, kudos to you; I know some people who wouldn't be able to handle it."

"I mean ... I rely on my faith too," I said, "but if I'm being honest, that has also been confusing. I thought on the other side of my LOA struggles was a promotion, but now I've been asking God what the point of all this was."

"Yeah, no I completely get it. I hope you figure it out soon. But you're really strong."

What I was, was tired. I don't know how I continued to work every day and do all the things I was doing. I woke up in tears every day and went to bed in tears. I was now infrequent at the gym, and it wasn't because of a lockdown. Cooking was no longer something I enjoyed, but a weekly chore I did on Sundays to prepare for the upcoming week so I wouldn't be tempted to order in. I went through the same routine every week, only looking forward to my next paycheck.

God undoubtedly sustained me because there's no way I could have gone through that time on my own, but at the same time, I wondered why things were happening this way.

"I'm at the end of my rope. I can't do this anymore. I am so tired," I told Him on days I could still pray for myself. Other days, I said a version of "from my tears to Your ears." I didn't want more strength, but I went to Him for rest.

And there I was, that Thursday afternoon, chatting with someone who thought I was strong for handling only a fraction of a story I shared with him. This had happened before, with different people. Although I've learned overtime to see these interactions as opportunities to share how I rely on my faith, I have also wondered why God allows so much more to come at me, if in fact a fraction of my experiences is already overwhelming.

———————⌇————————

The year 2023 was not all painful, though, which I confirmed when I did my year-in-review later in December. I accomplished a hundred percent of the three goals I set at the end of 2022, two of them earlier than initially planned. And I did even more.

One notable achievement, and the highlight of my year, was incorporating DCTMWT / RDRMDA. This was not my plan; it was never one of my goals. Once more, it's not that I didn't think I could own a company one day; I had just never planned for DCTMWT to become one.

I had no clue *Dreams Come True, and Mine Will Too* would evolve from a thought to a mantra to a book to a hashtag to brand to a company.

I cried tears of disbelief on the day I received the incorporation documents from the Canadian Revenue Agency. After taking a break in 2022 and spending the entire year outside of this project, I spent a lot of time in 2023 preparing for the book launch, whenever that was going to happen. I didn't write much; I focused on building The Business and finalizing The Website.

Switching from pen and paper to a project management tool was instrumental in this process, and I am so glad I did. Again, this doesn't mean I ditched my journals; I still wrote in them throughout the year and as I reflected on it.

At the end of 2023, I was still easing back into the habit of setting goals. Keeping in mind everything I'd learned and experienced over the past few years, I cautiously wrote a few goals, labeling anything I had no control over as a wish. I also intentionally left some blank space, both in my journal and in my project management tool, for God to accomplish any of *His* plans for me.

Anything I could never imagine or plan for myself.

Big or small.

CHAPTER 27:

DREAMS COME TRUE, AND MINE WILL TOO

I imagined all possible endings to this book, except this one. This is because, in all my imaginary scenarios, I ended up receiving an offer from McKinsey & Company, or at the very least, one from the Boston Consulting Group.

Sometime in 2021, I decided not to pursue Bain & Company, the other Big 3 (MBB) management consulting firm. My decision had nothing to do with ranking or prestige and everything to do with my personal and professional goals. Back in 2021, when I was striving to make my dream of working in consulting come true, I networked with professionals across different firms and attended as many events as I could.

Starting in the summer of that year, I had coffee chats practically every other day, a handful of which were with Bain consultants. Through those chats, my research, and the YouTube videos I watched, I realized Bain focused too much on private equity for my liking. It seemed most consultants did a rotation in the firm's Private Equity Group, which wasn't something I was interested in. Though my internship at CIVC Partners back in 2019 in Chicago sparked a flame in my heart for the world of finance, it also made me realize private equity wasn't something I wanted to do, at least not in the long run.

Bain is also a smaller firm, the smallest of all three, with a smaller global footprint. This is important because I often thought about relocating somewhere else in the world, and if I was going to do that through my job, I wanted to be at a company that gave me options. I specifically wanted to relocate to Africa, where Bain, at the time of writing, only has one office, compared to BCG's five and McKinsey's seven. And while I still lived in Canada, I didn't want to remain in Toronto. Again, Bain only has one office in Canada, compared to BCG's three and McKinsey's five. For these reasons, including reduced interview prep time in case my applications were successful, I decided to focus on McKinsey and BCG, with a strong preference for McKinsey.

⸺◦⊸◦⸺

In some of my imaginary scenarios, I started this chapter directly with an excerpt from my McKinsey offer letter. I went on to describe how much I'd dreamed of seeing the word "Congratulations!" in the subject line of a McKinsey HR email. I said how proud I was to have completed the multi-step recruiting process and passed all four case interviews. I explained how it felt to have finally made my dream come true, the dream I'd had since I was fifteen years old, the dream I did not give up on even after multiple failed attempts.

Depending on the year I imagined these scenarios, my feelings toward making this dream come true were different. Each year, a little less intense.

In 2021, specifically before October, realizing this dream would have been absolute bliss. I would've arrived at what I considered at the time to be my destination, or at least some version of it. Becoming a management consultant was the ultimate goal; it was my life's purpose. Everything after that was an add-on. I would've made a LinkedIn post sharing that my dream had come true and that I'd written a book about it. I would've attached a picture of me next to the McKinsey sign at the office, followed by two pictures of my book.

In 2022, I was on a break from setting goals and was trying to live outside of that dream. However, whenever I thought about it coming true, it was still bliss, but a toned-down version of it. I would be happy, but happier to have learned the biggest lesson of my life. At this stage, I would essentially be glad to have a job that afforded me a better lifestyle and helped me pay off my debt as quickly as possible, while still helping those around me as best as possible. I would've made a LinkedIn post somewhat similar to the one I would've made in 2021, noting that while I was proud of that accomplishment, I was prouder to have realized that there is more to life than accomplishing my goals.

In 2023, when I imagined receiving an offer from McKinsey, I knew I'd be ecstatic, ecstatic to be free. Especially toward the end of the year, most of that ecstasy would have come from finally being able to launch this book together with my very own company. I'd be happy to finally show the world what I'd been working on for years: the website I'd built, the book I'd written, the company I'd started. I'd be excited to now have the freedom to share my experience doing all this on my very own blog, focusing less on the fact that I was now a consultant. In fact, I was prepared to write something like this:

"While I may have passed all stages of the interview process at McKinsey, nothing compares to what I have built with my own hands."

I would've meant it. I even looked forward to the day I'd write it in this book. I secretly wondered what that would look like, especially to the firm. And I secretly didn't care. My LinkedIn post would be the announcement that I'd written a memoir, and I'd mention somewhere that I had accepted an offer to join McKinsey. There would be no picture of me next to a McKinsey sign on the post, though I'm sure I would've taken some for myself.

In 2024, I'd be grateful that McKinsey had saved me from Accenture, though I worried that my experience there would be the same or worse. Receiving an offer from the firm would still be a dream come true, but it would be an old dream, one that gradually mattered less until it didn't matter at all. My LinkedIn post would be a similar book launch announcement to the one I described for 2023, except this time, I would have made it a few months after joining the firm. The post would focus on my book, with a quick update that I had now been working at the firm for a few months.

In all these scenarios, however, I would've been proud of myself. I always looked forward to the day I'd tell my mom that my dream had come true, even when it became an old dream.

As I began to care less about McKinsey and more about my own company, I worried about how I would balance the two if I received an offer. I knew my workload would be significantly heavier, but I was starting to feel less comfortable with the idea of prioritizing my consulting job over my other passions. And if there were ever a choice to be made, I would've chosen my passions.

On the other hand, I was trying to hold onto the remaining flame of the bigger fire that used to burn for that dream. If I was still going to pursue it and go through the extensive interview process, I needed a certain level of emotional attachment.

But how did I get here? How did the flames go out?

Let's go back to March 2023. Now that I was nearing my one-year anniversary at Accenture, I began to look for ways to exit the firm, specifically to join McKinsey. I requested coffee chats with consultants on LinkedIn and registered for networking events hosted by the firm. I only had one coffee chat, though, partly because not everyone accepted my requests, but mostly because my goal wasn't to get a referral. I genuinely wanted to get a better understanding of what it was like to work at McKinsey, now that I had matured professionally and experienced another kind of consulting environment.

Additionally, I had asked God to help me make my dream come true without a referral if it was His will. Although I was no longer obsessed with this dream, I was still very passionate. This was a year earlier, on April 25, 2022, the very day I joined Accenture. I'd written my request in one of the two new journals I'd bought that year. So, as I looked for ways to leave Accenture, I wanted to be careful not to overstep or go too hard. More generally, though, asking for referrals was never something I felt comfortable doing, despite all the advice and culture around looking for jobs.

The McKinsey Black Network hosted an event in Toronto on June 1, 2023. I applied to attend, but by the time I did, the in-person phase of the event was already at capacity. However, the recruiter sent me the link to the virtual phase, which took place later that evening. At the time, all the flames of my dream of working there were still burning in my heart, and I could feel them rise and oscillate as I listened to people share their experiences. It also helped that most speakers were Black.

I stayed in touch with the recruiter after the event, reaching out to her on LinkedIn the next day to request a chat. She was happy to help, but introduced me to another recruiter who, in her opinion, was better suited to answer my questions. A few email exchanges later, that recruiter recommended I reach out again in September, as the firm had already recruited their 2023 class and wouldn't be looking for experienced professionals until the fall. I was disappointed, especially because I was ready to apply.

June 5th is when I was planning to apply. I was at my desk, working from home that Monday like every other day of the week. I'd uploaded my updated resume and filled out the application form. Just as I was about to click on the "Submit" button, I heard the notification sound of a new message on LinkedIn. Because that tab was already open in my browser, I instinctively moved my cursor over to see who had messaged me. It was the McKinsey recruiter, responding to my connection request from three days earlier and offering to introduce me to someone else. I let out a disappointed sigh.

"Does that mean I can't apply now?" I asked, slightly turning left to face the cross on my nightstand.

More than wanting to make that dream come true, I needed the money. My dad had recently passed, and I was going home to Cameroon soon. A little extra money wouldn't have hurt, especially with all that still needed to be done. A flame or two went out. Still, I put a reminder on my calendar to reach out to the recruiter again once I was back in Toronto. I closed the McKinsey Careers portal tab without applying. I went on with my day, the taste of disappointment souring my mouth, only partly offset by the realization that timing wasn't ideal.

Back from my leave of absence in August 2023, I was now dealing with everything I've shared earlier about my experience requesting a paid LOA at Accenture. When I reached out to the McKinsey recruiter again a month later in September, she informed me that their hiring priorities had shifted, and that they wouldn't be recruiting again until the new year. More flames went out. By then, I was fighting the mounting depression I'd been sensing since my return to Canada, combined with my LOA struggles with Accenture. I held on, telling myself these things were happening for a reason. That reason, I thought, was so I could get a promotion at Accenture and leverage it when I applied to McKinsey in 2024, though I was gradually losing interest in the firm.

You already know I did not get promoted at Accenture and had to pay my salary back to the firm in November 2023. I was tired of the corporate world and wanted to be free from it. McKinsey wasn't much of a dream anymore, more of an escape from Accenture, a source of higher income that would take care of my shaky finances and give me permission to end this book and finally be free. All these delays and challenges progressively wore me out. There was only one flame left.

On January 8, 2024, I diligently followed up with the McKinsey recruiter as the task on my project management tool reminded me to do. I didn't get a response until February, and the response was that the firm hadn't yet figured out their hiring plans for experienced professionals for the year. Meanwhile, stories of layoffs across companies–including McKinsey–were swamping my news feed.

The last flame wasn't burning very high anymore, but I needed it to still be alive. If it almost went out, I rekindled it with the memories of my fifteen-year-old self who dreamed of becoming a consultant, or with memories of my time at The Peninsula Hotel in Chicago, arranging accommodations for the consultants who were flying into the city and dreaming of being in their shoes one day. I rekindled the flame with memories of my failed attempts at getting into Monitor Deloitte, the firm's strategy consulting practice, or with the prayer I'd made to God who was now probably just testing my patience, or with the reminder that I still had three case practice sessions with my coach from the consulting bootcamp I'd enrolled in, in 2021, having used only three for interviews I never had. I rekindled the flame reminding myself that projects were more varied and short-lived in strategy consulting, or with the fact that I needed more money, or that I couldn't possibly finish this book if that dream did not come true.

All of this even though it was now absolutely clear to me that my only dream was to become an author, to hold in my hands the fruit of my labor: this white-and-yellow book with my name on it.

In addition to layoff news, several times over the first months of 2024, I came across horror stories from former McKinsey employees recounting how the firm had forced them out. Although their stories were disheartening, I convinced myself that either my experience would be different, or I'd be detached enough from the company not to care. I didn't intend to stay there very long, anyway. I wanted to pay off my debt, learn a few more things to help with my other professional goals, then leave. I didn't believe in being happy or fulfilled in a corporate environment anymore. I'd rely on my revived passion for writing and my other non-work passions for a sense of fulfillment, holding onto my job just enough until my debt was paid off.

Yet, I wondered how some people seemed to be happy and fulfilled at their jobs. The posts I saw on LinkedIn contrasted the stories I read on my news feed. Employees being proud of and celebrating their employers. Employers being proud of and celebrating their employees. Even some of the people I had coffee chats with seemed to genuinely enjoy their work and be happy at their firms. *But how?* I wondered. I wanted to experience that, but at the same time, I was too tired and hurt.

I'd already vowed to myself that 2024 would be my last time going after a consulting job; I didn't want my entire life to revolve around it. If this old dream didn't come true in 2024, I'd simply move on.

By February 2024, I just wanted a new job. It didn't matter which one, as long as I got to make my *real* dream come true.

The flame was out.

———— ⬦⬦⬦ ————

In the second of the two new journals I got in 2022, I've been writing monthly recaps since the beginning of 2023. They're usually not very long, depending on how I feel. I reflect on the month that just ended and look ahead to the next, noting any goals I want to achieve. Now, these are less accomplishments than simple reminders. They range from trying a new recipe, to getting a ticket to a concert, to filing taxes, to resigning from a job, or, you know, to finishing writing a book. Could be anything, really. I learned in 2022 that I will always need some sort of structure and organization in my life, but I can make things lighter and hold loosely to my plans.

Once more, and even if by then I'd already written a good portion of this book, the purpose of these reflections wasn't to serve as content. However, having recently re-read what I wrote about April 2024, I'd like to share it here.

May 1, 2024, at 12:10 a.m.

April Recap

So, Andrea Bocelli's concert was absolutely amazing, and I am so glad and grateful I went. It was the best night of my life! Also got to see a bit of Montreal and confirmed I definitely want to move there.

I resigned from Accenture, and it's been so liberating, although also very scary since I don't have a new job yet. This week is my last, and I feel great! I don't know ... it's weird because I'm excited but also very scared at the same time. I don't know what I'm doing or where I'm going next (still haven't applied to McKinsey and now even wondering if I will, if I even still want to work there...).

I told myself I was just going to trust God completely this time, no matter how blurry the road ahead looks. Whatever happens with my job or living situation, I am sticking by His side.

I feel ready to launch The Book and The Company.

I cut my hair on April 9th.

I want higher quality things and am tired of lower quality stuff.

I'd like to renew my wardrobe and learn to do my makeup.

I don't know what I'm doing.

Looking Ahead...

I don't even know what goals to have for May. Everything is a blur; the road ahead is completely dark. I'll continue to apply for jobs, but also chill a little bit.

— Trust God.
— Go back to therapy?

Yeah … I ended up resigning from Accenture without a new job. I made that decision on February 23, 2024. Nothing special had happened that day; I'd just been thinking, taking into consideration how unhappy I'd been feeling and how long I'd be able to keep waiting for any new job to come save me. Not very long.

My mood was starting to affect the quality of my work, and I was starting to resent the firm, which I didn't like. That apparently wasn't noticeable, as evidenced by the praise and positive feedback I received from the client and the manager on the project I was working on. More than that, my manager was now looking to train me to replace her, considering the progress I'd been making. The Manager level at Accenture was four to five levels above Analyst. I'd also shared with my manager during one of our calls that I didn't feel like I was growing anymore, having spent a year and a half already on that single project. While that was the truth, it certainly wasn't complete.

Additionally, it was now talent discussions season again. The fiscal year at Accenture ran from September to August of the following year, with the regular promotion cycle starting in September with talent discussions and ending in December when the results would take effect for people who had gotten promoted. Some years, mid-year promotions also occurred, with that cycle starting around March and ending in June.

In both instances, each employee and their people lead needed to prepare for talent discussions several weeks ahead. Part of that preparation included documenting self-reflections, gathering feedback from colleagues, managers, and client account managers, crafting a story that people leads would share during discussions on behalf of their counselees, and writing priorities for the upcoming year or season. Starting fiscal year 2024, each employee needed to have a reviewer for each of their priorities.

Mid-year talent discussions and promotions (or simply "mid-year," as we called them) were not guaranteed. If they were going to take place, we learned a few weeks earlier, with the expectation that we had already started preparing. Writing priorities for the year, on the other hand, was a requirement whether or not talent discussions took place.

So, as we came back to work in January 2024 after the Christmas break, my people lead and I started to discuss mid-year. Many times, she asked me to start gathering feedback and go into our HR portal to write my priorities for the year and assign reviewers. Each time, I pretended to have been so busy it'd been difficult to get to it. The truth is, I just didn't care anymore. Plus, I didn't like this new way of policing people's goals and priorities. I certainly didn't need it.

One afternoon in February, after weeks of avoiding that exercise and with the deadline approaching, I finally opened the HR portal to reflect and write my priorities for the year. I looked at what I'd written a year earlier and a few months earlier for the September 2023 talent discussions. There were priorities related to client work and internal priorities outside of client work. I had accomplished all my goals and more. I'd performed well above my level, yet that had gotten me nowhere.

I didn't have any other priority than to leave the firm. I couldn't write that, so I didn't write anything. I didn't reflect, didn't request feedback. Instead, I let the deadline pass. Whatever trouble that would get me into didn't matter to me. It couldn't possibly be worse than what I had endured so far. Around this time is also when I learned about analysts who had joined the firm after me and had gotten promoted.

My PL was eager to get me promoted, but that didn't matter to me anymore. Back in November when she shared the disappointing news of me not receiving a promotion, she'd suggested we could even try for a promotion two levels up next time. I was already unsure then of how feasible that was, so when she confirmed two months later that I would be going for senior analyst (one level up) instead of consultant (two levels up) for mid-year, I wasn't surprised. But with an MBA, another master's degree, and now almost two full years of continuous experience, I knew I was worth more than that senior analyst position. But even if it were possible to get promoted to an even higher level, possibly even the highest, that wouldn't have changed a thing. There was no title and no amount of money that would've convinced me to stay at Accenture.

I wanted to leave. I *needed* to leave. So, I left.

That Friday of February 23rd, when I decided to leave Accenture, I told myself I'd put in my resignation in April, giving a month's notice instead of the typical two weeks. This was in part because I wanted to free myself from the burden of carrying that decision until the last minute, while my performance expectations would remain the same or be even higher, and in part out of respect for the manager on my project. Although my experience at the firm wasn't great, I did enjoy, to a certain extent, the project that I was working on. It taught me a lot about digital product management, which was now an appealing career option. I also appreciated my manager's guidance and involvement in my professional growth.

I'd been wanting to move to Montreal since the summer of 2023, for no other reason than to experience a new city. I hadn't experienced half of Toronto, but I was already craving something new. When I applied to McKinsey, I thought to myself, I would select Montreal as my preferred office location, assigning ninety percent to that option and the remaining ten percent to Toronto on the application form. And if I got the job, I wouldn't have to worry about expenses related to my move because the firm would provide a relocation bonus in addition to the sign-on bonus.

I'd never been to Montreal. I used my trip to go see Andrea Bocelli there in April 2024 as an opportunity to also feel the city. My friend Michelle from Accenture gave me a tour of key sights of Montreal. We ate great food and braved the rain to walk around downtown, the Old Port, and Westmount. I had fun. By the end of my three-day stay in the city, I was sold; I was going to move to Montreal, and hopefully I'd get a new job to help with moving costs.

Moving to a new city wasn't the only change I wanted to see in my life. Especially as I entered 2024, I wanted to practically have a new life, and this wasn't the new year effect. I was just tired of everything. I mean … I even cut my hair and changed my nail shape from coffin to almond! That is a big deal!

My last day at Accenture was May 3, 2024, and I still felt good that day about my decision to leave as I did on February 23rd, possibly even better. It was a mix of excitement and freedom, but also deep fear of the unknown. As days and weeks went by, it became a seesaw of emotions. Some days I was riding the highest highs of excitement, while other days I was in the deepest depths of fear.

One night, I was at my desk working on my resume for my imminent job search. I updated my Work Experience and Leadership sections, ensuring to quantify my achievements and noting the results each time, as I'd been taught since my first year in the U.S. I wrote and rewrote bullet points, highlighting my accomplishments over the last two years at Accenture and over the last year volunteering in an executive position at a non-profit organization. I noted any accolade or special recognition for any project I'd worked on. These accomplishments, especially those outside of work, weren't something I was doing to specifically show on my resume. I genuinely enjoyed what I was doing.

Once I completed the update, I zoomed out of the document to look at it in its entirety. I was proud of myself. Truly. I stared at the file for a few more seconds. All these numbers. The efficiencies I had helped create. The objectives I had helped reach ahead of schedule. The events I had run and the events I'd been a speaker at. And yet there was so much more that was not on that one-page PDF document. Still, one question kept crossing my mind: *Am I finally enough?*

I finally had two years of continuous work experience, displayed on a results-driven resume. Was that finally enough? Would recruiters now care less about my employment gap? Was I finally competitive enough? The words escaped my mind and came out of my mouth: "Am I finally enough?"

———— ⌇⌇⌇ ————

Now that I wasn't waiting for McKinsey anymore and with my recent interest in product management, I was looking and applying for product manager roles. I had reached out one last time to the McKinsey recruiter on April 8th, who let me know the firm still hadn't worked out its hiring plans for experienced professionals for the year. I wasn't going to wait around until it did, especially now that my motivation to join the firm rested entirely on following through with an old dream and checking that box in my journals. But even as I was applying for product management roles at small and large companies alike, I was struggling to find attachment to any of them. After two months, all my applications had been rejected. I was unfazed. The very process of looking for jobs already required too much energy from me; the only thing that kept me going was my financial obligations, which I thought a lot about.

Something else I thought a lot about was God's approval. Having given my dream back to Him in October 2021, after trying with all my strength to make it come true but failing, I wanted to make sure I was not releasing this book prematurely. As trying and frustrating as the delays were, I was going to wait until He gave me the green light to proceed, however long that took. But with the evolution of my dream, it became increasingly unclear what exactly I was waiting for.

At around 10 p.m. on Sunday, May 19th, I sat in silence on my bed to think. I wasn't feeling very well that night. My heart was heavy with confusion about my next steps. I had about a month's worth of savings with no more income, but instead a burning desire to publish a book and move to a new city. The fire from my old dream was completely out, but I was starting to wonder if I even still wanted to find a job, considering how detached I felt from everything else. I thought God's green light to finish writing this book would come in the form of an offer letter. But if I wasn't passionate about anything anymore, then what was I waiting for?

I began to imagine different scenarios in which I could publish this book. Waiting to receive a consulting offer was definitely off the table. Waiting to receive a product management offer or something similar was probable, though I wouldn't be entirely fulfilled. And how about not waiting for any offer letter at all? Tears rushed down my cheeks as soon as I put myself in this last scenario.

"But how?" I asked God. "This doesn't make sense! I've already quit my job without a new one. I still need money to pay the bills. And what about my debt?"

I was now sobbing.

"I am so scared, I am so scared," I kept repeating. "I've never done this before; please don't leave me alone. Please don't let go of my hand. I am so scared."

————— ⬦ —————

The following Thursday, on May 23rd, I woke up with the same heavy heart. I wasn't well, and this time, I took out one of my journals to write. I picked the one in which I first started writing again five years earlier, after my prayer journal. I wrote about how confused and scared I was, and how a McKinsey or other job offer may have been a security blanket, how unsure I was that I'd be able to take care of myself without a steady paycheck. I wrote three full pages. Before closing the journal to put it back in my drawer, I mindlessly flipped through the pages until I stumbled upon one of the first entries I'd made about dreams; it was the one from July 7, 2019. That entry had stayed with me since the day I'd written it, a subtle reminder of what I was working toward. I didn't remember it entirely, but it was there, somewhere in the back of my mind.

I shared it earlier in this book, but here is an excerpt again:

That was the "I'm scared" part. I will say though (or rather write) that while I've been thinking about life and dreams and how some people get to make theirs come true and others don't, I realized I could/should have a different approach when it comes to my life and my dreams. Rather than just feeling sorry for other people all my life and thinking about how unfair it is, I should be thankful for the position I'm in, for every blessing and opportunity that comes my way. I want to realize how blessed I am to be able to do certain things, and I want to go after my dreams as long as they align with God's plan.

If He wants me to be a consultant, I will do everything in my power (with His help of course) to achieve that. At the end of the day, what's the point of living if you do not accomplish God's purpose for you? So, I want to do that and help people around me (and even those who are not) to the best of my ability. If I am blessed enough to be in a good/comfortable position in my life, if God allowed for my dreams to come true, why not share the proceeds with the people I share the gift of life with? That's what I want. Yes, life is unfair, but I don't want to just sit around complaining about how unfair it is and not realize what I could be doing with what I personally have and try to make someone else's journey on earth a little more enjoyable.

As soon as I read the words "and even those who are not" relating to people who aren't around me, tears once more rushed down my face, denying me any chance of holding them back. They were hot and wouldn't stop flowing. I remembered myself writing these words in my Chicago bedroom on South Morgan Street. I remembered how determined I was to make my dream of working in consulting come true, confident that it was what I'd been created to do. I remembered visualizing myself back then as a consultant, first at Deloitte, then at McKinsey. I was smart, well-dressed, and confident, going from one city or one country to another, advising companies on their next move, helping them through whatever dilemma they were facing.

I always thought the version of myself who had written those words in her journal wouldn't forgive her older version for not following through with her dream. I always felt like I needed to make that dream come true out of respect for my younger self, even if I did something else later.

The next paragraph in that journal entry was this one:

I really hope, (?) however, that my purpose is to become a management consultant. I hope my older self looks back at this journal and cries because she has accomplished/is accomplishing her purpose. I hope she cries as she remembers this day and can't believe she's now working her dream job, all while helping anyone that needs a little push in their life. I hope I become what I was ultimately created to be. 🖤 🖤

Five years later, in May 2024, I had no job and had never worked at Deloitte or McKinsey. I wasn't crying because I had accomplished my purpose. I was crying because I had let go of what I once thought was my purpose. And I wasn't sad. I'd let go of my old dream but hadn't realized I also needed to give myself permission to move on.

I wanted to hug myself from July 7, 2019, and tell her how grateful I was that she'd written those words. I wanted to hug her tight and let her know her passions had evolved, and that her own words are what eventually set her older self free.

I couldn't do that, so instead I pressed my closed journal to my chest, one arm over the other, my hands squeezing at the corners, my eyes letting the tears wash away the old, my heart grateful to finally be free. I was now convinced this was God's green light; I'd felt it. I thanked Him for it in-between sobs.

On May 23, 2024, I dreaded what lay ahead but was excited as well. I was ready to embrace the unknown.

Once I calmed down, I unsubscribed from all my job search alerts. I then opened my journal again to my most recent entry and wrote:

Maybe it was never about management or strategy consulting. Maybe it was never about Deloitte or McKinsey. Maybe my purpose isn't to be a consultant. Maybe The Dream is simply The Book. Maybe The Book is about <u>me</u>.

Dreams Come True, and Mine will Too.

I am going to be an author.

CHAPTER 28:

CONTINUING THE JOURNEY

Oh, hey! Today is Friday, July 5, 2024, and it's about 9:30 a.m. as I am writing these words. I am sitting on the balcony of my one-bedroom apartment in downtown Montreal, looking out to a city already buzzing with activity. It's a bit loud, so I have my noise-cancelling headphones on. I could go back inside where I won't hear much of what's going on outside once the balcony door is closed, but I'll have the entire eight months of winter for that.

My rental application for this apartment was approved in April—when I still had a full-time job—and I moved in last week, on June 24th. I'd hoped to receive or negotiate a relocation bonus as part of a new job offer, but with or without a new job, I was going to move to Montreal. So, without a new job offer, I started selling some of my furniture; on the weekend preceding my move, I packed everything else into boxes and suitcases.

I handed the boxes to the long-distance movers I had booked for the morning of June 24th. At 11 a.m. that day, I headed to Union Station to take the 11:32 a.m. train to Montreal. At 11:31, I was running on the platform, hauling my two suitcases and bags, watching as the crew were closing one door after the other.

A few minutes earlier, at the station, I'd been trying to redistribute the weight of my luggage. My large suitcase was overweight, while my carry-on was already full. The lady at the station wouldn't let me board the train, so I frantically looked for anything I could move from one bag to the other, or anything I could carry on me.

"You have four minutes," the lady at the station said, a reminder I might miss my train. At last, one of her colleagues came to rescue me. He affixed a **HEAVY** tag on my large suitcase and helped me close it. He ushered me up the stairs and onto the platform, aware that the train was about to depart. I was running but didn't know what car to board. I would've checked my ticket, but I couldn't find my phone. It wasn't in my pockets or in my handbag.

"Hurry!" a crew member screamed when she saw me on the platform. "What car are you on?" she asked. "I … I don't … car number 4!" I screamed back. This was the car I was on in April, when I took the VIA train to Montreal for the first time. I knew there was a chance I could be wrong, but that's all I had. Both times I had booked economy, and I knew I wouldn't get my $200 back if I missed this train.

"Ooh … right on time!" another crew member told me with a smile, as I lifted my suitcases up the stairs to car number 4. The lady on the platform helped me push the larger one. "This is heavy!" she exclaimed. "I know, I'm moving," I responded apologetically. She entered the car, lifted the stairs, and closed the door behind her. Several seats were still empty in the car, so I picked one by the window. I pulled out my phone, which I managed to find hiding at the bottom of another bag I was carrying. I was right in thinking I may have been wrong. My car was number 7. Still, I stayed there on seat 6A on car number 4, trying to collect myself before the passenger whose seat I'd taken boarded the train at the next stop.

After about five minutes, a slight shiver ran through my body before tears rolled down my cheeks on their own. I wasn't sad. Just barely realizing I'd almost missed my train to a city I was moving to without enough money or a new job. My back and knees hurt from stooping and crouching and bending and packing all weekend, and my arms hurt from carrying boxes and bags and suitcases. My head hurt from operating on little sleep; I was also hungry, though I was glad I'd gotten a Chick-Fil-A chicken sandwich one last time before leaving Toronto. Most of all, I was grateful to be on that train. This was one of those times I wished I didn't have to do it all on my own; regardless, I was proud of myself and grateful to be where I was. Plus, my friend Michelle had volunteered to help me unpack the next day. I wiped my tears, then headed to car number 7, leaving my suitcases in car number 4 to retrieve them once we arrived at Gare Centrale de Montréal.

----- ⚞⚟ -----

My apartment is beautiful. The building itself is beautiful. It has all the amenities I've ever had, and the ones I've never had. It has a pool. And a sauna. A gym and a yoga room. A sky lounge on the forty-sixth floor, and more. I take the elevator up to more than twenty floors before reaching mine. My apartment has a kitchen island and smart appliances. There's also a washer and dryer. My bedroom is big enough to comfortably accommodate a queen-size bed, and the walk-in closet leads to the bathroom, which can also be accessed from the main room. The rent is all-inclusive.

At my Toronto studio apartment on Spadina Road, the rent had gone up every year, reaching $1,825 in 2024 from $1,675 in 2022. I paid all bills separately, including laundry, and my building had no amenities. Adding everything up, I was paying close to the $2,100 I am now paying for my one-bedroom apartment in Montreal. More importantly, my new apartment has an AC and heating system I can control. I am no longer at the mercy of any roommate or centrally controlled temperature system. This means as soon as the first leaf turns slightly red at one corner, I'll turn the heater on in my apartment. And if it falls to the ground, then I'll know a snowstorm is coming, and I will dress accordingly.

Thank you for my apartment hotel, I've been telling God since moving into this apartment. In many ways, the building feels like a hotel; from the large lobby to the amenities, to the signage—including apartment numbers—to the lighting, finishes, and fragrance throughout the building, it all feels like a hotel. And I am grateful to be here.

I am also happy to report that I accomplished my two goals for May 2024. If you're reading this book, it means I did, in fact, trust God. At the time of writing, a professional is proofreading the first twenty-seven chapters of this book. I have also shared the news about my writing a book with close family and friends and have put in motion the many launch-related activities that had been on pause. And despite the initial hesitation expressed with a question mark at the end of the second bullet point in the Looking Ahead section of my April Recap, I went back to therapy. My hesitation stemmed from no longer having an income now that I'd quit my job and no longer having access to benefits. Going back to therapy would mean paying the entire cost out of pocket. I went back to therapy and paid the entire cost out of pocket, and I am glad I did.

At this point, you're probably wondering how I did all this considering I didn't have much savings and had no source of income. Well, that's a valid question or concern. When I said I only had a month's worth of savings, I was talking about liquid assets; in this case, cash. For most of my time at Accenture, I'd been saving for retirement using a registered retirement savings plan (RRSP), contributing a few hundred dollars every month that were invested in financial markets.

An RRSP is a retirement savings and investing account that residents of Canada–including international students–can use to prepare for retirement. To be eligible for an RRSP account, a resident (permanent or not) must have already filed an income tax return. The account is registered with the Canada Revenue Agency and provides certain tax advantages, as long as the money is not withdrawn before retirement[4]. Contributions to an RRSP can be made before income tax (directly from a paycheck) or after, and they are generally invested in financial assets.

Some companies contribute to their employees' retirement accounts by matching their contributions up to a certain amount. Accenture matched contributions up to 6% of employees' salaries for those who had been at the firm for at least one year, so I chose to make pre-tax contributions my RRSP. I started investing for retirement in December 2022, a few months after reviewing my finances. For the first five months before my first anniversary at Accenture, my retirement contributions were deducted directly from my paycheck but

---

4   Canada Revenue Agency. "Registered Retirement Savings Plan (RRSP)." Government of Canada, 15 Jan. 2024, https://www.canada.ca/en/revenue-agency/services/tax/individuals/topics/rrsps-related-plans/registered-retirement-savings-plan-rrsp.html.

were not matched by the firm. As soon as I became eligible, I updated my contributions to take advantage of the employer match.

I didn't intend to withdraw money from my RRSP this soon or at all before retirement, especially knowing the tax implications of doing so. But that's all I had. I wasn't thrilled to request the sale of my assets for the money to be transferred to my checking account; I'd been enjoying watching the numbers go up every few months, glad to be contributing to my future, even if my current financial situation didn't look great. That said, I also recognized that things could have been different, and I could have had nothing to fall back on. So, despite feeling like I had taken five steps back in my financial journey yet again, I was grateful I even had money invested somewhere. Balancing all my commitments over the past month has been tough, but it is not my first time. Each time, God made a way. And if He is with me this time like He was before, then I want to believe He won't have a problem giving me another $10, 071. 33. Well, after penalties, that amount decreased by $2,000; I also know I'll need to report it as income next year when I file my tax return, so it'll be taxed as such.

I may be in a new apartment in a new city that feels like a new country; I may be starting something new in my professional life, and I may have a new haircut and nail shape, but this is not a new beginning. I am continuing the journey.

It's the journey that began in March 1996 when I was born in my parents' car, eager to finally taste the authentic version of fried plantain. I spent the first twenty-one years of that journey (or technically, 20 years, 11 months, and 12 days) in my home city Yaoundé, Cameroon, before heading to Chicago, Illinois, in February 2017 to pursue a dream I'd had since I was fifteen. It's the same journey that brought me to Toronto, Canada, in December 2020 in pursuit of that childhood dream.

That journey took me to Punta Cana, Dominican Republic in March 2024. After years of hardships, many during which I did not celebrate my birthday or was alone in my room during the holidays, I wanted to do something special for my twenty-eighth birthday. I'd started planning for it about a year earlier, in April 2023. This was three months after becoming a permanent resident of Canada, and shortly after paying off my last subprime loan installment, using the settlement money I'd gotten from my landlord at the hearing with the Landlord and Tenant Board.

Now that I was a Canadian PR, I could travel to certain countries without applying for a visa. I checked the list of those countries and started planning from there. I also opened a separate high interest savings account in which I would put money every month starting in May. When my father passed away that month and with everything I went through in the second half of 2023, I almost thought I'd need to cancel my trip.

I arrived at Serenade Beach & Spa Resort on March 17th around 10 p.m. Punta Cana was fun. This was one trip I wanted to have, and one birthday I wanted to celebrate on my own. Even if friends or family were available, I would have still gone by myself.

I swam to my heart's desire. I ate breakfast, lunch, and dinner I didn't have to cook for myself. I walked along the beach in the morning and watched the stars appear and disappear at night. I had cocktails by the pool. I learned to dance bachata on a boat ride to Soana Island, possibly the most beautiful place I'd ever visited. I rode a horse along the beach, a light dew caressing my cheeks, my eyes marveling at the turquoise water and the beauty of nature, my mind wondering how it felt to live like this every day. I'd taken with me the camera I'd bought in the summer of 2022, when I decided to try my hand at photography. I took pictures of the white sand, the blue sky, the clear water. I took pictures of the sunset. I tried mofongo for the first time, which reminded me a lot of food back home. I practiced my Spanish, though I soon realized how different what I knew was from what they spoke there. I met new people, though most were from the U.S.

I was grateful.

On the morning of March 21, 2024, seating upright on my bed in my hotel room, I was crying tears of joy for the first time in twelve months. I was supposed to do my usual morning prayer, but I just didn't know what to say or how to say it.

"From my tears to Your ears," I said at last, remembering these same words I'd been saying months earlier when I was at the end of my rope.

The pain that you've been feeling cannot compare to the joy that is coming.

I believe You, God.

I spent seven days in Punta Cana and named my trip *Seven Days for Seven Years*. I wasn't just celebrating my birthday; I was celebrating myself for enduring the seven hardest years of my life.

Back in Toronto, I bought myself a slice of chocolate cake at the grocery store after church, together with a few candles. I spent the day doing regular Sunday things and once the night had fallen, I took out my slice of cake and placed it on my coffee table. I planted two candles in the cake, lit them up, and turned the lights to my studio apartment off. I sat on the rug by the coffee table, then sang happy birthday to the rhythm of my sobs.

I wasn't sad. I was grateful and proud of myself; it'd been quite a journey! I made a vow to myself, then blew out the candles. This was my first time blowing out birthday candles since 2016, when I celebrated my twentieth birthday back home with my family. I vowed to myself that moving forward, I would always celebrate my birthday. I would do so in whichever way possible, regardless of my circumstances, financial or otherwise. At the very least, I would buy a slice of cake from the grocery store and use the remaining candles from that day. Now, I just needed to finish my cake and continue the journey by following through on my decision from February 23rd to quit my job at Accenture once I was back from my trip.

It's the journey that has now brought me to Montreal, about to make a dream I didn't know I had come true after working on things I had never planned for myself. As I edited this book again over the past month, I realized it truly wasn't about strategy consulting. I am glad to have now at least tried most of the things I once postponed to when that old dream would come true.

———— ⌁ ————

I have learned and grown a lot on the journey so far, but in many ways, I am still the same. As I became more interested in mental health, started therapy in 2022, and continued to educate myself on the topic, I discovered I was a highly sensitive person (HSP). Yeah, I was shocked too; I would've never guessed! After years of believing I was inherently flawed, it was truly refreshing to learn about the positive aspects associated with high sensitivity. I learned it isn't just about feelings or emotions, but that it also plays a role in character traits such as integrity.

I also continue to attend Catholic church every Sunday, though I have formed my own beliefs on certain topics and no longer take part in certain practices. I continue to build my relationship with God in my own way, cautious not to compare my progress to anyone else's or be influenced by it.

As of October 2022, I have a new nose piercing. An old video of myself I watched that year inspired me, and I remembered how much I loved my nose rings and how good they looked on me. Nothing happened when I turned twenty-five, so I don't know … maybe I'll stop wearing nose rings when something magical happens the day I turn thirty.

An update from when I was twenty-five is I will no longer take the CFA. There's obviously nothing wrong with the exam, and I still have a lot of respect for charterholders, but I now have other interests and passions. Speaking of which, I have come to terms with the fact that I am a person of different interests and passions, many I know will continue to develop along the journey. To the extent possible, I will pursue each one, regardless of the outcome.

I continue to write my thoughts and feelings in my journals, as well as my dreams and plans and goals and wishes, careful not to hold them too tight. I have a new journal. If you're counting, you're probably at eighteen million, four hundred and seventy-six thousand, nine hundred and thirty-two. No kidding. My new journal is a hardcover, my first one since I was a child. The embossed triangle design gives dimension to the otherwise matte black cover. A turquoise light subtly illuminates a few triangles on the front. The journal is sturdy but smooth. Its pages are lined but not dated, and there are no prompts. On the back cover, at the bottom left, there's a logo; it reads #DCTMWT.

I don't know where the journey will take me next, but I know it'll end on the day God unilaterally decides it is time we meet. It'll happen after I have accomplished everything on His checklist for me and with no intervention on my part.

———— ⬥ ————

Our time together in this book is now coming to an end. When I first imagined closing this book back in 2021, I looked forward to writing about how everything had changed and how happy I was now that my dream had come true. I thought my skin would show no sign of ongoing or past acne; my body would be toned all around from my multiple trips to the gym every week. My debt would be paid off in full or in large part thanks to my sign-on bonus, my salary taking care of the rest soon after starting my dream job. My social calendar would be filled with trips and outings, and I would have found my purpose. A kind of happily ever after.

Three years later, things are looking *a bit* different. My skin has made tremendous progress, but it is far from perfection; I have learned to love it as is. My body has changed overall, and I have actually gained a little bit of weight. I am still adjusting to these changes, conscious of my history with body image, and appreciating the fact that I am now a twenty-eight-year-old woman. In doing so, I try not to compare my body to what it looked like when I was twenty-two years old in Chicago; I was certainly skinnier back then, but I was also depressed and unhealthy. I am a beautiful woman; this is an accurate statement, regardless of opinions. We've talked about my finances. And although my social life has improved, my calendar isn't quite filled with trips and outings yet. This book might be part of it, but I'm not sure yet what my purpose is; I do know what it is not. I suppose I will figure it out somewhere along the journey.

What I didn't consider, and what I didn't know in 2021, was how transformative writing this book would turn out to be. I didn't consider how proud I would be of the work I would do on myself and the person I would become. I didn't consider the skills and talents, the other passions and interests I would discover. I didn't consider how much the pain I'd felt at varying sizes and intensity over the years had satisfied my longing for relating to and understanding people's experiences and how it would continue to do so.

One thing that has remained constant since I began writing this book is my desire for you, my reader, to pursue your dreams regardless of your circumstances. As you do, I hope you hold on to them tightly enough to persevere through challenges, but loosely enough to let go and embrace those that better suit your journey.

It's 10:04 p.m. on July 8, 2024. I am sitting at my desk, looking at the triangular wooden sign on the table, the one I got for $3 the first time I went to Target in Chicago.

They absolutely do.

I was convinced the night I started this book, and I am convinced again tonight as I end it:

Dreams come true

And *yours* will too.

Believe.

POSTFACE

I am done striving. To be seen, to be heard,
to be valued, to be recognized.

I am enough.

THE END

This is the end of this book,
not the end of my story.

ACKNOWLEDGEMENTS

To the One without whom this book would not exist. Oh, God, thank You so much for this gift. I couldn't imagine when I started working on this project how much of a gift it would be, how much You would transform me through it. I don't know where to start to express my gratitude, and words will never be enough. I am so grateful for the journeys and for Your presence all along; You were there even when I didn't feel it. I am grateful for my relationship with You, for getting closer to You and learning more about You every year. I look forward to more years of knowing You better and learning to trust You with every part of my life. From the bottom of my heart, God, thank You. For seeing me, for hearing me, for loving me, for teaching me. You are amazing. And I love You, God. 🖤 Also, I hope You're happy with how everything turned out. ☺

To my mom, Ming Mang Moung. Where do I even start? Thank you for everything. The sacrifices, the love, the care, the resilience. I have thought about you a lot while writing this book, and I am sorry for the things you learned about me for the first time here. I am grateful to have you as my mom. You will always be the best. 🖤 🖤

To my sister, Sylvie. Thank you so much for your support and encouragement over the years. I owe many of my accomplishments to you, and I will always be grateful for everything you've done. Thank you for taking on additional responsibilities and for supporting me without judgement.

To my sister, Fanny. Thank you for your guidance and counsel, especially as I navigated my first year in the U.S. Thank you for your support.

To my dad. Thank you for wanting the best for us; I hope your soul rests in peace.

To my brother, Tony. My person! Thank you so much for your dedication, patience, and readiness to help. Thank you also for the multiple trips to Western Union over the years; they definitely helped!

To my sister, Lidia. I thought a lot about you too, while writing this book. Thank you for being there for me in your own way, in a way you didn't know helped. Thank you for all the TikToks you shared with me and for your light-hearted GIF-filled messages. Thank you for sharing some of your dreams with me and for inspiring parts of this book.

To my brother, Vicky. You, too, have helped in ways you didn't realize. From the videos you shared to the jokes you cracked, many came at a time I needed to laugh. So, thank you.

To my niece, Mia. You didn't know it then, but some questions you asked about my journey also inspired parts of this book. Thank you.

To my friends. You have each been there for me at different times in your own way, and I am grateful for your support. I am grateful for the old and for the new friendships, for the friendships lost, renewed, then strengthened. In no particular order: Jacky, Junior, Nadia, Ronald, Clara, Neil, Aristide, Marielle, Yves-Alain, Paola, Marie-Dominique. Thank you.

To you, my reader. I have thought about you too, while writing this book, in ways you did not see here. Thank you for reading this far.

Câlins,
Danielle

Printed in the USA
CPSIA information can be obtained
at www.ICGtesting.com
CBHW022049230924
14692CB00030B/52/J